Reading and Study Skills

English as a Second Language

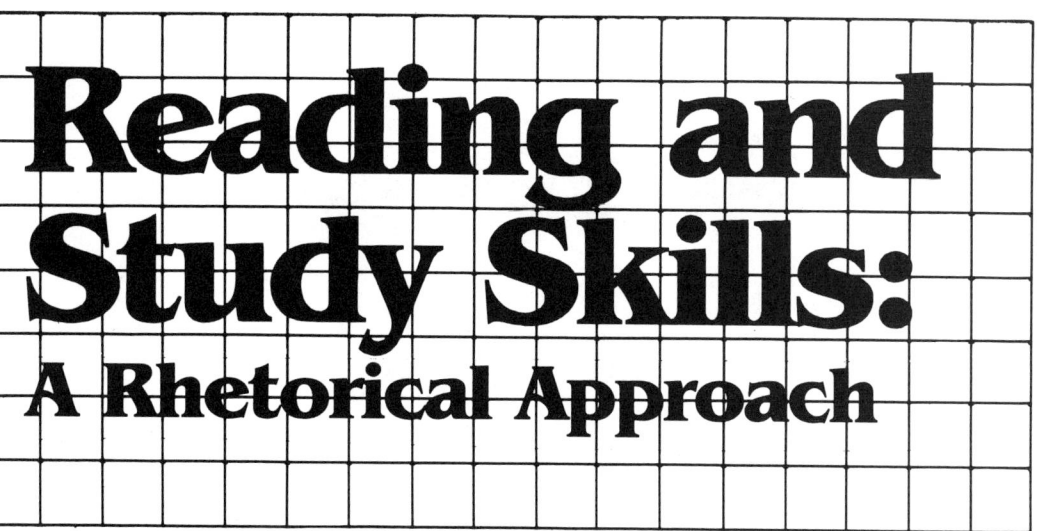

Reading and Study Skills: A Rhetorical Approach

Joan Kimmelman   **Harriet Krantz**
Charles Martin   **Sandra Seltzer**
Queensborough Community College
The City University of New York

Macmillan Publishing Company
New York
Collier Macmillan Publishers
London

Copyright © 1984, Macmillan Publishing Company, a division of Macmillan, Inc.

Printed in the United States of America

All rights reserved. No part of this book may be reproduced or transmitted in any form or by any means, electronic or mechanical, including photocopying, recording, or any information storage and retrieval system, without permission in writing from the Publisher.

Macmillan Publishing Company
866 Third Avenue, New York, New York 10022

Collier Macmillan Canada, Inc.

Library of Congress Cataloging in Publication Data

Main entry under title:

Reading and study skills.

    Includes index.
    1. Reading (Higher education)   2. Study, Method of.
3. English language—Rhetoric.   I. Kimmelman, Joan.
LB2365.R4C65 1984   428.4'07'11   83-14855
ISBN 0-02-364070-7

Printing: 7 8   Year: 9 0 1 2

ISBN 0-02-364070-7

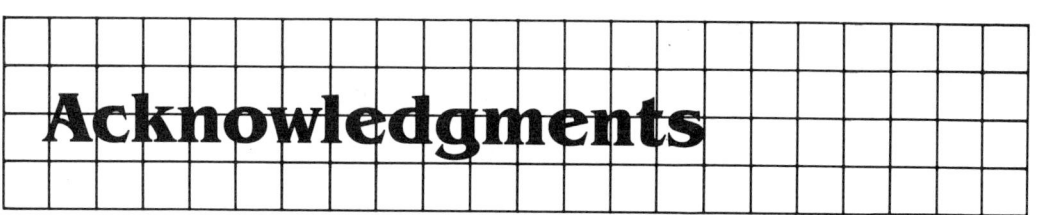

Acknowledgments

American Museum of Natural History. MARILYN COFFEY, "In Praise of Plains." Reprinted by permission from *Natural History,* Vol. 90, No. 11; Copyright The American Museum of Natural History, 1981.

The Benjamin/Cummings Publishing Company. BARBARA COMBS, DIANE HALES, and BRIAN WILLIAMS, *An Invitation to Health.* Copyright 1980 by Benjamin/Cummings Publishing Company, Inc., Menlo Park, Calif. Reprinted by permission of the publisher.

Harcourt Brace Jovanovich, Inc. Excerpt from ERNEST R. HILGARD, RITA L. ATKINSON, and RICHARD C. ATKINSON, *Introduction to Psychology,* 7th ed., 1979. Copyright © 1979 by Harcourt Brace Jovanovich, Inc. Reprinted by permission of Harcourt Brace Jovanovich, Inc.

Holt, Rinehart and Winston. LOUIS E. BOONE and DAVID L. KURTZ, "Private Enterprise" and other excerpts from *Contemporary Business,* 3rd ed. Copyright © 1982 by CBS College Publishing. Reprinted by permission of CBS College Publishing. One excerpt from *Contemporary Marketing,* 3rd ed. Copyright © 1974, 1977, 1980 by The Dryden Press. Reprinted by permission of Holt, Rinehart and Winston, CBS College Publishing. Excerpts from MARSHALL CASSADY and PAT CASSADY, *Theatre: A View of Life.* Copyright © 1982 by CBS College Publishing. Reprinted by permission of CBS College Publishing. Excerpts from WILLIAM HAVILAND, *Anthropology,* 3rd ed. Copyright © 1982 by CBS College Publishing. Reprinted by permission of CBS College Publishing. Excerpts from HERBERT B. MAYO, *Finance* by Herbert B. Mayo. Copyright © 1982 by CBS College Publishing. Reprinted by permission of CBS College Publishing. JAMES V. MCCONNELL, "Sleep Cycles," "Mind Over Matter," and other excerpts from *Understanding Human Behavior,* 3rd ed. Copyright © 1980 by Holt, Rinehart and Winston. Reprinted by permission of Holt, Rinehart and Winston, CBS College Publishing.

Steven Jantzen. STEVEN JANTZEN, "Prohibition: The 'Noble Experiment' that Failed." Copyright 1978 by Steven Jantzen. Reprinted by permission of Steven Jantzen, 62 Meadowbrook Road, Short Hills, N.J. 07078. "Prohibition: The 'Noble Experiment' that Failed" appeared originally in *Senior Scholastic Magazine.*

Macmillan Publishing Company, a Division of Macmillan, Inc. Excerpts from BARRY BERMAN and JOEL R. EVANS, *Retail Management, a Strategic Approach.* Copyright © 1979, 1983 by Macmillan Publishing Co., Inc. M. J. G. DE CRÈVECOEUR, "What Is an American" from *Lives of an American Farmer,* reprinted from *Anthology of American Lit-*

erature, Vol. I, edited by George McMichael. Copyright © 1974, 1980, by Macmillan Publishing Co., Inc. Excerpts from HENRIETTA FLECK, *Introduction to Nutrition,* 4th ed. Copyright © 1981 by Macmillan Publishing Co., Inc. Excerpts from BETH B. HESS, ELIZABETH W. MARKSON, and PETER J. STEIN, eds., *Sociology.* Copyright © 1982 by Macmillan Publishing Co., Inc. Excerpts from NICK NIGRO and ROBERT HANEY SCOTT, *Principles of Economics.* Copyright © 1982 by Macmillan Publishing Co., Inc. Excerpts from JAMES H. PICKERING and JEFFREY D. HOEPER, eds., *Concise Companion to Literature.* Copyright © 1981 by Macmillan Publishing Co., Inc. Excerpts from JOHN S. SINACORE and ANGELA C. SINACORE, *Health: A Quality of Life,* 3rd ed. Copyright © 1982 by Macmillan Publishing Co., Inc. All excerpts from these seven titles reprinted by permission of Macmillan Publishing Company.

Mayfield Publishing Company. Excerpts from PAUL M. INSEL and WALTON T. ROTH, *Core Concepts in Health,* 3rd ed. Copyright © 1976, 1979, 1982 by Mayfield Publishing Company. Reprinted by permission of Mayfield Publishing Company, Palo Alto, Calif. 94301.

The New York Times. JERRY BUCKLEY, "The Old-Time Bakery: A Still-Palpable Thrill." Copyright © 1982 by The New York Times Company. Reprinted by permission. MIGUEL C. [pseudonym], ". . . And, on Shaky Grounds." Copyright © 1978 by The New York Times Company. Reprinted by permission. GEORGIA DULLEA, "On the Pressures and Politics of Waiting in Line." Copyright © 1982 by The New York Times Company. Reprinted by permission.

Elise Piquet. ELISE PIQUET, "Welcome Back, Baby." Copyright 1981 by Elise Piquet. "Welcome Back, Baby" originally appeared in *The Reader's Digest.* Reprinted by permission of Elise Piquet, 28 South Wig Hill, Chester, Conn. 06412.

Random House, Inc. Excerpts from EDGAR Z. FRIEDENBERG, *Coming of Age in America.* Copyright © 1965 by the publisher, Vintage Books. Reprinted by permission of Random House, Inc. Excerpts from *The Random House College Dictionary,* Revised Edition. Copyright © 1980, 1979, 1975 by Random House, Inc. Reprinted by permission of Random House, Inc. Excerpts from CAMILLE WORTMAN and ELIZABETH LOFTUS, eds., *Psychology.* Reprinted by permission of Random House, Inc.

Rider in the Dark Productions. CAROLE CHAZIN, synopsis of "Rider in the Dark." Copyright © 1982 Rider in the Dark Productions, 205 Third Avenue, New York, N.Y. 10003.

Stein and Day Publishers. THOMAS BOSLOOPER and MARCIA HAYES, "The Feminine Physique" from *The Femininity Game* by Thomas Boslooper and Marcia Hayes. Copyright © 1973 by Thomas Boslooper and Marcia Hayes. Reprinted by permission of Stein and Day Publishers.

Taplinger Publishing Company. LINDA GOODMAN, "How to Recognize an Aries" and "Leo and Cancer Personalities" adapted from *Sun Signs* by Linda Goodman. Copyright © 1968 by Taplinger Publishing Company. Reprinted by permission.

Triangle Communications Inc. DENA KLEIMAN, "Cheating: Why It Is on the Rise Among Teens—and What Can Be Done About It." Copyright © 1981 by Triangle Communications Inc. Reprinted by permission of Triangle Communications Inc. All rights reserved. "Cheating: Why It Is on the Rise Among Teens—and What Can Be Done About It" originally appeared in *Seventeen* Magazine.

Tribune Company Syndicate, Inc. BOB GREENE, "Spending a Few Days with the Kid that You Once Were." Copyright © 1981 by Tribune Company Syndicate, Inc. Reprinted by permission of Tribune Company Syndicate, Inc. KITTY HANSON, "America in Solitary." Copyright © 1982 by Tribune Company Syndicate, Inc. Reprinted by permission of Tribune Company Syndicate, Inc. "Spending a Few Days with the Kid that You Once Were" and "America in Solitary" originally appeared in the New York *Daily News*.

William Morris Agency. JAMES A. MICHENER, "How America Lives." Copyright © 1981 by Family Media, Inc. Reprinted by permission of the author per the William Morris Agency as agents for the author and of the *Ladies' Home Journal*. "How America Lives" originally appeared in the *Ladies' Home Journal*.

Worth Publishers, Inc. IAN ROBERTSON, excerpts from *Sociology,* 2nd ed., pages 362–363. Copyright © 1981 by Worth Publishers, Inc. Reprinted by permission of Worth Publishers, Inc.

Photo Credits

Chapter 1
p. 18   Photo by Ray Fisher. Reprinted by permission of Time Magazine.

Chapter 2
p. 54   Photo by William McIntyre © 1981 by William McIntyre. Reprinted by permission of Photo Researchers, Inc.

p. 59   Courtesy of Carole Chazin.

p. 66   Reprinted by permission of The Bettmann Archive.

Chapter 3
p. 112   © 1977. Reprinted by permission of Photo Researchers, Inc.

p. 113   © 1977. Reprinted by permission of Stock/Boston.

Chapter 4
p. 140, 141, 144   Courtesy of James D. Anker.

Unit II
p. 169   © Sepp Seitz 1982. Reprinted by permission of Woodfin Camp & Associates.

p. 235   Drawing by Brian Schatell from an idea by Ray Forest.

p. 236   Drawing by Brian Schatell from an idea by Ray Forest.

p. 294   Photo by Jerome Wexler. Reprinted by permission of Photo Researchers, Inc.

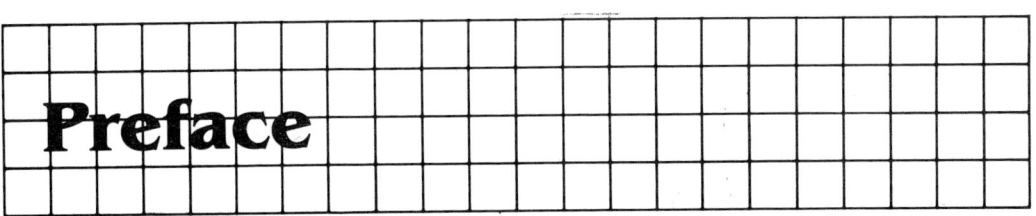

Preface

Reading and Study Skills: A Rhetorical Approach is a comprehension, study skills, and vocabulary text for native students and foreign-born intermediate students of English as a second language. We believe that these students can work most effectively when they learn skills presented in a logical and sequentially-developed manner, first acquiring skills presented through short, easy material and then applying the skills in more difficult passages.

The text is divided into three major units—Comprehension, Study Skills, and Vocabulary—to allow for flexibility in use. Each skill is presented inductively through short, easy examples, guided questions, and boxed skill guidelines. Students can work on any skill with the guidance of an instructor or independently, either in a lab setting or at home. In addition, students can apply the skills to writing exercises in the Comprehension Unit and to writing assignments that follow the longer readings and role-play exercises.

This text departs from the traditional approach of teaching comprehension skills separately. Rather, the skills are grouped within the framework of a particular rhetorical mode—narrative, descriptive, analytical, and argumentative—and, as a result, students develop skills appropriate to these modes. The instructor is free to present the modes in any way.

The text follows a holistic approach to comprehension rather than a compartmentalized one. For example, students can develop literal and general comprehension of narrative writing by focusing on its unique features: the chronological development of ideas, the sequence in which facts occur, the author's selection of ideas for development and use of the flashback, and the presence of sequence signal words and phrases. Students can then develop inference and critical reading skills related to the narrative (and to other writing styles): recognizing the narrator, the point of view the narrator presents, the facts and/or opinions being presented, and the predictions that logically follow from facts stated in a chronological order. Finally, students can apply these skills in four long selections and can complete a short narrative-type writing assignment. The role-play that follows reinforces the students' abilities to follow a chronological sequence, helps them to participate actively in class, and provides another reinforcement of writing narratively. Each Comprehension Unit follows this format and incorporates new skills.

The narrative, descriptive, argumentative, and analytical skill units contain brief writing assignments designed to help students develop comprehensions skills. The assignments are especially important in each of the sixteen long selections and four role-playing exercises. Students can reinforce their reading skills as they apply them to a specific writing assignment.

In the Study Skills Unit, students can follow a structured and sequential development of skills designed to strengthen their ability to recognize, record, and study the important ideas in expository writing. Students can identify and mark topics, main ideas, and details in single text paragraphs. After they develop their ability to preview text chapters and locate important facts, students can move to longer text passages, develop test-taking skills, answer objective test items, and write essay answers.

Some instructors may want to present the study skills material along with work in comprehension, since their students are actively involved in other subjects. Other instructors may want to focus on the comprehension skills before they present instruction in study techniques. However they wish to proceed, they can certainly present the last chapters on studying and taking tests at any time during the semester.

In the Vocabulary Unit, students can work with the dictionary and beginning context clue chapters in sequence. Once they begin to work with context clues, they can proceed in whatever order the instructor chooses. Some instructors may want to present the vocabulary skills along with work in comprehension and/or study skills. Others may want to focus on vocabulary skills as a specific unit during the semester. However they wish to proceed, they will have a sufficient number of exercises to allow for class and independent practice. Idioms have been defined so that students can apply their meanings in a variety of guided or independent practice exercises. Dictionary entries have been provided to allow uniform development and reinforcement of dictionary skills.

We gratefully acknowledge the assistance, both professional and personal, of our colleagues and friends: Susan Didriksen, our editor, for her guidance throughout the project; Pat Cabeza, our production editor, for her continued commitment to us and to the text; Holly Reid McLaughlin, for her excellent design; Rosalind Sackoff, for her advice and support; Amy Sonka, Boston University; Carol Cargill-Power, University of Southern Florida; Janet Klutho, Southern Illinois University; Ann Bachmann, Seminole Community College; Genevieve Cramer, Southwest Missouri State University, for their critical comments that helped shape the final text; Edith Grossman, Francine Stavis, and Terry Nicotra for their assistance in preparing the manuscript; our families, for their understanding and encouragement; our students, for their thoughtful evaluations of each portion of the manuscript.

Contents

UNIT I
Comprehension Skills — 1
Introduction — 1

CHAPTER 1
Understanding a Sequence of Ideas — 3
Recognizing Sequence in Narrative Writing   3
Recognizing Sequence Signals   4
Following Directions   6
Understanding Selectivity of Ideas   7
Recognizing Flashbacks   9
Determining Point of View   11
Distinguishing Between a Fact and an Opinion   12
Making Predictions   14
Applying Sequence Skills in Selections   17
  ". . . And, on Shaky Grounds"   17
  "The Old-Time Bakery: A Still-Palpable Thrill"   23
  "Welcome Back, Baby!"   30
  "Sleep Cycles"   36
Role-Playing   39

CHAPTER 2
Understanding a Descriptive Listing — 41
Recognizing Listing in Descriptive Writing   41
Identifying Listed Characteristics   42
Recognizing Listing Signals   45
Following Directions   47

xii   Contents

    Identifying Descriptions of Quality, Space, and Sequence   50
    Applying Fact/Opinion and Point of View Skills to
       Descriptions   54
    Making Generalizations and Assumptions   56
    Applying Descriptive Listing Skills in Selections   60
       "Spending a Few Days With the Kid that You Once Were"   60
       "Prohibition: The 'Noble Experiment' That Failed"   66
       "In Praise of Plains"   72
       "How to Recognize an Aries"   77
    Role-Playing   82

CHAPTER 3

Understanding Comparisons and Contrasts   84

    Recognizing Comparisons and Contrasts in Analytical
       Writing   84
    Recognizing Comparison and Contrast Signals   86
    Following Directions   88
    Understanding Shared Traits   90
    Identifying Comparisons and Contrasts of Parts, Space, and
       Sequence   94
    Applying Prediction and Assumption Skills to Comparisons and
       Contrasts   96
    Applying Fact/Opinion and Point-of-View Skills to Comparisons
       and Contrasts   99
    Applying Comparison and Contrast Skills in Selections   101
       "The Feminine Physique"   101
       "Leo and Cancer Personalities"   108
       "How America Lives"   112
       "What is an American"   118
    Role-Playing   121

CHAPTER 4

Understanding Causes and Effects   123

    Recognizing Causes and Effects in Argumentative Writing   123
    Recognizing Cause and Effect Signals   125
    Following Directions   127
    Identifying Causes and Effects and Distinguishing Between
       Them   130
    Applying Point-of-View Skills to Causes and Effects   134
    Drawing Conclusions   137

Applying Cause and Effect Skills in Selections   143
  "On the Pressures and Politics of Waiting in Line"   143
  "Cheating"   150
  "America in Solitary"   156
  "Mind Over Matter"   162
Role-Playing   166

UNIT II
Study Skills — 169
Introduction — 169

CHAPTER 5
Previewing — 171
Understanding Text Organization   171
Previewing the Textbook   172
Previewing Chapters in Psychology and Sociology   174

CHAPTER 6
Understanding Topics — 185
Identifying Topics of Lists   185
Identifying Topics in Text Paragraphs   187

CHAPTER 7
Understanding Main Ideas — 192
Relating Topics, Main Ideas, and Details   192
Identifying the Main Idea in Various Locations in the Paragraph   194

CHAPTER 8
Understanding Details — 198
Relating Main Ideas and Details   198
Identifying Main Ideas and Details in Text Passages   199

CHAPTER 9

Taking Notes — 203

Understanding Outline Form and the Relationships Among Ideas in an Outline   204
Outlining Lists   206
Outlining Text Passages   209

CHAPTER 10

Taking Tests — 217

Studying for Exams   217
Learning Approaches to Taking Tests   219
Taking Objective Tests   220
Answering Multiple-Choice Items and Following Directional Words on Tests   220
Answering True-False Items   225
Taking Essay Tests and Following Directional Words   228

UNIT III

Vocabulary Skills — 235

CHAPTER 11

Learning Idioms — 236

CHAPTER 12

Using the Dictionary — 259

Using a Word's Part of Speech to Determine Meaning   260
Understanding Multiple Meanings of Words   278

CHAPTER 13

Using Context Clues — 293

Using Sense-of-the-Sentence Context Clues   294
Using Synonym Context Clues   304
Using Example Context Clues   312
Using Antonym Context Clues   318
Recognizing Stated Definitions   324

Index — 329

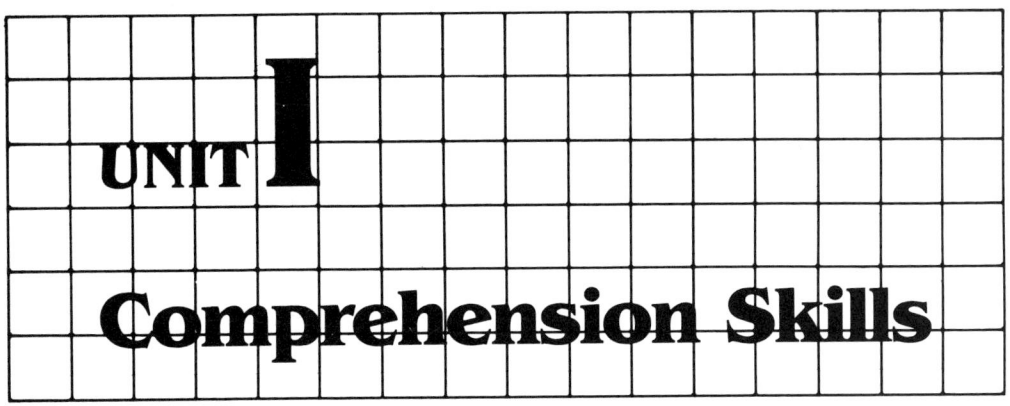

UNIT I

Comprehension Skills

INTRODUCTION

Understanding what you read requires many skills that build one upon another. They range from simple to complex skills. At the base, or literal level, is the skill of reading and understanding ideas stated in the passage. Once you understand stated ideas, you can begin to recognize how they relate to one another and what the author perceived their relationships to be. Another level of understanding comes when you can infer ideas or sense unstated relationships that the author wanted you to know.

In the following units you will focus on developing comprehension skills. You will work with passages grouped according to the different styles of writing: narrative, descriptive, argumentative, and analytical. In the remaining units you will work with expository material to develop comprehension and study skills related to text and test situations.

It is important to remember that reading skills neither exist in isolation nor apply to only one type of passage. Rather, many reading skills are necessary to comprehend the types of passages you read in school, at home, and at work. Also, you gain a deeper understanding of passages when you recognize the special relationships central to specific writing styles or rhetorical modes.

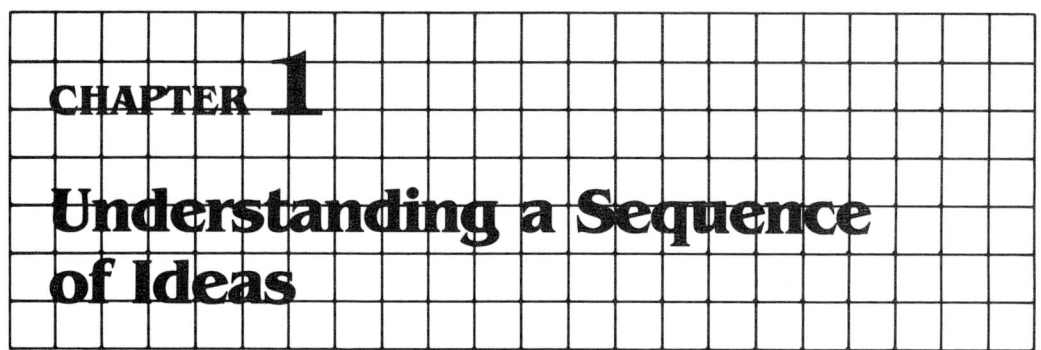

CHAPTER 1
Understanding a Sequence of Ideas

Recognizing Sequence in Narrative Writing

Much of what you read can be described as narrative; narrative writing is characterized by its quality of telling the events in a story in the order in which they occurred, that is, their chronological sequence. Authors write stories, news articles, essays, and text passages in which understanding the chronological sequence of ideas is essential for good comprehension. Read the following example to understand how literal, or stated ideas serve as a base for the chronological order of ideas in a passage.

Example

He then spent the next week in bed. John first became ill at lunch and went home immediately. John finally learned that he had weakened his condition and had wasted many days by trying to return to school not fully recovered. At last, he was well enough to return to school. He was not fully recovered when he insisted on returning to school. He had to return home that same morning.

Questions

1. How long did John's illness last? _____
2. When did John become ill? _____
3. What lesson did John learn? _____

4. Are the facts presented in an order that helps you to understand the incident? _____

5. What words signal the chronological order that the paragraph should follow? _____

Clearly, you can answer questions one, two, and three with facts stated in the paragraph. However, you may have experienced difficulty reading the paragraph and answering those questions because the facts were not presented in a chronological order. The words "then," "first," "finally," "not yet," "same," and "at last" are *signal words* that tell the chronological sequence of events in this incident, but they were not presented in the order in which the events occurred.

To make the incident more logical, rearrange the sentences in chronological order. Use the *signal words* and phrases and show your understanding of the literal or stated facts.

_____
_____
_____
_____
_____
_____
_____
_____
_____
_____

Recognizing Sequence Signals

> Recognizing the **chronological sequence of events** in the development of incidents, stories, articles, and text passages helps you to comprehend narrative writing. You will understand the development of an idea when you note the sequence it follows and the **words that signal** that sequence.

Practice

Rearrange the following groups of facts in a sequence that is logical and that helps you to understand them.

Group 1

kindergarten _____

high school _____

post-graduate _____

elementary _____

junior high _____

college _____

Group 2

childhood _____

middle age _____

infancy _____

adulthood _____

teen-age _____

old age _____

Practice

Use each sequence signal word in its logical place in the paragraph.

1. **next**   **finally**   **before**   **first**

    _____ I registered for my classes, I _____ read the college catalogue. _____, I checked my curricular requirements. _____, I went to registration and picked up my course cards.

2. **second**   **first**   **when**   **later**

    My career counselor told me that _____ I must fill out a job questionnaire. The _____ requirement was that I list my available hours by day and time. _____ I finished that, we had an interview. _____, we considered the opportunities that would suit me.

Following Directions

Sequence signal words help you to understand the chronological arrangement of events in essays, articles, and stories. Read the example to understand how sequence signals also help you to understand and follow an instructor's directions for work in class, on tests, and in texts.

Example

1. Before you bring up your paper, be sure to review the essay.
2. Trace the path that blood follows in the body.

Questions

1. In example one, what should you do first—review the essay or bring up your paper? _____
2. In example two, how does the instructor indicate that a chronological sequence is required? _____

When you recognize that an instructor's directions usually signal the order for completing work, you can better understand what your instructor requires. Following that order often simplifies the task required.

> Instructors often signal the specific order in which they want an assignment or test item completed. They use words and phrases such as "trace" and "develop" to indicate that they want a sequentially developed answer. Noting any **sequence signal words** can help you complete the assigned work according to your **instructor's directions.**

Practice

Read the following paragraph and answer the questions TRUE (T) or FALSE (F) based on your understanding of the chronological sequence of ideas.

Professor Martin wanted to be certain that his students finished all parts of the midterm exam. Thus, he wrote very specific directions for all parts of the test. For Part I, he told students to begin by answering only those questions known to them and to omit the rest. Part II, the essay section, required more time and thought. He told his students to read carefully the four essay choices and then to select one essay. Part III was a matching question. Professor Martin told his students to work on this next before going back to Part I. Students could then fill in the unanswered questions in Part I. Finally, he encouraged them to reread their essays before turning in their completed exams.

_____ 1. Students began by answering all questions in Part I.

_____ 2. The second instruction students received was to write an essay.

_____ 3. Students were told to review Part I before moving to the matching questions.

_____ 4. Because the essay section required time and thought, Professor Martin instructed his students to write the essay last.

_____ 5. Students worked on portions of the exam before they completed Part I.

Understanding Selectivity of Ideas

Read the following example to determine how the author selects important ideas for development in a sequence.

Example

It is very difficult to believe that I am finally graduating. Yet, I am sitting here, listening to speakers praise the class and urge us to continue in our pursuit of knowledge. It seems like only yesterday that I entered school, a recent newcomer to the United States. I remember how nervous and excited I was. My freshman year was filled with wonderful discoveries: new friends, courses, instructors, responsibilities, and new impressions of school life in America. By my sophomore year I had settled into a routine and began to concentrate on my courses. Perhaps I experienced my most difficult moments during the third year when I was required to make a career choice, one that would change the direction of my studies. I then settled into my senior year with a full schedule of interviews, job placement sessions, and job applications. And now, suddenly, it is all behind me. As I listen to the speakers and look at my friends and family, I am once again filled with excited anticipation about the future awaiting me.

Questions

1. List the years that were highlighted in this passage: _____
_____

2. Were the events discussed in a chronological order? _____

3. Were all the events in this student's college career discussed? _____

   Why? _____

Authors cannot write about every event as it develops in a passage. Therefore, they select key events or ideas to highlight the development of the story, incident, article, or text passage.

> Recognizing that authors are **selective** in presenting ideas and events in stories, essays, news articles, and text passages can help you to understand the ideas that are important in the development of the selection.

Practice

Check the key ideas that you might select to develop each example.

1. Baking a cake is not difficult if one follows certain guidelines.

   _____ Have the proper ingredients and utensils ready.

   _____ Follow the recipe directions.

   _____ Listen to the radio.

   _____ Invite friends to help select the type of cake you will make.

   _____ Allow enough time for the cake to cool.

   _____ Clean up afterwards.

2. There are many stages a child goes through in learning to socialize with others.

   _____ Sleeping through the night

   _____ Living with brothers and sisters

   _____ Learning to walk

   _____ Going to nursery school

   _____ Selecting a school

   _____ Going to kindergarten

   _____ Going to elementary school

Practice

For each sample statement, write the ideas you might develop in a chronological essay.

1. There are many stages one goes through in developing a relationship with a man (woman).

   _____
   _____
   _____
   _____
   _____

2. My weekday routine follows a very logical pattern.

   _____
   _____
   _____
   _____
   _____
   _____
   _____

Recognizing Flashbacks

Authors are selective when they interrupt the chronological order of the passage to provide a "flashback"—an episode or idea that occurred earlier and is inserted in the middle of the passage because it illustrates a character trait or a point of development. Authors use certain sequence words to signal the flashback when it interrupts the chronological order.

Example

   I was walking across Hyde Park to meet a British friend for lunch, and the gravel on the broad path crunched under my feet. Suddenly—I don't know why—I remembered the feel of hard sand on New Jersey beaches when I would run out of the cold ocean to wrap myself in a great towel. I remembered the endless hours spent building sand castles. Now, I was to meet a friend around the corner from the Royal Lancaster Hotel—*From* "Welcome Back, Baby!"

Questions

1. Where do the events take place that start and end the sequence? _____

2. What event causes the author to remember her past? _____

3. What does the author remember? _____

> You can better understand the special sequential relationship of ideas and events when you recognize the use of the **flashback**. The flashback helps to explain an idea, event, or character by interrupting the narrative with some incident that took place in the past.

Practice

In the following paragraphs, space is provided for a flashback. Consider the idea the author expresses and develop a flashback for that idea.

A. I now have an excellent chance of getting a promotion with my company. Besides my years on the job and my willingness to accept greater responsibility, I am careful performing those tasks assigned to me and take great pride in a job well-done. For example, I used to have a job as_____

_____

With this kind of experience, I feel confident that I will soon be rewarded.

B. I have lived in this town for two years and have learned a great deal about small-town life. It has taken me quite a while to become accustomed to the slow pace of living. I used to rush to _____

_____

_____

_____

_____

_____

I learned from that experience and believe that I will continue to learn from the people and their way of life in this town.

Determining Point of View

Narrative writing has a narrator, someone who tells the story. Read the following example to determine the importance of knowing who the narrators are and what personal feelings (opinions) the narrators may be expressing.

Example

Narrator A

Over the years my husband and I have seen our neighborhood grow and change in character. Twenty years ago the people with whom we socialized were involved in the same activities. We belonged to the same clubs, our children attended the same schools, and we shopped together. Then, some of our friends moved because of job relocations. A wonderful couple, newly arrived in this country, moved in next door and soon began to share some of their traditions with me: new foods, music, and customs. In the past few years, people from many parts of this country, and some immigrants, have enriched my experiences. Now, as I look around, I realize how many new and interesting activities I've become involved in.

Narrator B

Over the years my wife and I have seen our neighborhood change completely. Twenty years ago I knew everyone on the block. We belonged to the same clubs, shared the same ride to the office, and enjoyed each other's company at social activities. Then, some of my friends moved because of job relocations. Newcomers moved in and soon set up ethnic stores, special houses of worship, and even separate schools. In the past few years, more and more new people have taken over the neighborhood. Now, as I look around, I realize that I have nothing in common with these newcomers. I stay to myself and look forward to the day when I can get out of this neighborhood.

Questions

1. Who relates the experience in A? _____
2. Who relates the experience in B? _____
3. Are the same basic facts developed in A and B? _____
4. What is the key idea developed in A? _____
   _____
5. What is the key idea developed in B? _____
   _____
6. Does each narrator express the same or a different attitude about the key idea? _____

Authors often write stories, essays, and articles to express opinions about people, places, events, or ideas. By understanding who the narrator is and what the stated facts are, you can sense stated and/or unstated opinions developed by the author.

> Recognizing **who the narrator is** and the **point of view,** or **opinion** the narrator expresses can give you a better understanding of the author's attitudes about people, places, events, and ideas.

Distinguishing Between a Fact And an Opinion

Recognizing an author's point of view depends on your ability to distinguish between facts and opinions. Read the following example to note that distinction.

Example

I believe that most Americans would not want my job. I work from nine to five, six days a week. The room I work in is 14 by 20 feet. Ten people work in that space. There are no windows. We're given twenty minutes for lunch. There is no overtime pay.

Questions

1. What opinion about his job does the author express? Underline it.
2. Highlight the facts that the author uses to develop that opinion.

Understanding a Sequence of Ideas

When you understand the difference between a fact and an opinion, you can begin to understand statements that express a point of view. Statements that can be directly proven or disproven with evidence are considered facts. Opinions cannot be proven or disproven. A writer can, however, persuade the reader to accept an opinion by presenting supporting facts.

> A **fact** can be proven or disproven with direct evidence. Often a writer states an **opinion** and expresses an attitude or feeling about people, places, events, situations, or ideas. The author can use facts as a basis for persuading the reader that the opinion is correct. Distinguishing between facts and opinions will help you to understand a selection. You will achieve a deeper level of comprehension in your reading.

Practice

Read the following sentences. If a statement can be proven or disproven with direct evidence, write FACT. If a statement expresses the author's attitude, write OPINION.

_____ 1. The federal judge dismissed the discrimination case.

_____ 2. The mayor's landslide victory clearly shows the public's total support for his policies.

_____ 3. The plan to protect the people who live and work near the nuclear power plant is inadequate and may never be workable.

_____ 4. Dental schools across the country are finding that requests for applications are decreasing.

_____ 5. Our criminal justice system is in great trouble.

_____ 6. Three million credit cards are stolen every year.

_____ 7. Single head-of-household arrangements are becoming very popular in America.

_____ 8. Polls of sportswriters show a majority favor the new baseball rules.

_____ 9. The robbery suspects were arrested in a twenty-mile car chase.

_____ 10. I feel that the closing of the factory will destroy the economy of this region.

Making Predictions

Read the following example to see how your understanding of the chronological sequence of ideas helps you to predict probable future actions, that is, to make judgments about what is likely or not likely to occur.

Example

Jim and Barry are applying for the position of manager of a tool company. Jim is completing a four-year liberal arts degree and wants to secure any job immediately upon graduating. He works in the college bookstore and is captain of the basketball team. Barry has completed a two-year degree specializing in mechanical technology. He currently works at a local garage and has had experience in repairing equipment, selling auto parts, and purchasing equipment. Both men have met with career counselors, have filled out applications, and have forwarded letters of reference to the tool company. Jim's letters have come from the bookstore manager, his English professor, and the coach of his basketball team. Barry's references have come from two technology instructors and his supervisor at the garage. Both eagerly await the next step in the job-seeking process.

Questions

1. What three steps has each man taken in the job-seeking process?

   _____

   _____

   _____

2. What is the next logical step in the process? _____

3. Based on your understanding of the facts—each man's qualifications— state which man will probably get the job: _____

4. Explain your reasoning in Question 3: _____

   _____

   _____

Authors often limit their discussions about ideas or events and expect the reader to use the stated facts and chronological sequence of events to predict possible future actions.

Understanding a Sequence of Ideas 15

> Knowing the facts and following the sequence of ideas can help you to **predict** possible future actions based logically on ideas developed in the reading.

Practice

In the following exercise, be sure you understand the logical order of ideas, and, based on your literal understandings, predict what is likely to happen (LIKELY) or what is not likely to happen (UNLIKELY).

A. Two years ago Ralph began work as a supermarket clerk. In six months he was promoted to assistant manager of the market. He worked hard and one year later took over the position of market manager. Because of his continued efforts to provide excellent service, Ralph's work came to the attention of the market's administrators. They watched his work carefully and several months later made a decision.

unlikely 1. Ralph will be evaluated for five years before he is promoted.

_____ 2. When Ralph is promoted, he will become a good market manager in the company.

_____ 3. Ralph will move to the administrative offices shortly.

_____ 4. Ralph will be moved to one of the firm's smaller markets.

_____ 5. In two more years with the company, Ralph will have held every possible position.

B. Roberta and Joseph have applied for status as United States citizens. Joseph has a fine job, and Roberta is enrolled at a local college where she studies secretarial science. Each had an American sponsor, and each has studied hard for the citizenship exam.

_____ 1. Joseph will get a better job when he emigrates from the United States.

_____ 2. Both Roberta and Joseph will become citizens.

_____ 3. Roberta will begin her medical studies when she enrolls in college.

_____ 4. Roberta, but not Joseph, will pass the exam.

_____ 5. Roberta and Joseph will skip the next exam.

C. "For years we've discussed the advantages of owning our own home rather than renting an apartment," said Alison to her husband, Teddy.

"But I don't think we can pay that much for the mortgage. And besides, we will still have many other expenses," he replied.

"We pay as much for rent as we would for the mortgage. And remember, part of the mortgage payment is tax-deductible."

"I don't see how that will help us."

"We'll get some money back every April after taxes. We certainly don't have that benefit with our apartment."

"I see your point. Let me think this over. Hmmm. Money returned to us!"

_____ 1. Teddy will consider the advantages of owning a home.

_____ 2. Alison will claim their apartment rent as a tax deduction.

_____ 3. The taxes on a home and an apartment will be equal.

_____ 4. Alison will need further convincing about the benefits of home ownership.

_____ 5. Alison and Teddy will decide to buy their own home.

D. What some Americans consider necessity, others consider luxury. Consider the Jackson family. When Mr. and Mrs. Jackson were married, they moved into an apartment that was equipped with a stove, a refrigerator, an electric burglar alarm system, air conditioning, heating, a building phone system, and a dishwasher. In addition, their building had a laundry room equipped with washers and dryers. The Jacksons could listen to music as they took the elevator to their twentieth-floor apartment, and they could park their car in a heated, electronically protected garage. They could also enjoy the building's rooftop facilities which included a pool, a sauna, a steam bath, and a lounging area.

_____ 1. The Jacksons will soon move to another building.

_____ 2. The Jacksons will expect the same basic conditions if they consider any future moves.

_____ 3. If the Jacksons move, they will immediately order the necessary kitchen appliances, such as a stove.

_____ 4. When the Jackson children are grown, they can expect to enjoy more electronic conveniences than they do now.

_____ 5. All families in the United States will have these advantages in the near future.

Understanding a Sequence of Ideas 17

Applying Sequence Skills in Selections

You now have the opportunity to apply comprehension skills to passages similar to those you read daily in newspapers and magazines. Before you read a selection, familiarize yourself with the vocabulary that has been previewed. Then, as you read, be aware of the sequence of ideas, the use of flashbacks, and any stated or unstated opinions. Each selection is followed by questions that focus on the skills of understanding vocabulary, stated facts, sequence of ideas, author's point of view, and predictions. Finally, you will practice using these skills as you complete a writing assignment.

Selection 1: ". . . And, on Shaky Grounds"
by Miguel C.

Vocabulary Preview

The following terms appear in the reading. Knowing their meanings will help you to understand the selection.

Idioms	Meanings
nothing off	no amount of money taken from one's salary
piece-rate	money paid for each item worked on and completed rather than a set wage for the hours worked
suited for	qualified for a certain type of employment
take it for granted	assume as a certainty

Vocabulary	Meanings
arrested	stopped the symptoms of a disease either temporarily or permanently
benefits	conditions provided for the good of the person
deductions	money taken from one's salary
officially	legally authorized
raid	a surprise search for the purpose of seizing something
status	the position of a person before the law
sweatshop	a business employing workers at low wages, for long hours, and under poor conditions

I got my first job here in New York years ago, in a loft on Broadway, just up from 14th Street. A fur factory.

In those days, Immigration used to raid the 14th Street subway station. A priest warned me about this. He said: "When you get off the subway, make sure you're carrying a copy of The Daily News. And if anybody comes up to you and asks you anything, just say, 'Bull----.' "

The hours in that factory were eight hours a day, six days a week. The pay was all on a **piece-rate** that worked out to be less than minimum wage. We got paid in cash—**nothing off** for taxes or Social Security. Because the business didn't **officially** exist: It had no books, no accounts, nothing of that kind.

Since then, my wife and I have worked in many places—mostly in factories on Canal Street and Broadway that make some kind of women's clothing. The hours are still the same (though some places shut down at noon on Saturday). There are no **benefits**, no **deductions**, no union. I don't think too many Americans would want my job. The places, like us who work in them, don't officially exist.

Except, of course, for Immigration. Working in one of these factories, you will soon be in your first **raid**: Immigration coming down the lines, asking for your papers. Men and women diving into piles of clothes, or trying to hide in the toilets. In a restaurant uptown (other than the **sweatshops**, restaurants are where illegals find work), a friend of mine hid in the freezer for 20 minutes.

The possibility of being deported, and the fear of it, is for all of us the central fact. If Immigration shows up at your front door, you must be ready to crawl out the back window—abandon all your possessions and start over. You can never **take it for granted** that your home today will be your home tomorrow.

It makes us, my wife and me, fugitives. Which is not something life in Ecuador had prepared us for. There, we were part of Ecuador's middle class—she was a lab technician, I worked in a Government office. She had gone to a private school, and had won several folk-singing contests. We may not be what you think of as the "typical" illegal immigrant couple, but remember, getting from Ecuador to New York requires enough money that it is really a luxury of the middle class.

We came here partly because my wife had a lung condition that could not be treated in Ecuador. That got us our visas.

We also came to make money.

The visas have long since expired. Our one try at making our **status** legal, two years ago, ended with disaster. Immigration's doctors disagreed with all of us, and ruled that even though my wife's disease had not been cured, it had been "**arrested**," and so we would have to return home to Ecuador.

But over the years, most of our relatives had come to New York—some with our help. What would we be going "home" to?

We decided to move again. And so we disappeared, that time, out to Jersey City.

Our lives here have been difficult in so many different ways. My wife sings as often as she can for Ecuadorean groups; yet we will never be thought of as Ecuadoreans here—at best we will be called "Hispanic." No one can imagine that we might be literate; that we might be **suited for** work outside the sweatshops. And a real home is something we do not dare to even dream about.

Yet we will do anything, and everything, up to the last minute, to stay. A friend of mine, a woman, told me as she was about to be deported: "Just wait. When the plane stops in Miami, I'll walk over to the postcards, and then from there, when no one's looking. . . ."

Literal Comprehension

Check the following statements that reflect information in the selection.

_____ 1. Men and women hide anywhere to escape immigration authorities and possible deportation.

_____ 2. Miguel came to America in order to make money and to get medical treatment for his wife.

_____ 3. Miguel and his wife are now considered true Ecuadoreans by their neighbors.

_____ 4. The couple will escape when the plane stops in Miami.

_____ 5. Because they are poorly educated, Miguel and his wife can only hope to buy a small, inexpensive house.

Sequence

A. Number the following events in their chronological order based on your understanding of the sequence of events in the selection.

_____ The couple's visas expire.

_____ The couple moves to Jersey City.

_____ Miguel's wife is a lab technician, and Miguel is a government employee.

_____ Miguel and his wife make clothing in shops that don't officially exist.

_____ The couple obtains visas in order to get medical treatment for the wife.

B. Based on your understanding of the sequence of ideas in the selection, complete each of the following statements by writing the letter of the correct answer on the line.

_____ 1. Before the couple moved to Jersey City
   a) they were deported.
   b) they were recognized as true citizens.
   c) their visas had expired.
   d) they stopped to look at postcards in Miami.

_____ 2. Factory workers tried to hide
   a) after they had jobs in official businesses.
   b) when immigration authorities conducted a raid.
   c) before the authorities raided their businesses.
   d) when they arrived at the airport.

_____ 3. The fear of being deported
   a) decreases as the years go by.
   b) is felt more by people who own homes.
   c) increases for Miguel in Jersey City.
   d) is a constant factor over the years.

_____ 4. Before arriving in the United States, Miguel's wife
   a) won folk-singing contests.
   b) sang for her countrymen in Jersey City.
   c) was thought of as Hispanic.
   d) worked in illegal sweatshops.

_____ 5. Before arriving in the United States, Miguel
   a) was warned about immigration raids on 14th Street.
   b) was a lab technician.
   c) sent all of his relatives to New York.
   d) worked for his government.

Understanding a Sequence of Ideas 21

Fact and Opinion

A. The following statements appeared in the selection. If they can be proven or disproven with direct evidence, label them FACT. If they express the author's point of view, label them OPINION.

_____ 1. . . . getting from Ecuador to New York requires enough money that it is really a luxury of the middle class.

_____ 2. . . . she was a lab technician, I worked in a Government office.

_____ 3. Our lives here have been difficult in so many different ways.

_____ 4. But over the years, most of our relatives had come to New York. . . .

_____ 5. Our one try at making our status legal, two years ago, ended with disaster.

B. Each of the following statements is an <u>opinion</u>. If you think Miguel C. would agree, label a statement YES; if he would not agree, write NO.

_____ 1. There is pride in working in sweatshops.

_____ 2. The authorities treat newly arrived immigrants fairly.

_____ 3. The Department of Immigration should deport everyone who enters the country illegally.

_____ 4. State and local authorities should close all sweatshops.

_____ 5. People should stop coming to the United States, for there is no hope of succeeding here.

Predictions

Decide if each of the following statements is a likely outcome based on the facts and sequence of ideas in the selection. Place a check next to those that are <u>likely</u> predictions.

_____ 1. Miguel and his wife will have to move again.

_____ 2. Miguel will remain an "unskilled" laborer.

_____ 3. Sweatshops will continue to exist in the United States.

_____ 4. As more Ecuadoreans join the community, Miguel will be less fearful of deportation.

_____ 5. Miguel and his wife will find it difficult to become citizens of the United States.

Vocabulary

A. Use the correct idiom in each sentence:

piece-rate   nothing off   take it for granted   suited for

1. I have studied computer technology for three years and believe that I am _____ the job.
2. Don't _____ that Professor Stevens will quiz us on the lectures only.
3. The _____ is lower for the job of addressing envelopes than for ironing shirts.
4. My check was higher this month because there was _____ for taxes.

B. Match the split sentences that follow.

_3_ When I passed the exam

____ Because of the heavy rains

____ The benefits of this job include

____ The sweatshop owner did not give

____ The doctors think they have arrested

____ When the police heard of the illegal gambling house

1. the game was officially rescheduled for the next evening.
2. raises in salaries this year.
3. I achieved status as an American citizen.
4. the fever and can now treat the basic cause of the illness.
5. a free health plan, dental insurance, and free eye examinations.
6. they decided to raid it immediately.

Writing

Miguel and his wife faced new and uncertain experiences coming to and living in the United States. Similarly, each of you has faced and will face a totally new situation, whether in a new school, a new community, a new job, or in other circumstances. Think about a new experience you have had and relate it in a short, sequentially developed essay. Remember to select the key events to develop in chronological order. You can express opinions and use a flashback to help relate the events.

Selection 2: "The Old-Time Bakery: A Still-Palpable Thrill"
by Jerry Buckley

Vocabulary Preview

The following terms appear in the reading. Knowing their meanings will help you to understand the selection.

Idioms	Meanings
convenience store	a small store with a variety of items for sale
fast-food	food prepared quickly and cheaply for many people
honest-to-goodness	real; in an old-fashioned or original manner
winding our way	moving in and out along a path

Vocabulary	Meanings
casualty	any person or group harmed as a result of an act or event
era	a period of time marked by distinctive characteristics or events
homogenization	blending unlike elements to become alike
molasses	thick, dark-colored syrup made in the refining of sugar
palpable (see title)	easily seen, felt, or heard
picturesque	charming; pleasant; interesting
premises	a building and its land
puffy	swollen; inflated
vacate	give up possession or occupancy

WASHINGTON—For the first time that anyone can remember, in a place where people have pretty good memories, there is no **honest-to-goodness** bakery in Geneva, the small town in upstate New York where I was born 26 years ago. Two dozen churches, five funeral homes and two movie theaters but no bakery.

Oh, you can still buy baked goods in the supermarkets or in the smaller **convenience stores**. But it's not the same. Those stores have everything from breakfast cereals to antifreeze but they don't have a master baker such as Red Visco. And they don't give out free cookies to kids with their mothers.

When I was a kid, my father was paid on Thursday morning and that afternoon we would go to the Acme supermarket in the Plaza Shopping Center to buy enough groceries to last six children and their parents for a week. After **winding our way** through the aisles, we would go next door to the Plaza Bakery.

What I saw and smelled there made me quickly forget the other store. It started even before I was inside. The windows were filled with the baker's work: **puffy** jelly donuts and **molasses** cookies, chocolate cakes and cherry pies and bread freshly sliced. Once inside, the attraction grew. Glass display cases were filled with everything displayed in the windows and more. You could almost see the aroma coming from the kitchen in the back.

There was almost always a line, but that did not bother me. It gave me more time to think about what I would buy if I had the money. The cupcakes were tempting but I usually chose half-moon cookies, chocolate cookies topped with vanilla icing on one half and chocolate icing on the other. Standing in line also gave me a chance to study the women as they wrapped string around the white boxes that had blue lettering and a sketch of the bakery on top.

When it was my mother's turn to order, I made sure I was at her side and on my best behavior because even before my mother had a chance to speak, the woman in the white uniform would reach over the counter and put a big chocolate chip cookie in my hand. That was the policy of Red and Mary Visco's bakery: free chocolate chip cookies for the kids.

This policy and the bakery lasted 16 years. But one Saturday last December the last chocolate chip cookie was handed out to the last kid and Red and Mary Visco closed their bakery door for the last time. In doing so, they closed an **era**.

The Plaza Bakery did not close for lack of business and the Viscos had planned to stay open at least until they reached retirement age in a few years. But last November a notice arrived in the mail from the owner of the shopping center that changed those plans. The Viscos, who had been operating on a monthly lease for years, were told to **vacate** the **premises** by Jan. 1. The supermarket next door was expanding. The bakery had to go. Red Visco was offered another space in the Plaza. But moving would have cost at least $5,000 and the rent would have been tripled. So Red Visco, a baker for all his adult life, decided to close his business.

In an age when supermarkets have become "concepts in total shopping," traditional personal service does not seem as important as it used to be. Convenience is more valued than craftsmanship. The changes in Geneva since my childhood have not been dramatic but the **homogenization** that is evident in so much of our country today can be seen there, too. Red Visco is not the only **casualty**.

When I was a kid, we did not go to the store to buy milk; it was delivered by milkmen from one of the local dairies. They drove funny-looking trucks that did not go very fast and made strange sounds. The milkmen had names such as Andy Brown and Pete Snyder. Milk used to come in bottles, and as the trucks made their way through the streets, you could hear the clinking of the glass. The bottles went first. Now the milkmen are gone too.

Geneva is now a full-fledged member of the **fast-food** generation. McDonald's and Burger King and Dunkin' Donuts stand three in a row on one side of Hamilton Street, and Arthur Treacher's Fish and Chips is right across the street.

For most of the years I lived in Geneva, a **picturesque** restaurant called the Lafayette Inn occupied a spot on the hill overlooking the town. The restaurant was named for the Marquis de Lafayette, who stopped to rest across the road in 1825 on his 15-month tour of the United States.

But the inn burned to the ground a few years ago. The bulldozers came, then the carpenters and builders, and now there's a Ponderosa and a Pizza Hut on the site. I wonder how many of the next generation will ever hear the story of Lafayette's visit to our town or have the chance to go to a real bakery with mother?

Understanding a Sequence of Ideas   25

Literal Comprehension

Complete the following statements based on your understanding of the facts in the selection.

_____ 1. The modern stores in Geneva
   a) have no baked goods.
   b) offer traditional personalized service.
   c) are models of convenience shopping.
   d) usually specialize in one type of product.

_____ 2. As a child, Jerry Buckley
   a) went to the market to buy bread.
   b) received free cookies from the Viscos.
   c) couldn't wait to visit McDonald's and Dunkin' Donuts.
   d) met the Marquis de Lafayette.

_____ 3. A picturesque restaurant occupied the spot where
   a) the Plaza Bakery used to stand.
   b) the Pondorosa and Pizza Hut once stood.
   c) the Marquis stopped to rest.
   d) the shopping center was built.

_____ 4. Red and Mary Visco closed their business when
   a) the number of customers declined.
   b) Jerry Buckley was born.
   c) they were offered another space in the Plaza.
   d) the owner of the shopping center tripled their rent.

_____ 5. The changes in Geneva include
   a) a shift from convenience shopping to craftsmanship.
   b) a decline in individual services.
   c) a loss of total shopping services.
   d) all of the above.

Sequence

Complete the following statements based on your understanding of the sequence of ideas in the selection.

_____ 1. Jerry discovered wonderful sights and smells
   a) before he entered the bakery.
   b) for the last time sixteen years ago.
   c) twenty-six years ago in Geneva.
   d) both outside and inside the Plaza Bakery.

_____ 2. Fast-food restaurants have
   a) been replaced by a shopping center.
   b) replaced the Lafayette Inn and the bakery.
   c) carried on the tradition of personal service.
   d) continued to serve the same foods as the bakery had.

_____ 3. The Lafayette Inn
   a) replaced the Pondorosa and the Pizza Hut.
   b) burned to the ground in 1825.
   c) was a typically old-fashioned restaurant.
   d) is still enjoyed by the youth of Geneva.

_____ 4. Red and Mary Visco are noted for
   a) sixteen years of individual service and fine baking.
   b) opening Geneva's first convenience market.
   c) joining the Acme supermarket last November.
   d) supplying today's shopping center customers with every baked item imaginable.

_____ 5. Some highlights of Jerry's youth were
   a) getting free cookies at McDonald's.
   b) enjoying two movie theaters in town.
   c) knowing the delivery men and the store owners.
   d) stopping each Thursday at the Burger King.

Fact and Opinion

A. If the following statements from the selection can be proven or disproven with direct evidence, label them FACT. If they express the author's point of view, label them OPINION.

_____ 1. The cupcakes were tempting.

_____ 2. They don't give out free cookies to kids with their mothers.

_____ 3. In closing their bakery door, Red and Mary Visco closed an era.

_____ 4. Traditional service does not seem as important as it used to be.

_____ 5. The milkmen drove funny-looking trucks.

_____ 6. The milkmen had names such as Andy Brown and Pete Snyder.

Understanding a Sequence of Ideas

_____ 7. Oh, you can still buy baked goods in supermarkets.

_____ 8. The changes in Geneva since my childhood have not been dramatic.

_____ 9. There is no honest-to-goodness bakery in Geneva.

_____ 10. Convenience is more valued than craftsmanship.

B. If you think Jerry Buckley would agree with the following <u>opinions</u>, write YES. If he would not agree, write NO.

_____ 1. Old-fashioned bakeries provided warmth and charm to their customers.

_____ 2. Stores today seem cold and impersonal.

_____ 3. Today's youth can develop close relationships with the store owners who serve them.

_____ 4. Modernization has destroyed the friendly, small-town spirit.

_____ 5. Growing up today can be as rich an experience as it was twenty-five years ago.

Predictions

Based on the facts in the selection, check those statements that are <u>likely</u> predictions.

_____ 1. Traditional service will continue to decline as the concept of convenience grows in value.

_____ 2. In the future, most small stores will be replaced by convenience markets.

_____ 3. Tomorrow's generation will have none of the experiences that Jerry Buckley had as a child.

_____ 4. More businesses will experience the homogenization that bakeries and restaurants have gone through.

_____ 5. People will eventually lose their desire for homemade and traditionally crafted items.

Vocabulary

A. Each sentence has been divided into two parts. Based on your understanding of the new underlined words, first match the sentence parts in Group A, and then match the sentence parts in Group B.

Group A

_____ The construction crew ordered the building <u>vacated</u>

_____ We were eager to sample

_____ When a fire was discovered, we

_____ My eyes became <u>puffy</u> because I

1. stayed in the sun too long.
2. the <u>molasses</u> cookies grandmother had baked.
3. left the <u>premises</u> immediately.
4. and they began work on the new housing development.

Group B

_____ When milk is thoroughly blended

_____ A new <u>era</u> began with the use of

_____ The first <u>casualties</u> benefited from

_____ A <u>palpable</u> feeling of excitement

_____ From our balcony we saw a

1. <u>picturesque</u> village.
2. comes with any scientific discovery.
3. it is <u>homogenized</u>.
4. computer technology.
5. immediate medical treatment.

B. Use each idiom in a sentence:

honest-to-goodness **winding our way**
fast-food **convenience store**

1. _____

2. _____

3. _____
   _____
   _____

4. _____
   _____
   _____

Writing

Jerry Buckley discovered and wrote about changes in the lifestyle in his hometown. Can you imagine, or have you seen changes in the places where you spent your childhood? Trace one or more changes in the lifestyle in your hometown or in your current neighborhood. Remember to select key ideas, to follow a logical sequence, and, if you wish, to use a flashback as an illustration or explanation.

Selection 3: "Welcome Back, Baby!"
by Elise Piquet

Vocabulary Preview

The following terms appear in the reading. Knowing their meanings will help you to understand the selection.

Idioms	Meanings
a good run of luck	a series of favorable experiences
box score	the record of each team in a ballgame
cozy up to	get close to, comfortably
paid no heed	ignored
taken with	attracted to; overcome by an emotion

Vocabulary	Meanings
bristle	become stiff with anger or irritation
bulging	filled to capacity
constricted	tightened
deflated	depressed in spirit
discreetly	quietly; without drawing attention
exhilarating	stimulating
gravel	stones, pebbles, and sand
incoherent	without logic
jumpseat	a folding seat in the back of a taxi
skycap	a porter who carries baggage at an airport
thrusting	forcing acceptance of something
trigger	an act or event that starts a reaction
twitched	moved suddenly
vastness	great size

There is something about Americans: you can take us out of America, but you can't take America out of *us*. As sure as the sun will rise, a time comes when we know, just know, we must go home.

The **trigger** can be a World Series **box score** in a week-old American paper, windblown in a Paris gutter. It can be the wedding announcement of a high-school friend. Or news of a family reunion. Like a salmon that finds its way from the **vastness** of the sea to the river of its birth, we're **taken with** an irresistible urge.

For me, that moment arrived on a sunny August day in London, 3500 miles and five years from America. I was walking across Hyde Park to meet a British friend for lunch, and the **gravel** on the broad path crunched under my feet. Suddenly—I don't know why—I remembered the feel of hard sand on New

Jersey beaches when I would run out of the cold ocean to wrap myself in a great towel. I remembered the endless hours spent building sand castles. And the **exhilarating** rides on the local roller coaster.

I was to meet my friend around the corner from the Royal Lancaster Hotel, a flashy modern building with tall flagpoles fluttering flags of many nations. The end flag was mine. A piece of red, white and blue flag that I used to salute in school. "I pledge allegiance. . . ." Suddenly my throat closed, and my heart **constricted**. What was happening to me, anyway?

My elegant friend was **cozied up** to a table sparkling with white tablecloths and heavy silverware. As I sat down, my ears picked up an accent: "Back in Iowa, we get this kind of weather all summer long." I tried to look **discreetly** at the group two tables away.

My friend's eyes followed mine. She shook her head. "Just look at that jacket. And those ties. Where *do* American men buy their clothes?"

I **bristled** with unexpected, **incoherent** anger. "At Sears, Roebuck or Joe Blow's Clothing Store. And some of them have as much style as any Englishman. And at least American women can make decent coffee. Not to mention hamburgers. Why, you don't know what a real hamburger is, thick and juicy and dripping with mustard and ketchup on a toasted bun, with a milkshake—a chocolate milkshake—so thick you have to eat it with a spoon. And in summer we used to have cookouts where we'd barbecue thick steaks. Then we'd sit around on blankets, toasting marshmallows over the coals and necking our tiny hearts out."

What was I saying? Toasting marshmallows? Necking our hearts out?

"Oh, my dear," said Jane, her eyes wide with discovery and understanding, "you're homesick!"

I blew my nose, suddenly **deflated**, and nodded.

Somehow, as I always knew it would, my time had come. In less than a month I had given up my apartment and shipped my belongings to the United States. Now I peered through the little window as the jet circled Kennedy Airport. The sky was so blue over New York it hurt my eyes. My legs **twitched** with eagerness to get moving. Down the endless corridors, through passport control, into the mob at customs.

I pushed my two heavy suitcases and **bulging** carry-on bag to the end of the customs counter just as a tall, thin **skycap** went by with his cart. "Would you mind lifting all this onto your wagon?" I called. "I have a bad back."

"Sure thing," he said. "I'll put you in the taxi line."

"Oh, I can't do that," I said. "I'm taking the bus."

He **paid no heed**, headed straight for a cab and unloaded my luggage. I motioned that it should go right back on his trolley.

"Look, Mr. William Scott," I read from his badge, "I don't have a job yet. Or an apartment. Taxis cost a fortune."

William Scott laughed and shook his head. "You got to take care of that back," he said. "You're taking a cab." He reached into his pocket and took out a thick roll of bills.

"I've **had a good run of luck** lately," he said, **thrusting** three ten-dollar bills into my hand. "Now, you take a taxi into town, and someday when you're coming through Kennedy again, just leave 30 bucks with any of the guys here. Tell them it's for Scotty, the crazy skycap, and it'll get back to me."

Unbelievingly, I stared at him. You see, I'd forgotten how it was.

"Something wrong, miss?" he asked. "You okay?"

"I'm okay," I replied. "It's just that I've been away five years."

He grinned and held out his great paw. "Well, welcome back, baby!"

I couldn't say another word. Scotty whistled for a cab and then disappeared into the terminal.

"Okay, lady. Where to?" The driver turned around and looked at me. A half-smoked cigar was gripped in his teeth, and a tattoo on his forearm spelled MARILYN. "I said, where to?"

I settled back on the torn plastic seat, slipped off my shoes and put my feet up on the **jump seat**.

"Home. And I do mean home."

Literal Comprehension

Complete each statement based on your understanding of the facts in the selection.

_____ 1. The author was affected by
   a) news of a family reunion.
   b) gravel on the path and a flag on the pole.
   c) the World Series score in an American newspaper.
   d) the sight of the Royal Lancaster Hotel.

_____ 2. Elise defended
   a) the American style of dress.
   b) the food and eating habits of Americans.
   c) America's policies toward foreigners.
   d) both **a)** and **b)**.

_____ 3. Mr. William Scott promptly
   a) gave the author all his money.
   b) drove the author into the city.
   c) insisted the author take a taxi.
   d) recognized that the author was homesick.

_____ 4. From the airport, the author headed directly for
   a) home.
   b) the apartment she had previously rented.
   c) the taxi stand.
   d) the nearest Sears, Roebuck Store.

_____ 5. Scotty, the crazy skycap,
   a) said he would collect the $30 shortly.
   b) has had good fortune recently.
   c) gave the author his wagon.
   d) helped the author find an apartment.

Understanding a Sequence of Ideas   33

Sequence

A. Show your understanding of the person speaking by writing YES if the statement agrees with the facts in the selection and NO if it does not.

_____ 1. The phrase "we must go home" refers to Americans living in foreign countries.

_____ 2. The taxi driver said to Elise, "Welcome back, baby!"

_____ 3. Jane stated that Americans don't know how to make decent coffee or real hamburgers.

_____ 4. Scotty insisted that Elise take a taxi.

_____ 5. The taxi driver insisted on putting Elise's luggage on the taxi line.

B. Decide if the following statements are TRUE or FALSE based on the sequence of ideas in the selection.

_____ 1. Elise had lived in London for five years before she became homesick.

_____ 2. Before Elise met Jane, she had decided to return to the United States.

_____ 3. Elise packed her belongings before lunch.

_____ 4. Elise ran on the Jersey shores and built sandcastles before she came to London.

_____ 5. Elise met the friendly taxi driver on her way to the airport in London.

Opinion and Prediction

Complete the following statements by writing the letter of the most likely answer on the line.

_____ 1. Elise Piquet will probably
   a) return the money to Scotty.
   b) return to live in New Jersey.
   c) give $30 to the taxi driver.
   d) give $30 to a stranger.

_____ 2. Jane probably believes that
   a) the British cannot prepare food as well as the Americans.
   b) all Americans will return home someday.
   c) Americans, like the British, can become homesick.
   d) Elise will return to live in England.

_____ 3. Elise will probably
   a) never leave the United States again.
   b) stay in New York for a short time before returning to live in England.
   c) commute between London and New York.
   d) make occasional trips out of the States.

_____ 4. Had she not remembered the beach and seen the flag, Elise
   a) would not have noticed the people from Iowa.
   b) would still have reacted emotionally at the table.
   c) would have immediately packed her bags the next day.
   d) would have met Scotty under other circumstances.

_____ 5. Elise probably believes that
   a) Scotty is not typical of the American character.
   b) most Americans are trusting and generous.
   c) Jane is typically anti-American in her behavior.
   d) Americans are overly emotional people.

Vocabulary

A. Place a check next to each sentence in which the underlined idiom is used correctly and an X next to each sentence in which the idiom is not used correctly.

__✓__ 1. If I have a <u>run of good luck</u>, I can immediately pay all my debts.

_____ 2. Because I <u>paid no heed</u> to the test directions, I didn't have time to finish all the questions.

__X__ 3. The newspaper showed that the supermarket had a <u>box score</u>.

_____ 4. The kitten <u>cozied up</u> to my side and purred with delight.

_____ 5. I was so <u>taken with</u> her performance that I tore up the program and angrily walked out.

B. Complete each of the following sentences to show your understanding of the underlined word.

1. _____, we used the taxi's <u>jumpseats</u>.

2. Tasting the homemade apple pie <u>triggered</u> _____.

3. In the morning, nothing is more <u>exhilarating</u> than _____.

4. _____ deflated the team's spirit.
5. My leg twitched when the doctor _____
   _____.
6. The usher discreetly asked _____
   _____.
7. _____, I closed the bulging bag.
8. The cat bristled at _____.
9. _____ or I will not listen to your incoherent talk.
10. The skycap helped us to _____
    _____.
11. Workmen placed the gravel in _____.
12. The vastness of the desert is like _____.
13. The jacket collar constricted my _____.
14. _____, I thrust out my hand to her.

Writing

Just as Elise had an experience that triggered her desire to return home, so many of you have had experiences that triggered strong emotions, such as wanting to return to your hometown or remembering a particularly sad or wonderful time in your childhood. Write about an incident you have experienced that brought on an emotional response. Use a flashback to relate the experience.

Selection 4: "Sleep Cycles"
by James V. McConnell

As you read this portion of a psychology chapter, be aware of new vocabulary that the author previews for you and of the ordering of ideas—in a sequence, in a selective way, and with signal words.

Sleep is part of your daily activity cycle, but there are several different types or stages of sleep, and they too occur in cycles.

If you are an average sleeper, your sleep cycle will go something like this:

1. When you first drift off into slumber, your eyes will roll about a bit, your temperature will drop slightly, your muscles will relax, and your breathing will slow and become quite regular. Your brain waves slow down a bit too, with the alpha rhythm predominating for the first few minutes. This is called **Stage 1 sleep.**

2. For the next half hour or so, as you relax more and more, you will drift down through **Stage 2** and **Stage 3** sleep. The lower your stage of sleep, the slower your brain waves will be.

3. Then, about 40–60 minutes after you lose consciousness, you will have reached the deepest sleep of all. Your brain waves will show the **delta rhythm**. This is **Stage 4** sleep.

4. You may think that you stay at this deep fourth stage all the rest of the night, but that turns out not to be the case. Instead, about 80 minutes after you fall into slumber, your activity cycle will increase slightly. The delta rhythm will disappear, to be replaced by the **activity pattern** of brain waves. Your eyes will begin to dart around under your closed eyelids as if you were looking at something occurring in front of you. This period of Rapid Eye Movements lasts for some 8–15 minutes and is called **REM** sleep.

During both light and deep sleep, the muscles in your body are relaxed but capable of movement. However, as you slip into **REM** sleep, a very odd thing occurs—most of the **voluntary muscles** in your body become **paralyzed**. Although your brain shows very rapid bursts of neural activity during REM sleep, your body is incapable of moving. In more technical terms—as we will see later in this chapter—we can say that REM sleep is accompanied by extensive **muscular inhibition**.

Delta rhythm. The slow waves (less than 4 cycles per second) your brain shows when you are sleeping deeply.

REM sleep. Toward the end of each 90-minute sleep cycle, the eyes move about rapidly for 8–15 minutes. It is during this period that most dreaming seems to occur.

Voluntary muscles. Any muscles over which you have conscious control, such as the ones involved in talking, walking, or writing. **Involuntary muscles** are those over which you have little or no conscious control, such as the ones invovled in keeping your heart beating, your lungs breathing, or that help your stomach digest food.

Sequence

Complete the following statements based on your understanding of the sequence of facts in the selection.

_____ 1. The lower the stage of sleep,
   a) the greater the alpha waves will be.
   b) the greater the activity pattern of the brain.
   c) the slower the brain waves will appear.
   d) the closer one is to the initial Stage 1 sleep.

_____ 2. REM sleep is characterized by
   a) a lack of body movement.
   b) a drop in temperature.
   c) the appearance of delta waves.
   d) a loss of consciousness.

_____ 3. Before one reaches deepest sleep,
   a) muscular inhibition occurs.
   b) loss of consciousness has already occurred.
   c) one's body muscles become paralyzed.
   c) one's eyes begin to move as if looking at something.

_____ 4. Muscular relaxation, a temperature drop, and breath regularity are characteristics of
   a) Stages 2 and 3 sleep.
   b) REM sleep.
   c) delta rhythms.
   d) Stage 1 sleep.

_____ 5. An increase in the activity cycle indicates
   a) one is waking up.
   b) the beginning of the Rapid Eye Movement stage.
   c) a relaxing of body muscles.
   d) an increase in the body's delta rhythm.

Predictions

Complete the following statements based on facts in the selection.

_____ 1. Tonight, you will probably dream during
   a) Stage 4 sleep.
   b) Stage 1 sleep.
   c) REM sleep.
   d) Stages 2 and 3 sleep.

_____ 2. The average person will probably experience
   a) one sleep cycle tonight.
   b) muscular inhibition during Stage 1 sleep tonight.
   c) several sleep cycles tonight.
   d) no sleep cycles.

Vocabulary

If the underlined word is used correctly, place a check on the line.

_____ 1. I was so excited about getting the job that I went into a deep <u>slumber</u>.

_____ 2. My <u>delta rhythm</u> was most active during the ten-minute break between classes.

_____ 3. During <u>REM</u>, we vacationed for a week at the seashore.

_____ 4. <u>Voluntary</u> muscles are controlled muscles.

_____ 5. During sleep, <u>muscular inhibition</u> causes body paralysis.

Writing

Imagine that you have the ability to watch yourself sleep this evening. Briefly trace the pattern of sleep you will follow. Remember to select the key facts and to present them in a chronological sequence.

Role-Playing

Consider the following story in which a student is faced with a difficult situation that he must resolve. The activities that follow provide practice in speaking and in writing a narrative.

The Situation

Jose is a student at a college in an urban area. During his first two semesters he did very well, and at the beginning of the third semester, he was admitted to a special pre-med program. If he completes the program successfully, he will be guaranteed admission to a good medical school. He will be able to study to become a doctor.

Jose lives at home with his mother, father, two younger brothers, and a sister. His mother and father both have full-time jobs, and Jose works part time in a restaurant to help with the family finances. Several weeks ago Jose's mother began feeling sharp chest pains. When she went to a doctor, he told her that she would need heart surgery and would have to give up her job for at least one year.

Faced with large medical expenses and the loss of almost half the family's income for the next year, Jose's father wants him to drop out of school and go to work full time to help the family. Jose loves his family very much and knows the sacrifices that they've made for his education, but, if he drops out now, he will lose an entire semester's credit, and may even lose his place in the pre-med program. He doesn't know what to do. He speaks to his fiancée, Maria, who urges him to remain in school, since to withdraw now will place his entire future in danger. He also speaks to his cousin, Carlos, who tells him that his first duty is to help his family get through the difficult times ahead.

What should Jose do?

Directions

Choose students to play the roles of Jose, Maria, Carlos, and Jose's parents. The rest of the class will be divided into two groups of coaches, one to advise Maria, and one to advise Carlos. They must provide Maria and Carlos with arguments to use in the upcoming family discussion. After they are finished, the students playing the five main characters can step out of the classroom for a few minutes to plan how they will act out their roles. As soon as they return, the role-playing begins. It ends when Jose reaches a decision. Afterwards, the entire class can question Jose on his decision, or they can participate in a general discussion: Did Jose make the right decision? Why or why not?

Topics for Discussion and Writing

1. Have you or any of your friends ever faced a similar problem? Write a first-person narrative telling how you reached your decision.

2. How do you react when you are faced with an important problem? Using an example from your experience, describe the steps you usually take in order to come to a decision.

3. A year passes. Jose and Carlos meet on the street one evening. How have things turned out for Jose and his family? Complete this dialogue in which they discuss the events that have taken place since the time when Jose made his decision. Follow this form:

   Jose: Hello, Carlos! I haven't seen you for years.
   Carlos: Jose, I almost didn't recognize you. What's new?

4. Consider what happened during the role-playing exercise in class. Briefly write about what took place during the activity. Remember to follow a chronological order of events.

CHAPTER 2
Understanding a Descriptive Listing

Why is reading a book frequently more satisfying than seeing a movie version of the same story? When one considers some of the reader's tasks such as following a chronological order of events and visualizing characters, settings, and situations, reading a book seems a difficult task. A viewer of a movie has less to do: one must follow a sequence of events, but has no need to create a mental picture of characters or setting; these have been created on the screen. Perhaps actively working to create images provides greater involvement and satisfaction than passively viewing images on a screen.

Recognizing Listing in Descriptive Writing

When you read narrative writing you focus on the chronological order of events. Consider the following example to see how the author treats two similar topics, first descriptively and then narratively.

Example

Paragraph A

We entered the house and viewed our new living space. We looked into the parlor which held only an antique sofa and a beautiful grand piano in front of a bay window. In the kitchen we saw an old black coal stove, an old-fashioned icebox with two doors, and a table with three broken legs. We walked slowly into the living room. There we examined the worn red-flowered carpet. Indeed, the old house was in need of new furnishings.

Paragraph B

We entered the house through the front door. After moving through the hall toward the stairs, we climbed to the bedroom. There we quickly unpacked and dressed for an afternoon swim in the lake. Next, we went to the boat dock where we spent a relaxing afternoon sunning ourselves. Finally, we had a delicious barbecue on the lawn.

41

Questions

1. In which paragraph is the sequence of events important? _____
2. In which paragraph is a listing of characteristics presented? _____
3. In which paragraph could the author rearrange the ideas and still maintain the logical order of facts? _____

In narrative writing, the author emphasizes a chronological ordering of events or ideas. In descriptive writing, the author "draws a picture" for the reader by describing the characteristics, traits, or qualities of a subject.

> Understanding a **descriptive passage** requires that you recognize how the author builds a description by listing the characteristics of the subject, that is, the people, places, situations or events, and ideas. Recognizing these characteristics helps you build a solid base of literal comprehension.

Identifying Listed Characteristics

Understanding descriptive writing relies on your ability to identify and visualize those details the author uses to describe a character, situation, or idea. When you understand them you can create an image or picture of what the author is describing. Consider the following example to see how the author uses concrete descriptive words and phrases to create a visual image.

Example

A. It is not a good morning.

B. It is a very nasty morning.

C. The morning sky is filled with threatening dark clouds and sheets of rain are beating against my window.

Questions

1. Which sentence describes the morning in a way that best helps you to visualize it? _____

2. Write the words and phrases that help you to visualize the morning:

   _____

   _____

> Understanding descriptive writing requires that you focus on how the author uses **concrete details** to characterize a subject. Identifying and understanding those concrete or highly descriptive details enables you to visualize what the author is describing.

Practice

In each group, highlight the five words that best describe the underlined phrase. There are many possible choices.

1. <u>rock music</u>
   - marching
   - melodic
   - loud
   - notes
   - sour
   - rhythmic
   - soulful
   - awful
   - heavy
   - tuneful

2. <u>evening meal</u>
   - joyous
   - spicy
   - delicious
   - creative
   - filling
   - exotic
   - overcooked
   - nice
   - early
   - tasteless

3. <u>dating</u>
   - loving
   - closeness
   - social
   - good
   - walking
   - intense
   - two
   - angry
   - expensive
   - passionate

4. <u>school</u>
   - tall buildings
   - small classes
   - difficult subjects
   - exciting teachers
   - learning
   - challenging work
   - dull
   - friendly students
   - travel for hours
   - interesting

Practice

For each of the following, list four details that will help create an image. You may use a dictionary or thesaurus to help.

1. a fat person: _obese_, _____, _____, _____
2. good health: _____, _____, _____, _____
3. freedom: _____, _____, _____, _____
4. a good job: _____, _____, _____, _____
5. war: _____, _____, _____, _____
6. the president: _____, _____, _____, _____
7. family: _____, _____, _____, _____
8. a vacation: _____, _____, _____, _____
9. education: _____, _____, _____, _____
10. children: _____, _____, _____, _____

Practice

Imagine that you are considering a career. For each career listed, name four details that best describe an applicant's qualifications.

1. typist: _____, _____, _____, _____
2. nurse: _____, _____, _____, _____
3. salesperson: _____, _____, _____, _____
4. chauffeur: _____, _____, _____, _____
5. construction worker: _____, _____, _____, _____
6. teacher: _____, _____, _____, _____
7. accountant: _____, _____, _____, _____
8. scientist: _____, _____, _____, _____
9. dancer: _____, _____, _____, _____
10. artist: _____, _____, _____, _____

Recognizing Listing Signals

Authors usually signal a listing of details. Read the following example and note the words that draw your attention to the listed details.

Example

Although I have frequently complained to the new management company about the unsatisfactory building conditions, I continue to see numerous signs of disrepair in our public areas. For example, there are several things wrong with the hallways. The carpets and once-shiny wallpaper are worn, and pieces of plaster are falling from the ceiling. In addition, the overhead lighting is dim and five or six of the light fixtures are broken. Also, the daily garbage remains unremoved. Finally, the marble front entranceway has broken pavement.

Questions

1. What words and phrases signal the listing of details describing the building? _____

2. How many details are provided about the hall and entranceway? ____

Authors use words and phrases to **signal a listing of details** about people, places, situations, and ideas. Recognizing those signals helps you to notice the important facts in descriptive passages. Authors frequently use words and phrases such as "first," "next," "last," "also," "in addition," "too," "several," "moreover," and "many" to signal a listing of characteristics.

Practice

Use the following signal words correctly in the paragraph.

1. **next   first   many   also**

There are _____ unforeseen benefits to taking only twelve credits this fall semester. _____, I have five or six extra hours for my studies and family chores, such as cleaning my room and cooking dinner. _____, I can add extracurricular activities such as basketball to my schedule. I can _____ work at the local supermarket on a part-time basis.

2. **in addition   finally   many   first   too**

Everyone admired the _____ fine features of the newly decorated room. _____, we noticed the large rounded gray velvet sofa, the room's centerpiece. _____, we examined the heavy gray and burgundy curtains that had the same floral design as the corner chairs. The oil paintings, _____, complemented the softly toned room. _____, the quiet gray and violet pictures and rug of the same colors unified the entire room.

3. **here are some of   besides   in addition to**
    several   finally   also   furthermore

_____ financial considerations such as rent and real estate taxes, there are _____ reasons why young and even older people choose a particular place to live. _____ the reasons why we decided to settle in this small rural town we now call home. _____ finding the town's setting against a small mountain chain attractive, we _____ realized that the Main Street area had food, clothing, and houseware stores to satisfy our every imaginable need. _____, I was offered a high-paying job at the local home and factory construction company. _____, the public schools appeared to be excellent, and we knew that our three children would quickly establish new friendships with healthy and happy youngsters who seemed to play gaily on every corner.

Following Directions

Recognizing that authors use words and phrases to signal a listing of characteristics can help you to understand the ways ideas are developed in essays, articles, and stories. Read the following example to see how understanding such signal words and phrases can help in class and test situations.

Example

1. Name five qualities a good teacher has.
2. Describe the qualities that make your school a good or bad place to learn.

Questions

1. For which question should you write a list? _____
2. What word signals that a list is required? _____
3. For which question should you write a list of characteristics in paragraph form? _____
4. What word signals that a paragraph is required? _____
5. Does either question ask that you follow a sequential order? _____

When you are aware that instructors use words and phrases that signal listing in a required task, you can follow directions and complete assignments appropriately.

Authors use words and phrases that signal a listing, such as "list" and "name." They use other words and phrases such as "describe," "discuss," and "explain" to indicate that you should develop a listing of details in paragraph form. Recognizing these signal words and phrases can help you to complete an assignment according to the instructor's directions.

Practice

List five objects found in a room in your home. Then, next to each item, state two specific details about each. Finally, in the space provided, use the information to discuss the room briefly.

The Objects *Specific Characteristics of the Object*

1. _____ a) _____
   b) _____
2. _____ a) _____
   b) _____
3. _____ a) _____
   b) _____
4. _____ a) _____
   b) _____
5. _____ a) _____
   b) _____

There are many interesting features in my _____ (name the room).

_____
_____
_____
_____
_____
_____
_____
_____
_____
_____

Practice

Imagine that your have come upon an auto accident and must describe the scene. Complete the list provided. Then, using the information in the list, briefly describe the scene.

The Scene   *Details*
1. Car number 1   a) _____
                     b) _____
2. Car number 2   a) _____
                     b) _____
3. Driver number 1   a) _____
                     b) _____
4. Driver number 2   a) _____
                     b) _____
5. The telephone pole a) _____
                     b) _____

<u>Shortly before noon, I was on my way to lunch when I came upon the scene of an auto accident.</u>

_____
_____
_____
_____
_____
_____
_____
_____
_____
_____
_____

Identifying Descriptions of Quality, Space, and Sequence

Read the following paragraphs to see how the author describes people, settings, and situations.

Example

Paragraph A

My next door neighbor, a selfish woman, has little regard for anyone's privacy. She carefully watches friends, neighbors, and relatives who arrive at our door, and, at the first opportunity, rushes over to question rudely who they are and what they want at our house. She also stops by at times like breakfast and lunch for cups of coffee. During these visits she asks endless personal questions about my parents and my homelife. In addition, she relates confidences told her by others. She is a pest and a busybody.

Paragraph B

The most peaceful place in my house is the small, tree-shaded backyard. Although it is small in size, it provides many areas of space and privacy for our family. To the right is a large shade tree. Two chairs stretch out beneath it; they are perfect for my elderly parents when they need to relax. Farther back is another large tree and a wading pool for my sister. To the left is yet another large tree from which hangs an old rubber tire that is wonderful to swing on. Thus, everyone has a special, very private place in our yard.

Paragraphs C

Type lots of letters? Term papers? Manuscripts? If so, a computer (with a printer and a word-processing program) can make editing and correcting marvelously simple. The operator types in sentences and paragraphs, and the material appears on the video-display screen. If a typing error occurs, the operator moves a video cursor—a tiny square of light—to the offending letter or word and types in the correction. With the same dispatch, passages can be deleted, new material introduced, paragraphs rearranged. And material that is unaltered does *not* have to be retyped.

When the editing process is over, the operator presses a key or two, and the printer starts tapping out the entire corrected document. Alternatively, the material can be stored in the memory bank, to be retrieved later (Ross, 186).

Questions

1. List the neighbor's characteristics described in Paragraph A:

   _____   _____

   _____   _____

   _____   _____

   _____   _____

2. List the characteristics of the backyard described in Paragraph B:

_____   _____

_____   _____

_____   _____

_____   _____

_____

3. List the characteristics of the computer processing technique described in Paragraphs C:

_____   _____

_____   _____

_____   _____

_____   _____

_____   _____

Authors use a variety of techniques when they write descriptively. With people, objects, or ideas, they describe a representative part or parts of the whole; with settings, they describe the scene spatially, usually moving in a logical direction around the area relating parts to one another; with a situation, they describe the circumstances at each stage.

> Recognizing that authors describe persons, objects, and ideas by listing their characteristic qualities, settings by listing their spatial characteristics, and situations by listing their stages strengthens your comprehension of literal ideas in descriptive and other kinds of writing.

Practice

Read the following paragraphs and answer the questions based on the descriptions of people, settings, and situations.

Paragraph A

Not only are we Americans healthier than ever before, we are also far more health-conscious. The media bombard us with the latest medical breakthroughs, and books on diet and exercise climb the best seller lists. Jogging has become virtually a national mania; social conversations center on fitness, and we spend our money on sports clothes and equipment. As concerned citizens, we lobby our governments about such public health issues as radiation, pollution, pesticides, and toxic wastes (STEINMANN, 3–4).

Answer these questions TRUE (T) or FALSE (F).

_____ 1. Because of poor health, Americans are more health-conscious than ever before.

_____ 2. Americans focus attention on staying fit, reading about health-related issues, and being aware of medical advances.

_____ 3. Americans spend all their money on lobbying efforts.

_____ 4. Americans lobby their congressmen about physical fitness programs.

_____ 5. Americans love to jog, exercise, and diet.

Paragraph B

Most of the modern supermarkets, by the mid-fifties, were laid out in a carefully calculated manner so that the high-profit impulse items would be most surely noticed. In many stores they were on the first or only aisle the shopper could enter. Among the best tempters, apparently, are those items in glass jars where the contents can be seen, or where the food is actually out in the open, to be savored and seen. Offering free pickles and cubes of cheese on toothpicks has proved to be reliable as a sales booster. An Indiana supermarket operator nationally recognized for his advanced psychological techniques told me he once sold a half ton of cheese in a few hours, just by getting an enormous half-ton wheel of cheese and inviting customers to nibble slivers and cut off their own chunks for purchase. They could have their chunk free if they could guess its weight within an ounce. The mere massiveness of the cheese, he believes, was a powerful influence in making the sales. "People like to see a lot of merchandise," he explained. "When there are only three or four cans of an item on a shelf, they just won't move." People don't want the last package. A test by *The Progressive Grocer* showed that customers buy 22 per cent more if the shelves are kept full. The urge to conformity, it seems, is profound with many of us (PACKARD).

List four ways that designers of supermarkets have structured the setting to encourage shoppers to buy items.

1. _____

2. _____

3. _____

4. _____

Paragraph C

In a criminal trial, the complainant is always "The People of the State," and the person accused of committing the crime is the defendant. The People, who are represented by the District Attorney, make an opening statement which is not considered as evidence. The People offer evidence in support of the accusation against the defendant, and its witnesses are called first. After all witnesses are called, The People may offer further evidence before summing up. The People must prove the charges against the defendant beyond a reasonable doubt.

Answer the statements TRUE (T) or FALSE (F).

_____ 1. The person accused of committing the crime is called The People.

_____ 2. The defendant must prove innocence beyond a reasonable doubt.

_____ 3. The District Attorney's opening remarks are not offered as evidence.

_____ 4. The State brings charges of a crime in a criminal trial.

_____ 5. The District Attorney represents the defendant.

Applying Fact/Opinion and Point-of-view Skills to Descriptions

A fact can be proven or disproven with direct evidence. An opinion, though it may be correct, expresses an author's point of view and cannot be proven. Consider the following to see how descriptions can include both facts and opinions.

Example

Questions

1. List four details about this person shown in the picture:

   _____   _____

   _____   _____

2. Describe this type of worker: _____

3. Was your answer to Question 1 based on fact or opinion? _____

4. Was your answer to Question 2 based on fact or opinion? _____

> Recognizing that an author uses **facts and opinions** to describe people, settings, situations, and ideas can help you to determine the **author's point of view** about the subject of a selection.

Practice

Read the following descriptive paragraph and complete the exercise that follows. Decide whether each statement taken from the passage is a FACT or an expression of the author's VIEWPOINT.

   Nevertheless, "teen-agers" do have money, about ten billion dollars a year of it, though this comes to only about ten dollars a week as an average. They scrounge it from home or earn it at odd times, and this, too, contributes to their colonial status. The "teen-age" market is big business. We all share an economic interest in the dependency of the "teen-ager." The school is interested in keeping him off the streets and in its custody. Labor is interested in keeping him off the labor market. Business and industry are interested in seeing that his tastes become fads and in selling him specialized junk that a more mature taste would reject. Like a dependent native, the "teen-ager" is encouraged to be economically irresponsible because his sources of income are undependable and do not derive from his personal qualities. He can be very responsible in buying things that are closely related to his real skills and interests and his evolving sense of himself: sporting equipment, used cars, the things that mean something to him. But he cannot easily work out an entirely personal and responsible pattern of economic behavior because he has no serious economic status; he is treated like a plantation worker whose benevolent master allows him a few dollars to take into town on Saturday afternoon, though they both know he will only spend it foolishly (FRIEDENBERG, 7).

_____ 1. Teen-agers have money.

_____ 2. We all share an economic interest in the dependency of the teen-ager.

_____ 3. The school is interested in keeping teen-agers off the streets.

_____ 4. Teen-agers have about ten billion dollars a year.

_____ 5. The teen-ager is like a dependent native.

Practice

Read the description of the surface of the moon given by Neil Armstrong, the American astronaut. If the statements that follow it can be directly proven with evidence, label them FACTS. If they express the author's point of view, label them OPINIONS.

> *HOUSTON* (Duke): Roger, Tranquility. We copy. Over.
> *EAGLE* (Armstrong): Out of the window is a relatively level plain created with a fairly large number of craters of the five to fifty-foot variety and some ridges, small, twenty or thirty feet high, I would guess, and literally thousands of little one and two-foot craters around the area. We see some angular blocks out several hundred feet in front of us that are probably two feet in size. . . . There is a hill in view, just about on the ground track ahead of us, difficult to estimate but might be half a mile or a mile (ARMSTRONG, 294).

_____ 1. The plain is relatively level.
_____ 2. Armstrong is looking out of the window.
_____ 3. The blocks are several hundred feet away.
_____ 4. There is a fairly large number of craters.
_____ 5. The ridges are about twenty to thirty feet high.
_____ 6. There are craters on the plain.
_____ 7. There are probably thousands of small craters.
_____ 8. Armstrong can see the hill.
_____ 9. The hill might be a half mile away.
_____ 10. There is a plain outside the window.

Making Generalizations and Assumptions

Once you understand descriptions of people, settings, situations, and ideas, you know literally what the author has written and you can answer factual questions based on these descriptions. There are deeper understandings that you can draw from descriptive and other styles of writing. Consider this paragraph to see how you can assume certain ideas that the author did not directly state, but intended you to know.

Understanding a Descriptive Listing   57

Example

Once again, immigration authorities waiting at a specified area at the United States border have captured seventy aliens attempting to cross the border illegally. Each had paid $500 for transportation; each had been promised a job, housing, and working papers. Authorities stated that the seventy were crowded into three vans driven by other aliens. The group suffered from overcrowding, lack of food and water, and exhaustion. The agents added that there was no evidence of the promised jobs, housing, or working papers. The chief operators were merely interested in the $500 per head they had collected, their usual fee for these illegal trips. This time, the group never made it.

Question

List the conditions experienced by the aliens.

_____

_____

_____

_____

_____

_____

_____

The factual description of the people and their condition serves as a basis for further understandings. Consider these questions:

1. Can you assume that the operators intended to keep their promise of jobs, housing, and working papers? _____
2. Can you assume that this was the only group captured in this way? __
3. Can you generalize and say that most immigrants arrive in the United States in this manner? _____
4. Can you assume that this is an isolated incident? _____
5. Can you assume that all illegal aliens are captured at the border? ___
6. Do you think the operators of the scheme are captured or do they continue their illegal activities? _____

Based on the written descriptions of the people, settings, and circumstances, you can draw additional understandings from the passage. Understanding the literal ideas can help you to sense further ideas about the reading.

> Recognizing that you can draw ideas beyond what has been directly stated broadens your understanding of a selection. Making **logical assumptions** about the characters, settings, and situations helps you to understand essays, articles, stories, and text passages in a variety of writing styles.

Practice

Carefully consider the stated descriptions in the following paragraph. Check those assumptions that you can draw logically from the stated facts.

> Just as primitive people dressed up and gave rituals for entertainment and to please the gods, so do we in a variety of ways. One way is when we participate in parades. We also dress up to attend church services, which follow a pattern or ritual. We belong to organizations that have badges and uniforms and observe handshakes, passwords, and patterns of progression for advancement. In addition, at football games, fans wear the team's colors. There is the singing of the national anthem, the introduction of the players on each side, and a band show at halftime. Thus, these rituals are loosely structured, but they usually follow a set pattern (CASSADY, 10).

_____ 1. Most organizations have secret handshakes.

_____ 2. People expect to follow rituals in church.

_____ 3. Advancement in a business organization probably follows an unstructured pattern.

_____ 4. Primitive people had rituals that probably followed a set pattern.

_____ 5. Fans at a ballgame expect to see some form of ritual entertainment.

Practice

The following portion of a movie synopsis describes the main character. Based on your understanding of that description, answer the following statements YES if they are logical and NO if they are not.

Understanding a Descriptive Listing 59

 The central character is Tooney, an itinerant peddler, skilled gambler, and master gunfighter. He is blind, yet gifted with unusual perceptive powers. Tooney manages to confuse his opponents by resorting to his superhuman abilities. He can shoot a coin thrown up into the air by listening to its turning. He can feel the color and value of poker chips. He is even able to locate a delicate cactus blossom surrounded by thorns from its aroma.

 Accompanied by his faithful mule, Susie, Tooney becomes involved in the town struggles. Singlehandedly, he wipes out the hired killers through his unorthodox gunplay and unconventional fighting techniques, which constantly astound bystanders. Continuing his journey westward, Tooney fearlessly moves on with the satisfaction of knowing that the town is out of peril (CHAZIN).

_____ 1. Susie has been with Tooney for many years.

_____ 2. This is Tooney's first attempt at helping those in trouble.

_____ 3. Tooney will probably meet others who are faced with troubles.

_____ 4. Most unsighted people develop Tooney's abilities.

_____ 5. Tooney uses his clever mind to overcome the outlaws.

_____ 6. Tooney has probably been sightless for many years.

_____ 7. Before this story begins, Tooney has just learned to play poker.

_____ 8. Tooney probably asks for help in fighting the outlaws.

_____ 9. Tooney comes to town looking for a fight.

_____ 10. In years to come, Tooney will be a legend in the West.

Applying Descriptive Listing Skills in Selections

You now have the opportunity of applying comprehension skills in longer selections. Familiarize yourself with the vocabulary that is previewed for each selection. As you read, be aware of the listing of characteristics, the words that help you visualize the descriptions, the use of words that signal a listing, and the use of facts and opinions. Each selection is followed by questions that focus on the skills of understanding vocabulary, stated facts, lists of descriptions, the author's point of view, and assumptions. Finally, you will practice using these skills as you complete a writing assignment.

Selection 1: "Spending a Few Days With the Kid that You Once Were"
by Bob Greene

Vocabulary Preview

The following terms appear in the reading. Knowing their meanings will help you to understand the selection.

Idioms	Meanings
a touch	a decoration that adds a personal feeling
for the better part of	for most of the time
get the urge	suddenly want something very much
have the run of	be allowed to use everything
runs up	goes from bottom to top
turned loose	allowed to go about by oneself

Vocabulary	Meanings
banister	a hand rail on the staircase
cranny	a small opening (space) in a wall
exhilarating	stimulating
imposing	impressive in size
inherently	existing within; as a quality
jarring	shocking
lavish	extravagant; expensive
moving	touching the emotions
refurbish	renovate; remodel or refurnish
remote	at a far distance
stoop	the front steps of a home

BEXLEY, Ohio—Of all the places I have dreamed of visiting, I have been lucky enough to visit most. And yet the place that had been most on my mind always seemed an impossible destination. Not because it is **remote**; it is not that far a journey to central Ohio. Not because it is expensive, either; money was not even a factor.

But it remained unlikely, because people just don't do things like this. What I wanted to do was go back to the house in which I grew up; not just look at it from a car driving by, but spend time there, visit it, remember it as it was. Several families have lived there since my own family moved away; often I had thought about what would happen if I just showed up unannounced some day, but I always rejected that as fantasy.

This time, though, I did it. I didn't have the nerve to simply knock on the door. But I found out the names of the people who now live in the house—Stanley and Elaine Shayne and their children—and I wrote them a letter asking if they'd mind. The Shayne family couldn't have been more understanding; they let me know that it was OK for me to be there (they even put a "Welcome Home" sign on the big tree in the front yard), and **for the better part of** three days, I lived at 2722 Bryden Road again.

It was **jarring**, **moving**, weird. Think about what it would be like if you were **turned loose** in the house where you grew up. You would find that it had been redecorated several times as families had moved in and out; you would find strangers living in the rooms you always associated with your parents and brothers and sisters. Everything would be different, yet everything would be the same. One moment you would feel a thousand miles away, the next you would feel as if you had never left. It would be confusing and **exhilarating** and happy and sad, all at the same time.

My visit was all of those things. I found myself climbing the front stairs countless times, looking into bedrooms, sitting on the front **stoop** waiting for the paperboy to arrive. The Shaynes got used to me soon enough; they had their meals, and talked in the living room or the backyard, and just allowed me to **have the run of** the place.

I went to my old room, and the boy who lives there now was lying on his bed listening to music. What a feeling. That might have been me in there when I was his age, but now I was standing in the doorway, an observer, almost afraid to step inside.

In the upstairs hallway was a little **cranny** built into the wall to hold a telephone. I had forgotten about it completely, but seeing it again took me back to all the nights I had pulled the cord into my own room and locked the door for privacy. And sure enough, on this evening the phone had been pulled away, and was locked in one of the children's bedrooms.

The interior of the house looked completely different, but every few minutes I would come across **a touch** that almost made me shiver. The front door, for example; it had been painted and refinished, but when I went to open it, the knob and latch felt so familiar in my hand; I looked at them, and although I hadn't thought about them in years, I knew immediately that they were the same ones.

And the wooden **banister** that **runs up** the stairway and then curves around next to the bedrooms—as I walked I found myself letting my hand glide across the top of it, and I realized that this was a habit I had ever since I was a child. Everywhere I turned there was something like that; the bathrooms had been **refurbished** and decorated, but in the children's bathroom the old-fashioned heater was still built into the wall beneath the window; you wouldn't imagine that something like that would affect you, but believe me, it does.

The house seemed very small to me. Which is inevitable, I guess; when you are growing up, your house is your whole world, and once your world becomes the real world itself, one building can never seem quite so **imposing** again. As I stood at the top of the stairs I realized that, of course, there was nothing **inherently** romantic in this structure; it was just one house on one block in one small city.

Still, when the three days were over, I had a feeling of satisfaction that is hard to describe. I hope, someday, the people in the Shayne family will look back on their years at 2722 Bryden Road with the same warmth and joy that I do; and I hope, if they ever **get the urge** to come back, they won't be too shy to ask, and that the people who live there in that future summer will not be too protective of their privacy to say yes.

Because I can promise them this: It may not be the most **lavish** vacation they will ever spend, but it will surely be one of the best.

Literal Comprehension

Fill in the blanks with facts from the selection.

1. The young boy was lying on a bed in Bob Greene's _____.
2. The _____ of the house looked completely different to Bob.
3. Bob vacationed in _____.
4. The author wrote _____ to ask permission to visit.
5. Bob experienced _____ and _____ feelings when he returned home.

Descriptions

Complete each statement based on your understanding of the descriptions in the selection.

_____ 1. The Shayne family is characterized as being
   a) too protective of its privacy.
   b) extremely understanding.
   c) filled with the joy of new discoveries.
   d) too shy to return to their home.

_____ 2. All of the following describe Bob Greene's reactions except
   a) satisfaction.
   b) confusion.
   c) happiness.
   d) fear.

_____ 3. The house can be characterized by all of the following except
   a) the same basic features from the author's youth.
   b) the redecorated, yet familiar rooms.
   c) an imposing size.
   d) places where one can be alone.

_____ 4. A new feature of the house is
   a) the heater in the children's bathroom.
   b) doorknobs, latches, and a wooden banister.
   c) a cranny built into the upstairs wall.
   d) redecorated bathroom furnishings.

_____ 5. The house has
   a) been occupied only by the Greene and Shayne families.
   b) changed in size.
   c) lost the imposing quality it once had.
   d) had a welcome sign in the yard for years.

Point of View

Complete each statement based on facts in the selection.

_____ 1. Bob Green writes this story to
   a) revisit his childhood home.
   b) describe a moving experience.
   c) show how much has changed in his hometown.
   d) share the Shayne's unusual experiences.

_____ 2. The author feels that the Shayne family is
   a) warm and sharing.
   b) very different from his own family.
   c) inherently romantic.
   d) very private about their lives.

_____ 3. The statement that best expresses the author's attitude about his experience is:
   a) One can never recapture the memories of youth.
   b) Seeing the changes in one's childhood home brings a longing to stay there.
   c) Returning to one's childhood home carries with it mixed emotions.
   d) It is difficult to recapture one's childhood emotions during a short visit home.

_____ 4. The author believes that
   a) places may change yet maintain a familiar spirit.
   b) one should never see strangers living in one's childhood home.
   c) as things age, they lose their original spirit.
   d) changes in a house spoil its charm.

_____ 5. The author believes that
   a) families need to protect their privacy.
   b) compared with youth of years ago, today's teenagers experience different home environments.
   c) one's childhood home represents a very small portion of one's world.
   d) strangers can often show great understanding.

Assumptions

Based on your understanding of the facts, check those assumptions that can be logically drawn from the selection.

_____ 1. Most people never return to their childhood homes.

_____ 2. Bob Greene knew the Shayne family before he wrote to them.

_____ 3. Children consider their homes to be a large part of their world.

_____ 4. Bob Greene had not returned home before this trip.

_____ 5. Bob Greene knew how he would react before he made the trip.

Vocabulary

A. Complete each of the following sentences with the correct idiom.

| for the better part of | have the run of | a touch |
| runs up | get the urge | turned loose |

1. When I checked into the hotel, I decided to add _____ to the plain room by arranging my books and personal belongings on the tables.

2. Whenever I _____ for something sweet, I buy a chocolate bar.

3. _____ the exam, I wrote about the philosophers I studied this term.

4. Have you noticed the lovely ivy that _____ the sides of the library?

5. As a visitor, I asked if I could _____ the library for the day.

6. The children were taken to the park and _____ for the afternoon.

B. Based on your understanding of the vocabulary, place a check next to those sentences in which the underlined word is used correctly.

_____ 1. Hold the <u>banister</u> as you go down to the cellar.

_____ 2. I was so <u>exhilarated</u> after my morning run that I cried for ten minutes.

_____ 3. The strawberry preserves were <u>jarring</u> all day.

_____ 4. The director exceeded his budget when he gave a <u>lavish</u> party for the board members.

_____ 5. Listening to the soprano's beautiful interpretation of the song was a <u>moving</u> experience.

_____ 6. My <u>refurbished</u> kitchen needs new appliances.

_____ 7. If you can't find the keys immediately, search every <u>cranny</u> till you do.

_____ 8. The best place to play <u>stoop</u> ball is in a neighbor's field.

_____ 9. A person's <u>inherent</u> qualities are usually learned in his or her pre-teenage years.

_____ 10. The Grand Canyon is an <u>imposing</u> sight for any visitor.

_____ 11. Unmanned spaceships now travel to <u>remote</u> portions of the solar system.

Writing

Bob Greene described his childhood home in a way that enables the reader to visualize what he saw and felt at the moment. Select a room in your house and write about it in a way so that a reader can visualize what you see and can understand the feelings you have about it. Be sure to use descriptive words and phrases as you present your point of view.

Selection 2: "Prohibition: The 'Noble Experiment' That Failed"
by Steven Jantzen

Vocabulary Preview

The following terms appear in the reading. Knowing their meanings will help you to understand the selection.

Idiom	Meaning
running risks	taking chances

Vocabulary	Meanings
ban	forbid by law
brewery	a factory that produces malt liquors
crudely	improperly; lacking proper development
dismal	disastrous
hootch	liquor made and distributed illegally
ratify	approve formally
repeal	cancel a law by voting to end it
ruinous	destructive
stuff	any goods or products
vile	sickening

Thousands of products have been **banned** because government officials judged them to be "dangerous to your health." Because of these protective laws, you can't buy certain drugs and foods, chemicals and insecticides.

The question is: Do we need laws that prevent us from **running risks** with our lives? If so, then perhaps laws are needed prohibiting the sale of cigarettes and alcoholic drinks. Both products have been known to kill people. The hazards of drinking too much alcohol are as bad or worse than the hazards of smoking too many cigarettes. All right then, let's pass a law closing the liquor stores, the bars, and the **breweries** in this country. Let's put an end once and for all to the **ruinous** disease from which as many as 10 million Americans currently suffer—alcoholism.

But wait. We've already tried that. For 13 years, between 1920 and 1933, there were no liquor stores anywhere in the United States. They were shut down—abolished by an amendment to the Constitution (the 18th) and by a law of Congress (the Volstead Act). After January 20, 1920, there was supposed to be no more manufacturing, selling, or transporting of "intoxicating liquors." Without any more liquor, people could not drink it. And if they did not drink it, how could they get drunk? There would be no more dangers to the public welfare from drunkenness and alcoholism. It was all very logical. And yet prohibition of liquor, beer, and wine did not work. Why?

Because, law or no law, millions of people still liked to drink alcohol. And they were willing to take risks to get it. They were not about to change their tastes and habits just because of a change in the law. And gangs of bootleggers (liquor smugglers) made it easy to buy an illegal drink—or two or three. They smuggled millions of gallons of the outlawed beverages across the Canadian and Mexican borders. They hid the **stuff** under the seats of cars, in hot-water bottles, in the trunks of Christmas trees, and in large blocks of ice.

Drinkers were lucky to know of an illegal bar ("speakeasy") that served Mexican or Canadian liquor. In those bars, there was little danger of being crippled and blinded. But if you drank alcohol **crudely** distilled in a gangster's garage, you could be paralyzed or even killed.

Under the prohibition law, paint and chemical industries were permitted to make a poisonous kind of alcohol—denatured or wood alcohol—for their products. Gangsters quickly invented clever schemes for illegally obtaining millions of gallons of industrial alcohol. They added flavoring to the alcohol and removed most of the poisonous chemicals from it. But deadly doses of the poison sometimes remained in the bootlegger's "**hootch**." Anyone who unsuspectingly drank this **vile** stuff would become nauseous. His skin would turn bluish and cold. He would lose control of his muscles and maybe go blind. If he had drunk enough, he would die.

President Herbert Hoover once spoke of prohibition as a "noble experiment." The experiment may have been noble in purpose, but in practice it was a **dismal** failure. Crime and drunkenness were both supposed to decline as a result of prohibition. Instead people drank more alcohol than ever—often poisoned alcohol.

On December 5, 1933, they **repealed** prohibition by **ratifying** the 21st Amendment to the Constitution.

But that was just one experiment. And it was tried a long time ago. Does the failure of one experiment mean that all experiments like it will fail?

In a democratic society, citizens decide what kinds of laws they want and need. If a law does not work, they are free to change or repeal it.

Here is a list of products that are potentially dangerous to the consumer. Should people under 18 be free to buy them? Should an adult be free to buy them?

1. Cigarettes
2. Liquor
3. Beer and wine
4. Marijuana
5. Handguns
6. Cars without seat belts
7. Saccharine (artificial sugar that may induce cancer)

Literal Comprehension

Check the following statements that reflect information in the selection.

_____ 1. Laws have been passed that ban the sale of alcoholic beverages, cigarettes, and handguns.

_____ 2. People liked to drink and defeated Prohibition.

_____ 3. The liquor sold in speakeasies could kill or paralyze.

_____ 4. Hootch caused many deaths during the Prohibition Era.

_____ 5. President Hoover praised the success of Prohibition.

Descriptions

Complete the following statements based on descriptions in the selection.

_____ 1. Which of the following was not a characteristic reason for the proposal of the 18th Amendment to the Constitution and the Volstead Act?
   a) There would be no further danger to the public from alcoholism.
   b) There would be a rise in the cost of alcoholic beverages.
   c) Without liquor, people would not drink.
   d) People would not become drunk and create a public nuisance.

_____ 2. During Prohibition, illegal alcohol was
   a) sold openly.
   b) no longer a temptation.
   c) a major factor in the passage of the Volstead Act.
   d) brought across Mexican and Canadian borders.

Understanding a Descriptive Listing

_____ 3. Crude alcohol was characterized by its
   a) added flavoring.
   b) ability to cause nausea, blindness, or death.
   c) bluish, cold quality which was very appealing.
   d) use as wood alcohol.

_____ 4. The Prohibition Era was characterized by
   a) a decrease in crime and drunkenness.
   b) an increase in bootlegging and speakeasies.
   c) a decrease in the production of industrial alcohol.
   d) an increase in handguns.

_____ 5. During Prohibition, people
   a) lived in fear of the law.
   b) were willing to risk arrest for the pleasures of liquor.
   c) recklessly endangered their communities.
   d) were respectful of the legal sanctions placed on them.

Point of View

Place a check next to those statements the author would agree with.

_____ 1. The public needs laws to protect it from harmful products.

_____ 2. People often run risks no matter how strong the warnings.

_____ 3. Going to speakeasies was the worst way of obtaining liquor during Prohibition.

_____ 4. The Congress was wise to repeal Prohibition.

_____ 5. No one should purchase a handgun.

Assumptions

Complete the following statements based on descriptions in the selection.

_____ 1. One can assume that people who do not use car seat belts
   a) do not own seat belts.
   b) believe that there is no danger in a crash.
   c) either forget to use them or find them annoying.
   d) want to be arrested.

_____ 2. During Prohibition, speakeasies gained in popularity because
   a) people disliked the dangers associated with them.
   b) taking a risk meant more to people than breaking the law.
   c) crudely distilled liquor was served there.
   d) most Americans stopped drinking.

____ 3. When enacting the prohibition laws, government officials assumed that
   a) every American would buy alcohol illegally.
   b) all criminal activities would cease.
   c) patrols of the Canadian border would halt the sale of alcohol.
   d) the social threat from drunkenness would decline.

____ 4. The operators of the chemical plants probably
   a) wanted to stop the sale of illegal alcohol.
   b) knew that their products were safe for consumption.
   c) were aware of the dangers in drinking crude alcohol.
   d) never drank alcohol in speakeasies.

____ 5. In democratic societies, citizens
   a) are aware of the dangers in all drugs and foods.
   b) are free to use any product they choose.
   c) can set up health protections through the enactment of laws.
   d) never purchase items the government says are safe.

Vocabulary

The sentences in Group A and in Group B have been split. Show your understanding of the underlined words by matching the sentence parts in Group A and then matching the sentence parts in Group B.

Group A

____ A repealed law is

____ The ruinous law was

____ A crudely made kite will not

____ They voted to ratify the bill and

____ Vile-tasting foods can

____ Your dismal score on the exam will

1. make one sick.
2. count heavily in the final grade.
3. no longer in effect.
4. immediately put it into effect.
5. stay up in a strong wind.
6. the reason for the closing of many businesses.

Group B

_____ People like many things that should be

_____ The brewery closed last week and was

_____ You brought so much stuff that there should be

_____ Some people continued to

_____ How can you illegally

1. run risks even after the health bulletins were issued.
2. enough to last a month.
3. banned for health reasons.
4. buy hootch from that gangster?
5. torn down immediately.

Writing

Steven Jantzen described a controversial period in American history, one in which people rejected laws designed to benefit them. Select an experience you have had in which you rejected what others believed to be beneficial. Write about what you were asked to do, why you rejected it, and what happened as a result. Be sure to use descriptions that will help the reader to visualize what you experienced.

Selection 3: "In Praise of Plains"
by Marilyn Coffey

Vocabulary Preview

The following terms appear in the reading. Knowing their meanings will help you to understand the selection.

Vocabulary	Meanings
abound	occur in great numbers; are filled
churning	twisting violently
conquistadors	sixteenth-century Spanish conquerors in the Americas
crockery	earthenware; pots, jars, containers
entity	a distinct thing
gear	personal property that one carries
mountain chain	a connected series of mountains
pampas	large grassy plains
sheer	complete; total
steppes	a large area of grassland that has no trees
torrent	a violent downpour
trek	a difficult journey
veldt	open grassland with few or no trees
versatile	changeable

The Great Plains region of the United States, where I was born and raised, is part of an enormous strip of flatland that stretches alongside the Rocky **Mountain chain** for more than three thousand miles, from the plateaus of northern Mexico to the Mackenzie River in subarctic Canada. In **sheer** extent, this North American grassland has no equal on earth although similar areas exist on other continents: the **steppes** of Siberia, the **pampas** of South America, the **veldts** of Africa.

The Great Plains is justifiably famous for its violent thunderstorms, one of the most dramatic aspects of the region's changeable, highly **versatile** weather. The storms, typically of short duration, are characterized by downpours of three to six inches or more. Also, the rain tends to be local, drenching the earth in one spot while the surrounding area remains dry. In addition, most thunderstorms are caused when two of the region's three major air masses collide. Most rain falls from April to July, with storms reaching their maximum in May or June, the months when most early travelers began their long **treks** into, or across, the Plains. Characteristically, early journals **abound** with tales of travelers drenched to their skins, spending cold, sleepless, wet nights, unable to find a bit of dry bedding or clothing among all their **gear**.

Anyone who has seen a Great Plains thunderstorm in its full splendor knows that its most spectacular feature, the thing that distinguishes it most clearly from an equally violent downpour in the city, is that the storm can be seen coming from miles away. Indeed, the Plains area is so large that a storm, from a distance, can be perceived as all of the following: a single **entity**, its black clouds **churning**, its lightning jets leaping, its gray sheet of rain falling in a slanting **torrent** even while the sun shines directly overhead. Before the storm is seen, it can be heard, its thunder rumbling gently from a great distance. In addition, before it can be heard, it can be felt—a shift in the temperature of the air, a certain silencing of the wind.

Hail often accompanies these storms, although, curiously, the size of hailstones seems to diminish with the passing of time. In 1541 one of Coronado's **conquistadors**, Pedro de Castañeda of Náxera, reported hail in the southern plains "as large as bowls and even larger, and as thick as raindrops, that in places they covered the ground to the depth of two and three and even more measures." The huge stones did all of the following things: destroyed the Spaniards' tents, dented their armor, bruised their horses, and broke all their pottery, a problem for the Spanish army since the local Indians, who ate only fruit and meat, had no use for **crockery** and could supply them with none.

Literal Comprehension

Check the following statements that reflect facts in the selection.

_____ 1. The characteristic that distinguishes a Great Plains storm from a city storm is the duration of the rain.

_____ 2. In 1541, Indians replaced the Spanish army's crockery that had been destroyed by hailstones.

_____ 3. A rumble of thunder and a silencing of the wind signal a Plains storm.

_____ 4. The Great Plains is a flatland strip extending along the Rocky Mountains from Mexico to Canada.

_____ 5. The Great Plains is known for its typically stable weather.

Descriptions

Match the items in Column A with their characteristics in Column B.

Column A	Column B
1. The Great Plains	__2__ greatest from April to July
2. the rain	_____ appears as a single entity
3. the storm	_____ causes great discomfort to travelers
4. the hail	_____ capable of denting armor
	_____ greatest in May or June
	_____ causes local drenching
	_____ can be seen approaching from miles away
	_____ extent is unequal on earth
	_____ often accompanies the disturbance
	_____ typically of short duration
	_____ falls in slanting torrents
	_____ is heard and felt before it is seen

Point of View

Check the statements the author would agree with.

_____ 1. The Great Plains region is the most spectacular land of its kind in the world.

_____ 2. Storms on the Great Plains have a special beauty.

_____ 3. More people should settle on the Plains.

_____ 4. The visual effects of the storm are overshadowed by its sounds.

_____ 5. The greatest storms on earth are of short duration.

Understanding a Descriptive Listing 75

Assumptions

Decide if the following statements are likely or unlikely based on descriptions in the selection. Check those statements that are <u>most likely</u> to be true.

_____ 1. Today, travelers in the Great Plains region do not encounter storms like those in the 1500s.

_____ 2. The early Spanish explorers asked the Plains Indians for help in preparing food.

_____ 3. Current Plains storms begin with a windshift and a silencing of the wind.

_____ 4. Downpours of three to six inches create widespread flooding on the Plains.

_____ 5. Early Plains travelers chose the spring months to begin their treks in order to witness the changing weather.

_____ 6. When one sees sunshine on the Plains, one can be assured of good weather.

_____ 7. The Great Plains can be crossed in the springtime even though violent storms occur.

_____ 8. Flatlands in all parts of the world never have violent thunderstorms.

_____ 9. Not all storms on the Great Plains are violent.

_____ 10. Areas of Siberia, South America, and Africa have weather as dramatic as the Great Plains.

Vocabulary

Show your understanding of the underlined words by completing the following sentences.

1. My grandmother's <u>crockery</u> was beautifully _____.
2. _____ were known as <u>conquistadors</u>.
3. _____ hit the windows in <u>torrents</u>.
4. The _____ marched as an <u>entity</u>.
5. <u>Churning</u> _____ made steering the boat impossible.
6. Be sure to include _____ when you pack the <u>gear</u>.
7. After the rains, the fields <u>abounded</u> in _____.
8. _____ was the most enjoyable <u>trek</u> of the summer.
9. Singers show their <u>versatility</u> by _____.
10. <u>Veldts</u> provide little protection for _____.
11. You can see _____ on the <u>pampas</u>.
12. The <u>steppes</u> are a relatively _____ area.
13. The <u>sheer</u> weight of the package makes it _____.
14. We viewed the <u>mountain chain</u> from _____.

Writing

Marilyn Coffey vividly described an area of the country known well by her family and by travelers. Her descriptions enable the reader to visualize the area and its storms. Walk outside and study the area immediately surrounding your home. Write about this area in a way that will help the reader to see, hear, smell, and feel what is going on at that moment.

Selection 4: "How to Recognize an Aries"
by Linda Goodman (adapted)

Vocabulary Preview

The following terms appear in the reading. Knowing their meanings will help you to understand the selection.

Idioms	Meanings
get something off one's mind	say exactly what one thinks
make believe	pretend

Vocabulary	Meanings
cast	a tint or coloring
chronic	continuing for a long time or happening frequently
constitution	physical character of the body, including strength and health
intuition	a perception of the truth or facts independent of the reasoning process
lavish	give in great amounts
rash	acting quickly, without consideration
slump	walk in a bent position
zodiac	a band in the heavens within which are the apparent paths of the sun, moon, and principal planets; it is divided into twelve constellations and signs

Aries is the first sign of the **zodiac**. It represents birth. The Aries male or female is the infant of the zodiac whose needs come first. When he has an idea or something he wants **to get off his mind**, he'll call you at four in the morning. But is he truly selfish? He **lavishes** smiles and favors on those who satisfy his demands and is totally unaware that he is causing anyone an inconvenience.

Like a child, the Aries is fearless. Even when hurt, he'll trustingly try again, forgetting the hurt. The Aries can easily **make believe**, but cannot lie or act in a complicated way.

It is easy to recognize the physical appearance of an Aries person. Typically, he has sharp features. You may notice a reddish **cast** to the hair in sunlight and more color than the average complexion. Also, his movements will usually be quick and capable, with a mental process to match. The Aries normally has broad shoulders and may walk with the body slightly bent forward in a great hurry. Few Aries **slump** and their posture reflects their self-confidence.

The Aries looks you straight in the eye, with honesty and faith. He'll never show the tears that represent weakness. He is at the head of his chosen career, and has a liberal attitude and a generosity with time and things. Openness and honesty are Arien trademarks.

Although daring in actions, the Aries can't stand physical pain. **Rash** behavior sometimes causes injuries to the head and face. His **constitution** is strong, but he usually abuses it by ignoring physical discomfort. He has a forceful optimism and seldom falls victim to **chronic** and lingering diseases. He is seldom guilty of gloom.

Furthermore, the Aries is sure that no one can do anything as efficiently as he can; and this often leads to disaster. He learns modesty and humility only after many dismal failures. But once he has learned, he can make one success after another with creativity and **intuition**. He is not cruel; he just honestly believes that he can do anything better than anyone else. The Aries has a temper but seldom becomes angry with individuals; rather, his anger is directed toward an idea or situation he finds unbearable.

Literal Comprehension

Check the following statements that reflect information in the selection.

_____ 1. Aries are children between the ages of one and three.

_____ 2. The Aries person lives in a make-believe world.

_____ 3. Aries people have easily recognizable features.

_____ 4. Some people believe they can do things better than anyone else.

_____ 5. The zodiac represents birth.

Descriptions

Complete the following statements based on descriptions in the selection.

_____ 1. The Aries person is characterized as
   a) honest, yet weak.
   b) lacking self-confidence.
   c) fearless and trusting.
   d) gloomy.

_____ 2. Physically, the Aries is described as having
   a) a slumping body posture.
   b) an inability to maintain eye contact.
   c) chronic suffering and illness.
   d) quick movements that often lead to injury.

_____ 3. The Aries is convinced that he
   a) will usually fail at tasks.
   b) is more efficient than anyone else.
   c) can inconvenience others.
   d) must plan his actions carefully.

_____ 4. The Aries' anger is
   a) usually directed at individuals.
   b) a reaction to intolerable situations.
   c) directed at his chronic ailments.
   d) a cruel expression of displeasure.

_____ 5. When confronting failure, the Aries
   a) makes believe it never happened.
   b) lavishes smiles on those who caused him to fail.
   c) openly shows his anger at those he distrusts.
   d) uses what he has learned to create new successes.

Point of View

Check those statements that represent the author's opinions.

_____ 1. The author believes that Aries people are cruel.

_____ 2. The author believes that all Aries people exhibit the characteristics described.

_____ 3. The descriptions are factual and do not represent a point of view.

_____ 4. The author believes that Aries people are self-centered and childlike.

_____ 5. The author shows that Aries people exhibit more positive than negative qualities.

Assumptions

Decide whether the following assumptions about Aries people are logically drawn from the selection. If they are, label them LIKELY; if they are not, label them UNLIKELY.

_____ 1. He is slow to forgive another's mistake.

_____ 2. He sees doctors and dentists infrequently.

_____ 3. As a child, he wakes his parents to satisfy his hunger.

_____ 4. He may criticize the food in a restaurant, yet leave a generous tip.

_____ 5. When sick, he becomes depressed and withdrawn.

_____ 6. Most drug addicts are Aries.

_____ 7. When taking on a new project, he plans each step carefully and builds a realistic system of work.

_____ 8. He has no time to gossip about others.

_____ 9. Most Aries are shy and uncertain about where they stand.

_____ 10. Aries' honesty and quick actions are carefully designed to meet any possible situation.

Vocabulary

Check those sentences in which the underlined words are used correctly.

_____ 1. Now that you've thoroughly explained the reason for your actions, you should get it off your mind.

_____ 2. My intuition is that the stolen jewels can be found at the airport.

_____ 3. Make believe that you like her cooking; it's something you've always enjoyed.

_____ 4. Aries, the Ram, is one of the twelve signs of the zodiac.

_____ 5. Rash statements may cause others unnecessary pain and suffering.

_____ 6. If you lavish gifts on your children, you will be accused of neglecting them.

_____ 7. Has your back recently begun to bother you, or is it a chronic condition?

_____ 8. Although you are experiencing headaches, your general constitution appears to be excellent.

_____ 9. The ballerina's slumped posture emphasized her grace, poise, and strength.

_____ 10. The fabric of the chair gave the walls a reddish cast.

Writing

Linda Goodman has created a clear image of the typical Aries personality by using descriptive words and examples of behavior. You can find Sun Signs and many similar books in a library or bookstore. Locate your sign according to your birthdate and select the characteristics that represent your personality. Use these characteristics to write about your personality. Be sure to use descriptions that give the reader a clear picture of your personality and behavior.

Role-Playing

Consider the following situation in which a woman is faced with a difficult situation that she must resolve. The activities that follow provide practice in speaking and in writing a descriptive essay.

The Situation

Maria is a housewife who has been married for twenty-two years. She has three children, a girl who is fifteen, and two boys, aged eighteen and twenty. They live at home with Maria and her husband, Mario. Maria is approaching forty and has recently found herself growing dissatisfied with her life. Mario has an interesting job as an X-ray technician in a large hospital, and their older children are attending a local community college. What they are doing seems interesting to Maria, while her own situation seems boring and limited.

Recently she has been thinking of going back to school to prepare her to re-enter the job market. Maria graduated from high school many years ago when her children were much younger. She had enrolled for a semester at the same community college where her older children are now studying, but the demands of her family forced her to withdraw. Now she thinks she would like to start over again.

When she mentioned this to Mario, he was opposed. "I'm making enough money to support the family comfortably," he said. "There's no need for you to go to work." "Besides," he added, "you've been away from the books for so many years, Maria—how will you manage to handle schoolwork and housework at the same time?"

Maria mentioned her idea to her close friend, Nancy, who was very encouraging. Nancy raised two children by herself, and she managed to find time to go back to school and work, too. She is now a licensed real estate broker. "It won't be easy," Nancy told Maria, "but you can do it if you really try. Your family will have to make sacrifices."

Maria has invited Nancy to dinner with her and Mario. During the dinner, they will discuss Maria's problem. She hopes that she will hear enough to enable her to resolve her dilemma.

Directions

Choose three students to play the roles of Maria, Mario, and Nancy. The rest of the class will be divided into two groups of coaches, one to advise Mario and one to advise Nancy. They must provide Mario and Nancy with arguments to use in their upcoming discussion with Maria. After they are finished, the students playing the three main characters may withdraw from the room to plan how they will act out their roles. As soon as they return, the role-playing begins. It ends when Maria reaches a decision. Afterwards, the entire class can question Maria about her decision or engage in a general discussion.

Topics for Discussion and Writing

1. One of the most powerful recent forces for social change has been the desire of many women to change their traditional roles. Describe a woman in your family who is either traditional or nontraditional in her role.

2. Imagine that five years have gone by. Complete this dialogue in which Maria and Nancy discuss the way things have turned out for Maria. Follow this form:

   Maria: Nancy, it's great to see you after all these years.
   Nancy: I've thought of you so often. Tell me what's happened.

3. Many women like Maria wish to re-enter the academic world or the job market after a long absence. What kinds of personal characteristics do they need in order to be successful? Write a descriptive essay.

4. What kinds of support services are available for women in Maria's situation at your school or in your community? Describe these services.

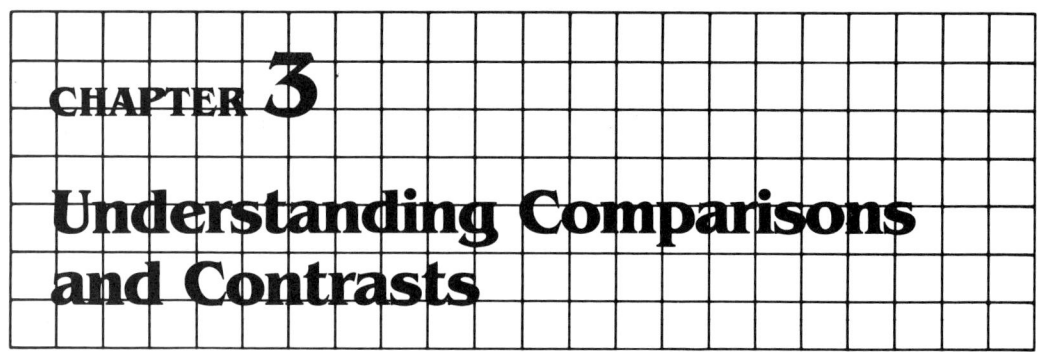

CHAPTER 3

Understanding Comparisons and Contrasts

Recognizing Comparisons and Contrasts in Analytical Writing

When you read narrative and descriptive writing, you must understand chronological sequences and descriptive lists. Now, as you read a different kind of writing, you will continue to use those skills. Understanding the chronological ordering of ideas and the descriptive listing of characteristics will help you as you read selections that use comparison and contrast. Consider the following paragraphs to see how the author treats two different subjects, first by describing and then by comparing them.

Example

Paragraph A

When I arrived in America, I decided to buy my own home. I was fortunate and quickly found a small one-story house in a lovely neighborhood. My new home has two bedrooms, each with its own bath. The kitchen, though small, has two large windows and is equipped with modern appliances. Next to the kitchen is a dining area that opens onto the living room. From the living room I can see the trees and flowers that grow plentifully around the house.

Paragraph B

There are many similarities between owning and renting one's home or apartment. For both, one makes monthly payments to a landlord or bank. Both styles of living allow for individuality in decoration. The owner and renter must meet monthly financial obligations, such as paying electric, gas, and telephone bills. Finally, the owner and the renter must keep their homes in good repair.

Questions

1. Which paragraph describes only one situation? _____ What is it? _____

2. Which paragraph describes two situations? _____ What are they? _____ and _____

3. Which paragraph offers a descriptive list? _____

4. Which paragraph offers a comparison? _____

> Authors often describe two or more subjects (such as people, places, situations, or ideas) for the purpose of **comparing** or **contrasting** them—that is, showing how they are similar or different with respect to a specific trait. Recognizing those comparisons and contrasts in essays, stories, articles, and text passages provides a basis for literal comprehension.

Practice

If the following items are appropriate subjects for a comparative essay, place a C on the line. If they would be developed best in a descriptive essay, place a D on the line. And if they should be discussed in a sequentially-developed essay, place an S on the line.

_____ 1. Applying for a Job

_____ 2. The Advantages of Leasing or Buying a Car

_____ 3. College Life

_____ 4. Obtaining Permanent Citizenship

_____ 5. Physical Requirements for Male and Female Firefighters

_____ 6. American Exports and Foreign Imports

_____ 7. A Country Picnic

_____ 8. Establishing a New Frontier in Space

_____ 9. City versus Country Living

_____ 10. Public versus Private Property

Practice

Match the pairs of items that one could compare or contrast in an essay.

Group A

_____ pets   1. nature preserves
_____ high school classes   2. candy stores
_____ zoos   3. wild animals
_____ natural food stores   4. movies
_____ books   5. college courses

Group B

_____ oil power   1. ocean mining
_____ space exploration   2. old age
_____ primitive cultures   3. private education
_____ infancy   4. atomic energy
_____ public education   5. modern civilization

Recognizing Comparison and Contrast Signals

Consider this example to see how an author signals comparisons and contrasts in a discussion of the features of computer and pinball games.

Example

Although the computerized games of the 1980s share many similarities with the pinball games of the 1930s and 1940s, they have many different features. Both capture the player's imagination with flashing lights, high-scoring possibilities, tests of quick reflexes, and repeated playing opportunities. Although both are electronically operated, the older-style pinball machine responds to levers and buttons with a simple system of bells and lights. On the other hand, the newer computerized games offer a variety of moving objects that are programmed to respond to the player. Both games hold a hypnotic fascination for the player, and one sees players standing for hours before both kinds of games, using one coin after another in an attempt to achieve the highest possible scores.

Question

What words or phrases signal the comparisons or contrasts in the example? _____, _____, _____, _____, and _____

> Recognizing that authors use **comparison/contrast signal words** helps direct your attention to those comparisons and contrasts. Authors frequently use signal words such as "like," "both," and "similarly" to show similarities. They use signal words and phrases such as "on the other hand," "but," and "although" to show differences.

Practice

Select the signal word that best completes each sentence.

(but, and)   1. I like chocolate ice-cream, _____ I don't like chocolate cake.

(On the other hand, Similarly)   2. Some people like to play with dogs. _____, some people dislike dogs intensely.

(while, like)   3. Some people pay high income taxes _____ others pay none at all.

(Although, Both)   4. _____ dog owners should keep their pets on leashes, many do not.

(different, alike)   5. Arty and Barry are _____ in their great fondness for playing practical jokes on others.

Practice

Select the phrase that best completes each sentence.

_____ 1. While farming offers a life in the outdoors,
   a) city living offers a life in the outdoors.
   b) city living requires more indoor work.

_____ 2. Both people were involved in the accident, yet only one
   a) agreed to pay his own expenses.
   b) was not involved in the accident.

_____ 3. Even though I work in another state, I still
   a) pay my local taxes.
   b) don't pay my local taxes.

_____ 4. The difference between our approaches is that
   a) we have similar attitudes toward problem-solving.
   b) we have opposite attitudes toward problem-solving.

_____ 5. Just as you distrust strangers,
   a) I also like them.
   b) I don't care for them either.

Following Directions

Understanding the words and phrases that signal comparisons and contrasts can help you to comprehend important ideas in essays, stories, articles, and text passages. In addition, you can follow an instructor's directions more exactly when you are aware of specific signals. Consider this example.

Example

1. Name two qualities that you admire about your teacher.
2. Name two powers that state and local governments share.
3. Write about the differences (or similarities) between the place where you grew up and your present home.

Questions

1. Which question(s) require(s) that you make a comparison? _____
2. Which question requires that you list similarities? _____
3. Which question requires that you make a comparison or contrast in paragraph form? _____

Understanding Comparisons and Contrasts

> Recognizing that instructors provide specific directions helps you to answer questions and **follow those directions**. Instructors usually **signal comparisons and contrasts** in short-answer questions by using one of these phrases: "name the difference," "list the common characteristics," and "what is the difference or similarity between." They signal comparative essays by using phrases such as "discuss the differences between," or "describe the similarities shared by two subjects."

Practice

Be aware of words and phrases that signal comparison and contrast in the following sets of directions.

1. Name one quality that a movie star must have. Then name two of your favorite movie personalities, and, in the space provided, discuss how they are similar or different in that quality.

    Quality of a movie star _____

    Two movie personalities a: _____

    b: _____

    All movie stars should be _____

    _____
    _____
    _____
    _____
    _____
    _____
    _____
    _____
    _____
    _____
    _____

2. Name one characteristic that plane and railroad travel have in common and one they have in contrast. Then, using that information, describe how they are similar in one respect and different in another.

Similarity _____

Difference _____

Airplane and railroad travel are alike in _____

_____

and they are different in _____

_____
_____
_____
_____
_____
_____
_____

Understanding Shared Traits

As you have seen, authors frequently use comparison and contrast to point out the similarities and differences between two people, places, situations, or ideas. Read the following example to see how the author analyzes the common or shared traits of two subjects in order to compare or contrast them.

Example

   Last week we were informed of a proposal to renovate the abandoned warehouse and to create a disco club in its place. The warehouse, for years an ugly sight and a deserted, dangerous place, will be completely remodeled. The new disco will be attractive inside and out, with bright and flashing lights, loud music, a constant flow of people, and complete parking facilities. In contrast to the dark, silent, and lonely warehouse, the disco will be a lively and cheerful place. The warehouse was a frightening place and the scene of many robberies. Now, the disco owners have assured us that they will provide adequate security for local residents and disco patrons. What a difference the new club will make!

Question

Consider the traits common to the warehouse and the disco: attractiveness, safety, numbers of people, and noise level. Does the author describe similarities or differences when comparing these traits? _____

> Authors analyze people, places, situations, or ideas by naming **common characteristics** and by describing how the subjects are similar or different with respect to each characteristic. Identifying the characteristics and recognizing the stated similarities or differences helps you to understand important facts in readings that present comparisons and contrasts.

Practice

The common or shared characteristic is underlined in each sentence. Complete each sentence by filling in the similarity or difference required.

Similarity 1. Urban residents <u>pay taxes for their schools</u>, and suburban residents _____.

Difference 2. Some four-year colleges <u>have dormitory facilities</u> while others _____.

Similarity 3. Both men and women <u>like</u> clothing that is _____.

Difference 4. In the United States, students <u>must attend school until they are sixteen</u>, while in other countries _____.

Similarity 5. Both my parents are <u>strict</u> about _____.

Practice

Read the following conversation and consider the stated comparisons and contrasts. If the two people are similar with respect to a characteristic, place a check in the chart. Then, note any differences.

Lester: Look at Aaron and Anita. They've been happily married for twenty years and continue to grow closer each day.
Steve: They may be very happy, but they still have their differences.
Lester: What do you mean? They like all the same things.
Steve: Name one.
Lester: Well, they enjoy travel.
Steve: True. But Anita likes the mountains, and Aaron enjoys the beach.
Lester: Okay. Then what about shows and movies? They're always talking about something they've seen.
Steve: Yes, but Aaron prefers serious drama, and Anita likes musical comedy.
Lester: Well, what about food? They both enjoy a variety of dishes.
Steve: On the one hand, Aaron likes to eat out, and on the other, Anita adores cooking new dishes at home. So you see, they are alike in their general interests but very different in the particulars.

	Similarity	Difference	
Characteristics		**Aaron**	**Anita**
1. Happiness	_____	_____	_____
2. Closeness	_____	_____	_____
3. Travel	_____	_____	_____
4. Entertainment	_____	_____	_____
5. Foods	_____	_____	_____

Practice

Think about your two closest friends. From the list that follows, select four traits. Then, in a phrase, describe the trait for each friend. Finally, use the information to compare or contrast your friends briefly.

Traits (select four)	Friend #1	Friend #2
Intelligence	_____	_____
Popularity	_____	_____
Loyalty	_____	_____
Aggressiveness	_____	_____
Sensitivity	_____	_____
Ambition	_____	_____
Athletic Ability	_____	_____
Sincerity	_____	_____

_____ and _____ have some qualities that are very similar and some that are very different.

_____
_____
_____
_____
_____
_____
_____
_____
_____
_____

Identifying Comparisons and Contrasts of Parts, Space, and Sequence

You now recognize how authors use comparisons and contrasts to point out similarities and differences between two subjects. In order to focus on the most important ideas, consider the following paragraphs in which the author compares or contrasts different types of characteristics. Note the type of comparison and contrast in each.

Example

Paragraph A

Carol and Ross enjoy going to the beach, but while they are there, they behave very differently. Carol has fair skin and cannot stay in the sun for long. Ross, on the other hand, is dark-skinned and can stay outdoors all day without burning. Carol, who is not a good swimmer, cannot fight the strong waves and ocean currents, while Ross, an excellent athlete and a fine swimmer, enjoys the challenge of the ocean. They bring food to the beach each day. Ross eats several sandwiches while Carol eats very little. One thing they have in common is their fondness for reading books on the beach and talking to their friends.

Paragraph B

Although Diane and Beverly both applied for the same type of job, each went about it in a different way. Beverly first updated her résumé and had it typed professionally, while Diane used her current résumé. Diane first called professional placement counselors and then waited to hear about possible job opportunities. Beverly, on the other hand, answered newspaper ads and went for as many interviews as possible. Each took different first steps to secure a new position.

Paragraph C

When Patti's company was bought by a larger firm, she and her co-workers moved to a new office which is unlike the old one in many ways. For one thing, the new office is much smaller. Before the move, Patti had a private office adjoining several others. The secretarial desks were grouped together in a central area where they were accessible to the executives. In the new office, the secretarial desks are jammed together in one small room. Where the old office had a separate area for supplies, copying equipment, and computers, the new office has no such space. The equipment and supplies must be squeezed in wherever there is room. Patti is dismayed at the new management's apparent disregard for efficiency and comfort in its headquarter. Their attitude is in shocking contrast with the former owner's concern for the staff.

Questions

Although the three paragraphs offer comparisons and contrasts, each concentrates on a different type. Fill in the letter of the paragraph that matches the type of comparison or contrast listed:

_____ 1. Comparison or contrast of sequence

_____ 2. Spatial comparison or contrast

_____ 3. Comparison or contrast of characteristic parts

> When authors compare or contrast two or more people, objects, or ideas, they analyze their **common characteristics**, that is, the **parts that contribute to the whole**. When they compare or contrast two or more situations, events, or processes, they analyze the **common steps or stages** in each. And when they compare or contrast two or more places, they analyze the **scenes spatially**. Identifying the specific types of comparisons and contrasts helps you to understand the important ideas in selections that develop comparisons and contrasts.

Practice

Reread the paragraphs in the example and answer the statements TRUE (T) or FALSE (F) based on the comparisons and contrasts in each.

Paragraph A

_____ 1. Ross's skin is darker than Carol's.

_____ 2. Carol enjoys the water more than Ross does.

_____ 3. Both Carol and Ross eat a large lunch at the beach.

_____ 4. Despite their physical differences, both Carol and Ross enjoy the beach.

_____ 5. Both enjoy talking with friends, but Carol likes reading more.

Paragraph B

_____ 1. Before Diane completes her résumé, Beverly will have sent hers to possible employers.

_____ 2. Both Diane and Beverly are consulting professional career counselors.

_____ 3. Beverly is beginning to interview while Diane has finished that stage of finding a new job.

_____ 4. Both Beverly and Diane have résumés.

_____ 5. Beverly, not Diane, is checking the job ads in the newspapers.

Paragraph C

_____ 1. The previous owner of Patti's firm showed less regard for the comfort of workers than the new owners do.

_____ 2. Patti's new office has less space than the old office had, but the work area is set up more efficiently.

_____ 3. Patti has less privacy now.

_____ 4. In the old office, secretaries had better access to office equipment than they do now.

_____ 5. The new management provides the same working conditions as the old management did.

Applying Prediction and Assumption Skills to Comparisons And Contrasts

Recognizing the differences between facts and opinions and making assumptions and predictions are comprehension skills that are as important to analytical writing as they are to narrative and descriptive writing. Remember that you build reading skills one upon another and that you apply each skill in a variety of situations. Consider the following example to see how you can use stated comparisons and contrasts to help you make predictions and assumptions.

Example

Two opposing groups, one which favors raising taxes, and one which favors keeping them at their present level, have put a major effort into winning support in the upcoming vote on the town's school budget. While the anti-tax group (opposing the tax) has contacted students, the local teachers' union, and concerned parents, the pro-tax group (in favor of the tax) has relied on randomly phoning as many town residents as possible. Both have sent mailings, but only the anti-tax people included a list of the ways the proposed taxes will be used. Both groups are claiming widespread support and victory in next week's voting.

Questions

1. Name four similarities that the pro- and anti-tax groups share:

   _____   _____

   _____   _____

2. Name two differences between the groups:

   _____   _____

3. Which group will probably win the vote? _____

4. Can you assume that the proposed budget is smaller than last year's budget? _____

> **Identifying similarities and differences** between compared or contrasted subjects can help you to understand the special characteristics of those subjects. You can use your understanding of the subjects to make **logical predictions** about future actions and **logical assumptions** about the nature of the subjects.

Practice

Check the assumptions or predictions that can be drawn logically from each statement. There may be more than one answer for each statement.

1. Most boys and girls are satisfied with their allowances.

   _____ a) Girls expect larger allowances than boys do.

   _____ b) Most children probably receive reasonable allowances.

2. City and suburban land values have been steadily increasing for the past twenty years.

   _____ a) Many people are probably buying land for investment purposes.

   _____ b) Land values will continue to increase in the next decade.

3. The financial responsibility for social programs is shifting from the Federal to state governments.

   _____ a) Local governments will soon be bankrupt.

   _____ b) Till recently, the Federal government paid for many of the social programs in this country.

4. As the industrial capacity of the Northeast declines, the Sun Belt states are becoming more attractive to Northern workers.

   _____ a) The Sun Belt region will become overpopulated if the current trend continues.

   _____ b) The Eastern portion of the country is similar in many respects to the Sun Belt region.

Practice

Read the following paragraph and answer the questions TRUE (T) or FALSE (F) based on stated comparisons or contrasts.

Natural and economic disasters share similarities and basic differences. Just as a hurricane, a flood, or a cave-in at a coal mine disrupts the economic, social, and psychological stability of a town, so the decision to close the town's major industry affects the total community. In a natural disaster, people may lose their homes in an instant; similarly, out-of-work employees are in danger of losing their homes, for without a paycheck they cannot meet monthly mortgage payments. Natural disasters destroy food, communication, and health facilities; business closings destroy tax revenues, employees' earning power, and seriously weaken the community's ability to provide social services. In both instances, Federal assistance is available. For the unemployed, that assistance is limited, whereas for the disaster victim, the aid is usually extended. Finally, victims of disasters usually stay to rebuild the area, whereas the victims of a collapsed economy must often leave in order to seek employment.

_____ 1. Entire towns have "died" as a result of natural or business disasters.

_____ 2. Over the years, the closing of a large business may have more severe effects than a natural disaster.

_____ 3. During times of economic disaster, salaries and tax revenues are more assured than Federal assistance monies.

_____ 4. Most natural disaster victims relocate to safer areas.

_____ 5. Many communities exist because of the operation of one large company.

_____ 6. Unemployment benefits are more limited than disaster benefits.

_____ 7. People usually have more advance warning about natural disasters than economic disasters.

_____ 8. State and Federal governments are prepared to meet all local crises swiftly and with equal assistance.

_____ 9. Most people are not prepared to deal with either a natural or an economic disaster.

_____ 10. Some families will never recover from natural or economic crises.

Applying Fact/Opinion and Point-of-view Skills to Comparisons and Contrasts

Now consider an example and note how the author compares or contrasts two subjects to express an opinion.

Example

1. In contrast to people of other countries, Americans are more demanding and more wasteful in terms of fuel and energy consumption.

2. Americans use more fuel and energy than people of other countries do.

Questions

1. Which statement expresses facts? _____

2. Which statement expresses the author's opinion? _____

3. Does either statement explain why other nations use less fuel and Americans use more? _____

Because authors describe people, places, situations, and ideas as they view them, they are making comparisons that may express facts or their points of view. Your ability to recognize that authors may describe only one aspect of a situation, as in the example, is another important skill.

> Authors use **facts and opinions to express views** when they compare and contrast subjects. Frequently they present a limited or one-sided description. You can build your understanding of a passage by recognizing the way an author approaches a comparison or contrast of subjects.

Comprehension Skills

Practice

Read the following paired statements. Show whether each expresses a fact or an opinion by circling the correct choice. Then check the comparison or contrast in each pair that expresses the more complete statement.

(Fact) / Opinion _____ 1A. The judge released Tom and Jerry after they had been taken into custody for robbery.

(Fact) / Opinion ✓ 1B. The judge released Tom for lack of evidence and also released Jerry in his parents' custody pending the robbery trial.

Fact / Opinion _____ 2A. Because of a poorly written and badly directed production, neither the male nor female star could sustain any emotional quality in their roles.

Fact / Opinion _____ 2B. Neither the male nor female star could achieve the emotional quality so necessary for a truly great performance.

Fact / Opinion _____ 3A. The Great Marcusi was cheered by the crowd, while his opponent was loudly booed.

Fact / Opinion _____ 3B. The Great Marcusi, boxing champion and a native of this town, was cheered by the crowd while his opponent was booed.

Fact / Opinion _____ 4A. The quality of the team's performance this year is far below their achievements last year.

Fact / Opinion _____ 4B. Because of injured or traded players, the team's performance is now lower compared with last year's.

Applying Comparison and Contrast Skills in Selections

You now have the opportunity to practice the comprehension skills developed in this unit. First, preview the new idioms and vocabulary for each selection. Then, as you read the selections, be aware of the development of comparisons and contrasts, the use of signal words and phrases, the use of different types of comparisons and contrasts such as parts, sequence, and space, and the expressions of points of view. The questions that follow each selection focus on your comprehension of vocabulary, stated facts, comparisons and contrasts, and points of view. You will also draw logical assumptions and make predictions. Finally, you will use these skills as you complete a writing assignment.

Selection 1: "The Feminine Physique"
by Thomas Boslooper and Marcia Hayes

So far as the excellence of a performance depends mainly on the kind of muscles, bones, size, and strength that one has, women can be dealt with as fractional men.

—Paul Weiss, *Sport: A Philosophic Inquiry*

Vocabulary Preview

The following terms appear in the reading. Knowing their meanings will help you to understand the selection.

Idioms	Meanings
has a lot to do with	greatly relates to
have a natural edge on	have an advantage
to be suited	have the necessary characteristics
to draw the line	to set a limit
to put up with	to tolerate

Vocabulary	Meanings
assets	qualities having monetary value
belies	misrepresents; hides
build	body development; structure
buoyancy	tendency to float
burly	muscular; strongly built
endurance	ability to continue in a difficult situation

exertion	a great effort; strenuous effort
gap	difference; inequality
orthopedic	relating to the bones, spine
ossify	to harden
peripheral	at the edge of one's vision; not central
physique (see title)	body structure
sedentary	accustomed to sitting; not moving around
stimuli	things that attract attention or cause a response
ultra-	extreme

Feminine strength and **endurance** have always been economic **assets** for men—a source of cheap labor for business and industry, of unpaid labor in the home. For centuries women have toiled on farms and in factories. Crawling on their hands and knees, stripped to the waist, they have pulled loads through coal mine tunnels too narrow to accommodate a horse. In Russia today, women build roads, lay bricks, and operate heavy equipment. Back in our own frontier days, every pioneer woman had to be able to do "a man's work."

Today, most people—certainly most men—quote physical differences between the sexes as evidence of barriers to athletic equality. Because of these differences, women are said **to be more suited** to some sports than others—and unfit to compete directly with men in *any* contact sport.

As for muscle mass, women do indeed, according to some studies, have roughly half the muscle mass of men. And men are, on the average, a third stronger than women. Most women are in poor physical condition, **sedentary**, and often overweight. Were they given the opportunities men have to keep fit, the strength **gap** would narrow considerably. The petite **build** of many top women gymnasts **belies** their extraordinary strength. Muriel Davis Grossfeld, the 1960 U.S. Olympic gymnast, is just over five feet tall. Yet fitness tests at the University of Illinois revealed that she was as strong as the average male college athlete.

So strength is relative, often misleading and frequently irrelevant in comparison to skill. But what about bones? It's true that women's bones **ossify** sooner than men's. That's because girls reach puberty earlier. But this is a plus, not a minus. Adolescent boys take a greater chance of injury because their bones aren't fully ossified until their late teens. At the 1972 conference on women in sport at Penn State University, it was reported that girls and women have fewer **orthopedic** injuries than men—partly because of earlier ossification, partly because, at maturity, women's bones are harder than men's.

Other so-called disadvantages women have **to put up with** are smaller hearts, higher pulse rates, smaller lung capacity, lower aggressive instincts, bad spatial orientation, and more body fat—all of which supposedly combine to give them less endurance.

First of all, taking on this impressive list in order, women's smaller hearts can work relatively harder than men's without any ill effects. At the Penn State conference, medical researchers reported that a pulse of 200 could be attained without risk in a fifteen-year-old girl, while adult women athletes can reach 180 easily during **exertion**— about 20 beats faster than a man.

Going on to the lungs, we find that the average adult male has a 30 per cent greater "aerobic capacity" or "vital capacity" (the volume of air that can be exhaled from the lungs after breathing in deeply) than the average woman. This is partly because men, being bigger, have bigger lungs; partly because the statistics are arranged to favor men. There have been no large-scale studies done on female respiration.

As for aggression, men apparently do **have a natural edge** here. Studies of infant male primates and little boys indicate that males play rougher and show a greater preference for bruising physical contact than do female apes and little girls. On the other hand, little boys are encouraged from infancy to be aggressive and little girls are punished for displays of aggressiveness; so it's hard to know where **to draw the line**.

Our current feminine body ideal is the thin, delicate build characteristic of most fashion models. In the past, the feminine body ideal was often pear-shaped—certainly heavier and more rounded than the **ultra**-thinness for which many women now starve. The muscular build typical of most men has never been the Western world's ideal for women. Muscular women have, in fact, been consistently discriminated against as unfeminine.

The **burly** woman athlete image has persuaded a lot of women that strenuous athletic activity leads to unattractive muscles. It isn't so. "Proper training is the answer," says Walter Kostric, trainer of Canadian track and field star Debbie Van Kiekebelt. "Some exercises can develop large muscles, but others don't. A good coach knows the difference."

Most women have more body fat than men. And where fat exists, muscle obviously doesn't. Conditioning **has a lot to do with** this, of course, but even physically active women do have more fat than men. In some areas of athletics—endurance swimming, for instance—a little extra fat can be an advantage, providing warmth and **buoyancy**. But when a woman is in top form, the extra fat doesn't affect her performance at all, in *any* sport.

Another difference between the sexes is spatial orientation. Men are supposedly better at orienting themselves in space—at "keeping their eye on the ball," using their own physical positions as a reference point to activity around them.

Women tend to use **peripheral** objects as points of reference and are easily distracted by visual **stimuli**. Men, for instance, can pick a figure out of a complex pattern more readily than women. Perhaps, it has been suggested, this is like prehistoric times when life depended on a man's ability to keep his eye on a deer running in the bushes. More likely, it's a psychological difference, resulting from greater self-confidence on the part of men.

When it comes to endurance, men, because of their greater strength and lung capacity, supposedly become exhausted less quickly than women. "Look at all the male long-distance runners that women haven't begun to catch up to," we're often told. But there are many more men than women running marathons, and in the Olympics women aren't allowed to run more than 1500 meters, so this evidence is only relative. Furthermore, women have greater *tolerance* for fatigue, which tends to even things out.

It seems clear from these examples that differences in reaction time, muscle mass, bones, hearts, lungs, endurance, strength, spatial orientation, and body fat—when they exist—don't necessarily make much of a difference where relative performance is concerned.

Literal Comprehension

Check those statements that agree with facts in the selection.

   _____ 1. A little extra body fat can be an advantage to endurance swimmers.

   _____ 2. Historically, women were considered too weak to do heavy labor.

   _____ 3. All exercises develop large muscles.

   _____ 4. In the Olympics, women are not allowed to run more than 1500 meters.

   _____ 5. Many people discriminate against muscular women.

Comparisons and Contrasts

Check those statements that agree with comparisons or contrasts made in the selection.

   _____ 1. If women and men had the same opportunities to keep fit, they would have the same strength capabilities.

   _____ 2. Generally, women have more body fat than men.

   _____ 3. Male athletes have fewer orthopedic injuries than women athletes.

   _____ 4. Men have larger hearts than women do.

   _____ 5. After breathing deeply, men can exhale a greater volume of air than women can.

   _____ 6. Little boys and girls have the same preferences for rough physical contact.

   _____ 7. A good coach knows which exercises develop large muscles.

   _____ 8. Women have a greater tolerance for fatigue than men do.

Understanding Comparisons and Contrasts

_____ 9. Generally, men are less distracted than women by peripheral objects.

_____ 10. Boys' and girls' bones harden at the same age.

Assumptions and Predictions

Based on your understanding of the comparisons and contrasts made in the selection, check those statements that are likely to be correct and mark an X for those statements that are unlikely to be correct.

_____ 1. Male athletes have less self-confidence than female athletes.

_____ 2. Male athletes have been the subjects of more research than female athletes.

_____ 3. Professional male athletes have earned more money than professional female athletes.

_____ 4. In the future, scientists will make every effort to create drugs that will ossify boys' bones at an earlier age.

_____ 5. The burly female athlete image will become the model for women in the Western world.

Point of View

If the following statements can be proven with direct evidence, mark them FACT. If they express a point of view, mark them OPINION.

_____ 1. In Russia today, women build roads, lay bricks, and operate heavy equipment.

_____ 2. Women's bones ossify sooner than men's.

_____ 3. Differences in reaction time, muscle mass, bones, hearts, and lungs don't necessarily make much of a difference in athletic performance.

_____ 4. Most women are in poor physical condition.

_____ 5. Women are more suited to some sports than others.

Vocabulary

A. Review the meaning of each idiom used in the selection. Then show your understanding of the idiom by completing each sentence.

1. Today's weather has a lot to do with whether or not I _____ _____.

2. If you _____, you will have an edge on the other students.

3. Because of my _____, I am suited for gymnastics.

4. Till now, I've agreed with your rules. However, I must draw the line at _____.

5. I enjoy eating dinner at your house, but I can't put up with _____ _____.

B. Choose the word that best completes each sentence and write it on the line.

orthopedic–ossify   1. Women's bones _____ sooner than men's.

peripheral–stimuli   2. Women tend to use _____ objects as points of reference.

buoyancy–build   3. A little extra fat can provide warmth and _____.

sedentary–endurance   4. Feminine strength and _____ have always been highly valued.

exertion–gap–physique 5. Adult women athletes can attain pulse rates of 180 during periods of _____.

burly–ultra-   6. Many women starve to attain _____ thin bodies.

assets–belies   7. The petite build of many top women athletes _____ their tremendous strength.

Writing

Thomas Boslooper and Marcia Hayes have compared and contrasted the physical characteristics of male and female athletes. What sport do you enjoy watching or playing? Consider the characteristics discussed by the authors. Compare and/or contrast how well you and a friend of the opposite sex can succeed in that sport. Remember to discuss one characteristic at a time.

Selection 2: "Leo and Cancer Personalities"
by Linda Goodman (adapted)

Vocabulary Preview

The following terms appear in the reading. Knowing their meanings will help you to understand the selection.

Vocabulary	Meanings
absorb	take in
astute	highly capable of understanding
crabby	complaining; irritable
deceptively	in a misleading way; falsely
expressive	conveying or showing emotion
gregarious	sociable; fond of being with others
melancholy	sad; depressed; thoughtful
rationalize	explain in a reasonable way
shrink from	avoid; draw away from
vulnerable	able to be hurt

Can one really describe a person's characteristics according to a Sun sign, that particular zone of the zodiac in which the sun was located at the moment of one's birth? Experts state that the personality characteristics influenced by one's Sun sign will be approximately eighty percent accurate when one describes that individual. Let us consider two signs, Leo (the lion) and Cancer (the crab) to see what characteristics are typical of persons born under those Sun signs.

The Leo personality is characterized by a desire to rule those around him and by his energetic and **gregarious** nature. The Cancer personality is characterized by the display of a variety of passing moods. The Cancerian enjoys laughter and is often the funniest in a room; he secretly loves attention. While he doesn't actively pursue fame, he also does not **shrink from** it. Similarly, the Leo enjoys being in the spotlight, and, unlike the Cancerian, actively achieves attention with bold and dramatic statements.

Both are sensitive to others. Leos have **vulnerable** egos that can be wounded by those who do not respect their wisdom and generosity. Cancerians, when hurt, seek solitude; their feelings are sensitive and their tears are real. Known for their changing moods, they may appear happy, **melancholy**, or **crabby** at times.

Both personalities have distinctive physical features. A typical Leo may have thick, wavy hair, a **deceptively** lazy look, a walk that is straight and proud yet smooth and gliding like a cat's, and a commanding appearance. The typical Cancerian may have a large skull, brow, and cheekbones, long arms and legs, an extremely thin body, and enormously **expressive** features that show his many moods.

Cancerians' moods are intense and they can make one feel them, too. They are known for their secrecy, compassion, and intuition; people often confide in them. Likewise, Leos are **astute**, but they act in a more commanding way; they love to teach and tell others how to manage their lives. They are especially good at **rationalizing** and smoothing out someone's problems. Leos often behave dramatically and act in a superior or commanding manner as they direct others or organize matters. Similarly, Cancerians take in all there is to know about others with compassion, and they never reveal their inner thoughts. Unlike Leos, they rarely judge; rather, they gather, **absorb**, and reflect. They help others, but cautiously decide how to distribute their time, money, and emotions.

Literal Comprehension

Check those statements that factually reflect information in the selection.

_____ 1. A person's general characteristics can be described according to all the signs of the zodiac.

_____ 2. Leo personalities tend to be sociable.

_____ 3. Cancerians walk in a straight and proud manner.

_____ 4. Dramatic statements often make Leos the center of attention.

_____ 5. Revealing their inner feelings draws Cancerians close to friends.

Comparisons and Contrasts

Complete the following statements based on your understanding of the comparisons and contrasts made in the selection.

_____ 1. Although both are known as astute judges of others' feelings,
   a) Leos are unconcerned with others' problems.
   b) Cancer personalities never get involved in others' problems.
   c) Leos, more than Cancerians, act to work out a friend's problem.
   d) Cancerians, not Leos, want to rule others' emotions.

_____ 2. Cancerians, but not Leos, are typically known for their
   a) astute insights into others' behavior.
   b) range of emotions and moods.
   c) sensitivity to others.
   d) deceptive laziness.

3. A conscious desire for attention is characteristic of
   a) the funny Cancer personality.
   b) both the Leo and the Cancerian.
   c) neither the Leo nor the Cancer.
   d) the bold and dramatic Leo personality.

4. Leos, rather than Cancerians,
   a) prefer an active role in managing the affairs of others.
   b) prefer to listen and quietly absorb what they hear.
   c) have long arms and legs.
   d) express a wide range of moods.

5. Cancerians, rather than Leos,
   a) need respect for their wisdom and generosity.
   b) are known for their deceptive tears.
   c) do not seek fame openly, yet they will not reject it.
   d) are typically straight and proud in stature.

Assumptions and Predictions

Check the statements that can be logically drawn from the selection.

1. A typical Cancerian might well be a collector of antiques and old treasures.

2. Many Leos become educators, politicians, and psychiatrists.

3. Cancerians probably can't help feeling superior to those around them.

4. Many Cancerians create beautiful gardens.

5. Many Leos enjoy being hosts at elegant parties.

Point of View

Check those statements the author would probably agree with.

1. A person's Sun sign is a good indicator of general behavior traits.

2. The Cancer personality is more appealing than the Leo personality.

3. Seeking attention is a negative personality trait.

4. The Leo is more physically interesting than the Cancerian.

5. Both personalities have the ability to help others in trouble.

Vocabulary

Match the term with its best descriptive example.

_____ gregarious
_____ shrink from
_____ vulnerable
_____ melancholy
_____ crabby
_____ deceptive
_____ expressive
_____ astute
_____ rationalize
_____ absorb

1. One can always tell what Jenny is thinking by looking at her eyes.
2. Paul enjoys visiting people and inviting them to his house.
3. Jamie doesn't want any responsibility and never volunteers for committee work.
4. The old woman has complained all morning.
5. Can you understand and remember all the points the instructor made today?
6. Jim can usually sense the real reason for people's behavior.
7. Betty looks so unhappy sitting alone in the corner.
8. Alvin can usually provide a clear explanation of what is happening.
9. My arm has been especially weak since I fractured it a year ago.
10. Cynthia usually says one thing but means something else.

Writing

The general characteristics of Leo and Cancer personalities have been adapted from Linda Goodman's complete analysis of the twelve Sun sign personalities. Hers and similar books are available in libraries. Using your birthdate and that of a close friend, read about the characteristics of the two signs. Then, compare or contrast yours and your friend's characteristics. Remember to write about one trait at a time.

Many people believe in astrology while others do not. Do you believe in astrology? Talk with someone of the opposite opinion. Then, briefly contrast that person's opinion with yours.

Selection 3: "How America Lives"
by James A. Michener

Vocabulary Preview

The following terms appear in the selection. Knowing their meanings will help you to understand the selection.

Idioms	Meanings
a turn to the right	a move in a conservative direction; keeping the established social, political, and economic direction
cling to	remain attached to an idea
dole out	measure or divide carefully among several people
put the brakes on	slow down or stop

Vocabulary	Meanings
allege	declare positively as if under oath
appall	fill with horror
binge	a time of excessive giving in to desires
destitution	complete poverty
impotent	completely unable to do something
integrity	a perfect or whole condition
Puritanism	strictness in moral matters
radically	extremely
rigorous	strict

Americans still follow many of the old ways. In a time of rapid change it is essential that we remember how much of the old we **cling to**. Young people still get married (2.41 million couples last year as opposed to only 1.52 million in 1960). Of course, many do get divorced, but they remarry at astonishing rates. They have children, but fewer than before. They belong to churches, even though they attend somewhat less frequently, and they want their children to have religious instruction. They're willing to pay taxes for education, and they generously support institutions like hospitals, museums and libraries. In fact, when you compare the America of today with that of 1950, the similarities are far greater than the differences.

Americans seem to be growing conservative. The 1980 election, especially for the Senate and House of Representatives, signaled a decided **turn to the right** insofar as political and social attitudes were concerned. It is as if our country spent the 1960s and 1970s joyously breaking out of old restraints and now wishes **to put the brakes on**, as cautious people often do after a **binge**. We should expect to see a reaffirmation of traditional family values, sharp restraints on pornography, a return to religion and a rejection of certain kinds of social legislation.

Patterns of courtship and marriage have changed **radically**. Where sex was concerned, I was raised in an atmosphere of suspicion, repression and **Puritanism**, and although husky young kids can survive almost anything, many in my generation suffered grievously. Without reservation, I applaud the freer patterns of today, although I believe that it's been difficult for some families to handle the changes.

American women are changing the rules. Thirty years ago I could not have imagined a group of women employees suing a major corporation for millions of dollars of salary which, they **alleged**, had been denied them because they had been discriminated against. Nor could I imagine women in universities going up to the men who ran the athletic programs and demanding a just share of the physical education budget. But they're doing this—and with the support of many men who recognize the justice of their claims. At work, at play, at all levels of living women are suggesting new rules.

America, is worried about its schools. If I had a child today, I would send her or him to a private school for the sake of safety, for the discipline that would be enforced and for the **rigorous** academic requirements. But I would doubt that the child would get any better education than I did in my good public school. The problem is that good public schools are becoming pitifully rare, and I would not want to take the chance that the one I sent my children to was inadequate.

Some Americans must live on welfare. Since it seems obvious that our nation can produce all its needs with only a part of the available work force, some kind of social welfare assistance must be **doled out** to those who cannot find jobs. When I think of a typical welfare recipient I think of a young neighbor woman whose husband was killed in a tragic accident, leaving her with three young children. In the bad old days she might have known **destitution**, but with family assistance she was able to hold her children together and produced three fine, tax-paying citizens. I like that kind of social assistance and am willing to support it. America is essentially a compassionate society.

America cannot find housing for its young families. I consider this the most serious danger confronting family life in America, and I am **appalled** that the condition has been allowed to develop. For more than a decade, travelers like me have been aware that in countries like Sweden, Denmark, Russia and India young people have found it almost impossible to acquire homes. In Sweden the customary wait was 11 years of marriage, and we used to ask, "What went wrong?" It seemed to us that a major responsibility of any nation would be to provide homes for its young people starting their families. Well, this dreadful social sickness has now overtaken the United States, and for the same reasons. The builders in our society find it profitable to erect three-bathroom homes that sell for $220,000 with a mortgage at 19 percent but find it impossible to erect small homes for young marrieds. For a major nation to show itself **impotent** to house its young people is admitting a failure that must be corrected.

Our prospects are still good. I find our chances to be at least as good as those of any other nation and probably better. We have a physical setting of remarkable **integrity**, the world's best agriculture, a splendid wealth of minerals, great rivers for irrigation and an unsurpassed system of roads for transportation. We also have a magnificent mixture of peoples from all the continents with varied traditions and strengths. But most of all, we have a unique and balanced system of government.

I think of America as having the oldest form of government on earth, because since we started our present democracy in 1789, every other nation has suffered either parliamentary change or revolutionary change. It is *our* system which has survived and should survive, giving the maximum number of people a maximum chance for happiness.

Literal Comprehension

Check those statements that reflect information in the selection.

_____ 1. Americans are characterized as conservative in their political beliefs.

_____ 2. Currently, America's sexual patterns are radical.

_____ 3. A unique quality of the American people is the survival of their balanced form of government.

_____ 4. One weakness of the American government is its inability to provide reasonably priced housing for newly married couples.

_____ 5. Sweden, Denmark, Russia, and India have solved the problem of housing their young people.

Comparisons and Contrasts

Complete the following statements based on your understanding of the comparisons and contrasts made in the selection.

_____ 1. In contrast to the youth of today, the youth of years ago
   a) were sexually restrained.
   b) had fewer children.
   c) were infrequent churchgoers.
   d) were less concerned about having fun.

_____ 2. Americans are more concerned than ever about
   a) the physical setting of minerals.
   b) revolutionary changes in their government.
   c) housing and education.
   d) culture and transportation.

_____ 3. A major difference in American beliefs compared with years ago is found in
   a) a rejection of religion.
   b) a new willingness to educate its youth.
   c) the concern for survival of the American form of government.
   d) the new attitudes displayed by women.

_____ 4. The patterns of family life, courtship, and marriage have become
   a) radicalized to a point where most people cannot accept them.
   b) altered in the direction of individual freedom and responsibility.
   c) more strict than in the 1950s.
   d) Puritanic and characterized by high marriage rates.

_____ 5. American politics reflects a
   a) stabilization of traditional values.
   b) breaking of old restraints.
   c) concern for dangers in the future.
   d) strong effort to reject all past legislation.

Assumptions and Predictions

Check the ideas that can be logically drawn from the selection.

_____ 1. The number of American marriages, divorces, and remarriages will increase in the next ten years.

_____ 2. Most foreigners want to live in America.

_____ 3. Americans are only interested in having fun.

_____ 4. The American system of government has never experienced the changes and turmoil as other forms of governments have.

_____ 5. The American government will continue to provide welfare assistance.

Fact and Opinion

The following statements appear in the selection. Check those that are facts rather than expressions of the author's opinion.

_____ 1. The 1980 election, especially for the Senate and House of Representatives, signaled a decided turn to the right.

_____ 2. Young Americans have children, but fewer than before.

_____ 3. Americans seem to be growing conservative.

_____ 4. Because it seems obvious that our nation can produce all it needs with only a part of the available work force, some kind of social welfare assistance must be doled out to those who cannot find jobs.

Point of View

Check those statements that the author would probably agree with.

_____ 1. Good public schools are the equals of private institutions.

_____ 2. Social, economic, and moral dangers to the American society are threatening the stability of the country.

_____ 3. Americans are considered unstable by other peoples of the world.

_____ 4. The best place in the world to live is America.

_____ 5. Sexual freedom in America is out of control.

_____ 6. In America, traditional values have died and have been replaced by nonrestrictive ways of thinking.

_____ 7. Social legislation should be enacted to provide continued welfare assistance.

_____ 8. Legislation should be enacted to provide tax supports for landlords and builders.

_____ 9. There is very little wrong with the United States.

_____ 10. Compared with other countries, the United States has a compassionate approach to housing its youth.

Vocabulary

A. Check those sentences in which the idioms are used correctly.

_____ 1. If you <u>cling to</u> your old way of computing these figures, you will be <u>here for</u> hours.

_____ 2. Radical movements usually <u>turn</u> a country <u>to the right</u>.

_____ 3. Before you have no money left, <u>put the brakes on</u> your spending for a while.

_____ 4. <u>Dole out</u> what is left of the ice cream to the children.

B. Highlight the word that best completes each sentence.

1. The six (alleged, appalled) offenders were ordered to rise when the judge entered the courtroom.

2. After last night's (destitution, binge) I awoke with a headache and blurred vision.

3. The (Puritanism, integrity) of the building was not damaged after the storm.

4. You have the (rigorous, impotent) honor of escorting the beauty queen to the party.

Writing

James Michener compared and contrasted modern American life with life here decades ago. Consider the city you now live in and the city where you grew up. Briefly compare or contrast the similarities and differences between each place. Write two or three paragraphs. Remember to focus on one characteristic at a time.

Selection 4: "Letters From an American Farmer; Letter III": Adapted from "What is an American"
by Michel-Guillaume-Jean de Crèvecoeur

Vocabulary Preview

The following terms appear in the reading. Knowing their meanings will help you to understand the selection.

Vocabulary	Meanings
contemplation	observation; consideration
haughty	snobbish
herd	crowd
toil	do hard and exhausting work

He (the Englishman) arrives on a new continent; a modern society offers itself to his **contemplation**, different from what he had seen. It is not composed, as in Europe, of great lords who possess everything, and of a **herd** of people who have nothing. Here are no aristocratic families, no courts, no kings, no bishops, no great manufacturers employing thousands, no great refinements of luxury. The rich and the poor are not so far removed from each other as they are in Europe. He views not the hostile castle and **haughty** mansion, but a pleasing uniformity of decent comforts appears throughout the communities. Lawyer and merchant are the only titles in towns; that of farmer is the only name of the rural inhabitants of the country. There are no princes for whom to **toil**, starve, and bleed; we are the most perfect society now existing in the world.

Literal Comprehension

Check those statements that express the correct factual content of the selection.

_____ 1. Europe was composed of mainly the rich and the haughty.

_____ 2. The new continent offered no luxuries.

_____ 3. The rural inhabitants of the new land were called lawyers and merchants.

_____ 4. In Europe, only the privileged few held power.

_____ 5. Princes ruled the most perfect society in the world.

Comparisons and Contrasts

A. Complete the following statements based on your understanding of the comparisons and contrasts made in the selection.

_____ 1. One difference between Europe and early America was that
   a) only Europe had granted titles such as lawyer and merchant.
   b) only Europe had rural areas in which farmers worked.
   c) America had no hierarchy of royalty as Europe had.
   d) people shared most of the power equally in Europe, but in America they did not.

_____ 2. The rich and the poor classes were
   a) found in Europe alone.
   b) far removed from each other in Europe.
   c) more separated in Europe than in America.
   d) unknown in the most perfect society in the world.

B. Match (1) Europe or (2) America with each description at the right.

1. In Europe,   _____ courts, titles, and luxuries existed.
2. In America,   _____ the rich and the poor were far removed.
                   _____ the majority possessed nothing.
                   _____ the rich and the poor were not as separated.
                   _____ power was held by a few.
                   _____ the aristocracy ruled.
                   _____ fair housing was had by all.
                   _____ the highest titles were merchant, lawyer, and farmer.
                   _____ titles such as prince and bishop existed.
                   _____ no royalty existed.

Assumptions and Predictions

Check those statements that can be drawn logically from the selection.

_____ 1. The Englishman was viewing the American continent.

_____ 2. When he wrote the letter, de Crèvecoeur did not foresee the growth of American industry.

_____ 3. At that time, the American people would not have wanted an aristocratic form of government.

_____ 4. European society was based on a system of equality.

_____ 5. Princes and lords were fair to their servants.

Fact and Opinion

The following statements appear in the selection. Label them FACT or OPINION.

_____ 1. Here are no aristocratic families, no courts, no kings, no bishops.

_____ 2. He views not the hostile castle and the haughty mansion.

_____ 3. A pleasing uniformity of decent comforts appears throughout our communities.

_____ 4. We are the most perfect society now existing in the world.

_____ 5. A farmer is the only appellation of the rural inhabitants of our country.

Point of View

Check those statements the author would probably agree with.

_____ 1. America is a better place to live compared with Europe.

_____ 2. It is better to be a prince, lord, or king than to be a lawyer, merchant, or farmer.

_____ 3. Being a poor, hard-working farmer is highly honorable.

_____ 4. The American style of equality followed the European tradition.

_____ 5. Americans were right to rebel against the hierarchy of power and wealth.

Writing

Michel de Crèvecoeur wrote his impressions of the differences between eighteenth-century European and American economic and social lifestyles. Using those characteristics, write about the similarities or differences between life in America today and life in another country.

Role-Playing

Consider the following story in which a student is faced with a difficult situation that she must resolve. The activities that follow provide practice in speaking and in writing an analytical essay.

The Situation

Paula is a student at your school. She lives at home with her parents and her younger brother, Richard. Since the family arrived in this country, Paula has become concerned about Richard's behavior: he used to be serious about his studies and about the part-time job he had, but now he spends little time studying, and Paula has learned that Richard was fired from his job. Furthermore, Paula has seen him hanging out with a group of local teenagers who have a bad reputation in the neighborhood.

The other night, while Paula's parents were out, she went into her brother's room to discuss her concern with him, and discovered that he had been drinking. At first he was angry with her for interfering in his business, but then he claimed that he had only been trying it out for the first time. When Paula threatened to tell her parents about the incident unless he agreed to stop fooling around with alcohol, Richard agreed.

Now Paula is confused. She has put herself into a situation in which she cannot tell her parents about Richard's drinking. She suspects the problem is more serious than he had admitted. However, if she breaks her agreement with Richard and tells her parents, she is afraid that they will react angrily and perhaps even throw Richard out of the house.

She goes to talk with two of her friends who came to this country when she did. Her friend, Susan, has seen one of her own brothers ruin his life with alcohol and drugs, and she feels that Paula is justified in doing anything she can to save Richard. However, her friend Arnold does not drink and has a more tolerant attitude toward people who do. He feels that Richard is going through a phase and will straighten himself out if Paula just leaves him alone.

What should Paula do?

Directions

Choose three students to play the roles of Paula, Susan, and Arnold. The rest of the class will be divided into two groups of coaches, one to advise Susan and one to advise Arnold. They must provide Susan and Arnold with arguments to use in their upcoming discussion with Paula. After they are finished, the students playing the three main characters can withdraw from the room to plan how they will act out their roles. As soon as they return, the role-playing begins. It ends when Paula reaches her decision.

Afterwards, the entire class can question Paula about her decision or engage in a general discussion.

Topics for Discussion and Writing

1. What facilities are available in your school or community to help young people with problems of drug or alcohol dependency?

2. Imagine that Paula decides to tell her parents about Richard. How do they respond? Complete this dialogue to be spoken by characters playing the roles of Paula and her mother. Follow this form:

   Paula: Mom, I need to talk to you about Richard.
   Her Mother: Oh, Paula! What's the matter?

3. Should Paula tell her parents? Write an essay in which you describe her situation. Discuss the reasons for and against her decision, and then present your own conclusion.

4. Some cultures are tolerant of the use of drugs and/or alcohol while others are not. How is the use of such substances regarded in your culture? Compare your country's views toward drugs and/or alcohol with the American view.

Chapter 4
Understanding Causes and Effects

Recognizing Causes and Effects in Argumentative Writing

In daily situations, you read passages that develop a listing of ideas, a chronological sequence, and a comparison or contrast between two subjects. When you read descriptive, narrative, and analytical writing, you should recognize an author's use of facts and opinions to present a point of view. In argumentative writing, the author presents a point of view, that is, takes a position or a stand on a topic and offers support for that position. Consider the following paragraphs to see how the author takes a position on job opportunities and uses a different type of support in each paragraph.

Example

Paragraph A

It is difficult for workers to find employment this year. One reason is that many industries are not hiring new workers. In addition, industries are reducing their current staff levels because of a decline in national economic conditions. Another reason is that workers who once might have considered early retirement are now staying at their jobs. Finally, other workers who used to view their jobs as optional now must keep their positions in order to meet their minimum financial responsibilities.

Questions

1. What statement does the author make about job opportunities?

2. What evidence does the author use to support the statement?

___

Paragraph B

It is difficult for workers to find employment this year. As a result, many recent college graduates are unemployed or are taking part-time jobs to meet expenses. Unemployment among high school graduates has meant that large numbers of teen-agers are seeking unemployment benefits. The unemployment figures are the highest in decades. Finally, the Federal government must contribute large amounts of money to support the growing numbers of people who are receiving welfare assistance.

Questions

1. What statement does the author make about job opportunities?

___

2. What evidence does the author use to support the statement?

___

In both paragraphs, the author takes a position about job opportunities, namely, "It is difficult for workers to find employment this year." However, in Paragraph A, the author supports the argument with four causes of the unemployment problem. In Paragraph B, the author develops a different approach to the position by giving the effects of unemployment on individuals and on the nation.

> Recognizing that an author makes a statement and then offers support for his or her position can help you to understand argumentative writing. When you identify the **causes that support a position** or the **effects of that position**, you focus on the important facts in argumentative writing.

Recognizing Cause and Effect Signals

Understanding argumentative writing depends on your ability to recognize an author's position on a topic and his or her use of facts and/or opinions to support that position. Authors usually use words that signal the type of support they are presenting. Read the following paragraphs to see how the author uses different words and phrases to signal causes and effects.

Example

Paragraph A

There are several important reasons why Mike, a high school senior, was rejected by the hiring supervisor at the local electronics company. Mike's first problem was his poorly prepared job application. Because he filled it in during the bus ride to the interview, Mike made many errors. The paper was filled with erasures, crossings out, and blank spaces. Another reason was Mike's poor appearance; he wore faded jeans and an old flannel shirt to the interview. In addition, he was late, thereby making both himself and the interviewer uncomfortable. As a result, Mike made a bad impression during the interview and never had the opportunity to demonstrate his fine abilities.

Questions

1. What phrase in the first sentence signals a paragraph developed with causes? _____

2. Name five additional words or phrases that signal the causes for Mike's failure.

_____

_____

_____

_____

_____

Recognizing that authors **signal** that **the causes** of a position will be developed as part of an argument helps you to focus on those causes. Some frequently used signals are: "several important reasons," "factors," "leads to," "because," "one reason," and "since."

Paragraph B

Mike's rejection by the hiring supervisor led to several changes in his attitude toward seeking a job. He made an effort to have a well prepared application which he checked for its thoroughness and appearance. He was determined to look presentable, and so he chose his clothing carefully the evening before the interview. Arriving late for the first interview affected his planning for the next one; he arranged for a ride to the plant and left extra time for unexpected delays. As a result of his efforts, Mike arrived on time, looked presentable, and appeared confident throughout the interview. The effect was so positive to Mike's attitude that he was able to demonstrate his abilities during the interview. As a consequence of his efforts, Mike was offered a position at the plant.

Questions

1. What word in the first sentence signals a paragraph that develops effects? _____

2. Name four additional words or phrases that signal effects in the paragraph. _____
_____
_____
_____

Recognizing that authors **signal** that **the effects** of a position will be developed as part of an argument helps you to focus on those effects. Some frequently used signals are: "led to," "as a result," "effect," and "as a consequence."

Practice

Each of the following statements contains a word or phrase that signals how the author might develop a position statement in a paragraph. Read each statement and decide whether the paragraph would best be developed using causes or effects. Write either CAUSES or EFFECTS on the line.

_____ 1. Temperatures reaching the nineties have lasted for ten days and have led city officials to initiate actions in the public interest.

_____ 2. A panel of dentists is exploring why there has been a sharp increase in the number of teenagers who are experiencing dental problems.

_____ 3. Parent groups are seeking to understand the effects of television violence on youngsters.

_____ 4. There are many reasons why people choose to work outdoors rather than in offices.

_____ 5. The increase in the number of families in which both parents work is having a wide range of consequences on American family lifestyles.

_____ 6. Economic inflation has forced many families to change their spending patterns.

_____ 7. People choose to own pets for a variety of reasons.

_____ 8. Bodily pain affects people in a variety of ways.

_____ 9. Misreading or ignoring test directions can lead to a variety of problems for the test-taker.

_____ 10. Why have so many of today's youth abandoned the traditional values followed by their parents?

Following Directions

Your instructor uses words and phrases to signal causes and/or effects in directions for tests and assignments. Consider the following example.

Example

1. Discuss the factors that led to a rise in home mortgage rates this year.
2. Explain what happened when you combined two acids in your experiment.

Questions

1. Which question requires that you develop causes? _____
2. Which question requires that you develop effects? _____

> When you understand that instructors write **specific directions** for tests, reports, and assignments, you can complete those assignments according to the specific requirements the instructor wrote. Directions that require the development of **causes** include specific words and phrases: "what led to," "what influenced," "what are the factors," and "what caused." Those that require the development of **effects** include specific words and phrases: "what are the effects," "result in," "consequences of," and "what are the results."

Practice

Each of the following sample items states a position that you must support with either causes or effects. First, list four ideas that support the position. Then, use the position statement and the supporting ideas to develop a paragraph.

A. There are many reasons why some people cheat on their income tax returns.

1. _____
2. _____
3. _____
4. _____

B. Taking a part-time job while attending college greatly affects a student's schedule.

   1. _____
   2. _____
   3. _____
   4. _____

C. Joining a campus club has influenced my life in several ways.

   1. _____
   2. _____
   3. _____
   4. _____

D. There are many reasons why students should wait a semester or two before choosing a career major.

1. _____
2. _____
3. _____
4. _____
_____
_____
_____
_____
_____
_____
_____
_____
_____
_____

Identifying Causes and Effects and Distinguishing Between Them

You have seen that in argumentative writing authors make statements and support their positions with arguments that develop causes and/or effects. In order to strengthen your literal comprehension skills, you must be able to recognize and distinguish between causes and effects. Consider the following paragraph in which the author makes a statement about memory and uses both causes and effects to support the statement.

Example

Your memory also misplaces or mis-files things occasionally. A "forgotten item" may thus be stored somewhere in your memory banks—wherever those banks may be—but you simply can't find the item "on command." Old experiences are often hard to retrieve because you have to scan the millions of similar index cards you've made since then to recover that one unique memory. The new memories thus *interfere* with your ability to recall older ones. Brand new experiences are sometimes hard to remember because you have such a limited number of cues as to their location in your long-term files, or because you must learn a whole new set of relationships between familiar items ("mental categories"). For instance, if you were to learn Chinese, you would have to prepare "mental index cards" in Chinese for every memory category that you have in English (MCCONNELL, 432).

Questions

1. Why are old experiences hard to remember? _____

   _____

2. What effect do new memories have on older ones? _____

   _____

3. What are two reasons why you can have a hard time remembering new experiences? _____

   _____

Authors support their position statements by developing causes, effects, or a combination of both. **Recognizing and distinguishing between causes and effects** helps you to comprehend the important ideas in essays, stories, articles, and text passages.

Practice

Consider the causes stated at the left and consider what logical effects they could have. Check those effects at the right. Do not check other causes or illogical effects.

Cause

A. Winning the state lottery could lead to

Possible Effects

_____ 1. Being fired from one's job

_____ 2. Paying old bills

_____ 3. Buying one's first lottery ticket

_____ 4. Hearing from friends and relatives

B. Earning a college degree could result in

_____ 1. Entering a career
_____ 2. Being prepared for the college entrance exam
_____ 3. Being accepted in a graduate program
_____ 4. Achieving passing grades

C. Writing a research paper could lead to

_____ 1. Deciding on a topic
_____ 2. Earning credit for the assignment
_____ 3. Organizing one's ideas
_____ 4. Registering for an advanced course

D. The effect(s) of overcrowding in prisons might be

_____ 1. Receiving effective classroom instruction
_____ 2. Not getting adequate medical attention
_____ 3. Early release for some prisoners
_____ 4. An increase in the crime rate

E. Installing computers in an office could lead to

_____ 1. Billing customers quickly
_____ 2. Slowing down the production rate
_____ 3. Hiring more file clerks
_____ 4. Lengthening the work week

Practice

First, consider the stated effect at the left and decide what could have led to that effect. Check the logical causes at the right. Do not check other effects or illogical causes.

Effect

A. Losing weight might be caused by

Possible Causes

_____ 1. Being worried about exams

_____ 2. Joining a health club

_____ 3. Becoming too thin

_____ 4. Being sick

B. Earning an A for your research report could be attributed to

_____ 1. Earning an A in the course

_____ 2. Carefully labeling the experiment

_____ 3. Doing the wrong assignment

_____ 4. Checking the report for its accuracy

C. Meeting with a career counselor might be the result of

_____ 1. Being sent on a job interview

_____ 2. Seeking career advice

_____ 3. Being unsure of how to write a résumé

_____ 4. Getting brochures from the counselor

D. Dropping a course could be a consequence of

_____ 1. Failing the first two tests

_____ 2. Changing your work hours

_____ 3. Enjoying the class greatly

_____ 4. Losing your standing as a full-time student

E. Comprehending a passage could be affected by one's

_____ 1. Understanding the stated facts

_____ 2. Understanding the vocabulary

_____ 3. Sensing the implied ideas

_____ 4. Choosing another book by that author

Applying Point-of-view Skills to Causes and Effects

Authors use facts and opinions to develop a point of view. Consider the following paragraphs to see how the author takes a position that expresses a point of view and then supports that position in different ways, first with causes and then with effects.

Example

Paragraph A

Many of my students have difficulty taking tests. For some, the test situation causes great stress and tension. The minds of these students "go blank" when they receive the test booklets. Others do not know how to study and, thus, come to the test ill-prepared to answer the questions. Some students study correctly but do not follow directions on the test. They usually do not finish the exam. These are some of the factors that contribute to the poor performance of certain students on tests.

Paragraph B

Many of my students have difficulty taking tests. As a result, they get poor grades on their quizzes. They must, therefore, work harder in class to communicate their understanding of the course content to me. In addition, they usually devote great periods of time to writing term papers and reports, in the hope that these assignments will raise their averages. Finally, many offer to do extra assignments in an effort to raise their grades. The effects of doing poorly on even one quiz can be stressful to most students.

Questions

1. In Paragraph A, what point of view about students does the author express? _____

Understanding Causes and Effects   135

2. Are the supporting statements in paragraph A causes or effects? _____
   Facts or opinions? _____

3. In Paragraph B, what point of view about students does the author express? _____

4. Are the supporting statements in Paragraph B causes or effects? _____
   Facts or opinions? _____

Recognizing that authors use facts and opinions to develop **a point of view** can help you to understand argumentative writing in which authors support their positions with causes and/or effects, any of which may be a fact or an opinion. A **fact** can be proven or disproven with evidence; an **opinion** represents the author's point of view and cannot be proven. However, the author can use facts to persuade the reader of the correctness of his or her opinion. Distinguishing between facts and opinions is basic to understanding argumentative and other writing styles used in essays, stories, articles, and text passages.

Practice

Read the following statements and supporting ideas. Determine whether each statement and its supporting ideas expresses the author's viewpoint (OPINION) or expresses a fact (FACT).

__OPINION__ 1. Living in the Northeastern part of the United States is clearly undesirable.

   __FACT__   The average yearly snowfall exceeds that of most of the Southern states.

   _____ The Northeastern cities are more densely populated than cities in the rest of the country.

   _____ People in the Northeast are less friendly than people from other parts of the country.

   _____ Schools in the Northeast are larger than schools in the rest of the country.

_____ 2. Because of continued research, we have refined our understanding of the physical properties of the human brain.

    _____ The brain weighs approximately three pounds.

    _____ The brain is made up of fifteen billion nerve cells.

    _____ The cortex of the brain is one-quarter inch thick.

    _____ The central fissure is a deep groove that runs down the center of the brain from front to back.

_____ 3. There are many difficulties connected with acting.

    _____ Jobs are hard to find.

    _____ Only a small percentage of people make a decent living as actors.

    _____ Actors spend time learning their roles.

    _____ Some shows close a few nights after they open.

_____ 4. What prevents some people from sharing their feelings with others?

    _____ Expressing their feelings may bring up a great deal of anxiety.

    _____ Many people don't recognize the feelings when they occur.

    _____ Some people have learned that certain emotions are acceptable while others are not.

    _____ Some people feel that they don't want to burden others with their problems.

Drawing Conclusions

Once you can identify the causes and effects the author uses to support a position, you can understand the literal or stated ideas in the passage. However, there are deeper understandings you can draw from argumentative and other writing styles. The following paragraphs appeared at the beginning of this chapter. Read them now to see how your understanding of the development of an argument supported by causes and/or effects can help you to form conclusions about a person.

Example

Paragraph A

There are several important reasons why Mike, a high school senior, was rejected by the hiring supervisor at the local electronics company. Mike's first problem was his poorly prepared job application. Because he filled it in during the bus ride to the interview, Mike made many errors. The paper was filled with erasures, crossings out, and blank spaces. Another reason was Mike's poor appearance; he wore faded jeans and an old flannel shirt to the interview. In addition, he was late, thereby making both himself and the interviewer uncomfortable. As a result, Mike made a bad impression during the interview and never had the opportunity to demonstrate his fine abilities.

Questions

1. What general statement does the author make about Mike? _____

2. Does the author develop the paragraph with causes or with effects?

3. Did Mike take the interview seriously enough? _____

4. List three reasons to support your conclusion in Question 3:

Paragraph B

Mike's rejection by the hiring supervisor led to several changes in his attitude toward seeking a job. He made an effort to have a well prepared application which he checked for its thoroughness and appearance. He was determined to look presentable, and so he chose his clothing carefully the evening before the interview. Arriving late for the first interview affected his planning for the next one; he arranged for a ride to the plant and left extra time for unexpected delays. As a result of his efforts, Mike arrived on time, looked presentable, and appeared confident throughout the interview. The effect was so positive to Mike's attitude that he was able to demonstrate his abilities during the interview. As a consequence of his efforts, Mike was offered a position at the plant.

Questions

1. What general statement does the author make about Mike? _____

   _____

2. Does the author develop the paragraph with causes or with effects?

   _____

3. Did Mike take the interview seriously enough? _____

4. List four reasons to support your conclusion in Question 3:

   _____

   _____

   _____

   _____

You can develop an understanding of places, situations, people, and ideas that the author intended you to have but did not state directly. Being able to **form conclusions** that are logically drawn from stated facts broadens your understanding of the subjects of essays, stories, articles, and text passages.

Practice

Read each statement and the two possible conclusions that follow it. Based on information in the statement, check the conclusion(s) that can be drawn logically from that statement.

1. Henry has been late to class six times, absent four times, and has missed two of three quizzes.

    _____ Henry is unconcerned about his grade in this class.

    _____ Henry enjoys the class.

2. There was no way of knowing when we had crossed the border—no markings, no border posts—but it must have happened sometime around midnight.

    _____ The author is unfamiliar with the area.

    _____ The author is traveling alone.

3. When I got back to the compartment, the only other passenger had awakened.

    _____ The other person had been sleeping.

    _____ The author is traveling by car.

4. Dr. Tobias, Chief of Surgery, requested clamps and sutures from the attending head nurse. They both glanced at the clock and quickly finished closing the wound. They smiled when they realized they had finished well within the critical time limit for such a surgical procedure.

    _____ The experienced surgeon and his nursing assistant performed the complicated operation.

    _____ During the operation, each was aware of the time.

5. The instructor read Sam's paper and saw that Sam had scored perfectly on the multiple-choice, true-false, and fill-in sections of the test. However, Sam had not finished the major essay and had lost fifteen points on that section.

    _____ The instructor believes that Sam generally understands the work.

    _____ The instructor fails Sam.

140   Comprehension Skills

Practice

The following pictures contain information about two people. From the information in each picture you should be able to draw a logical conclusion about what is happening between them.

_____ 1. From this picture, you can logically conclude that
   a) the young man and woman are interested in each other.
   b) the couple has just had a fight.

_____ 2. From this picture, you can logically conclude that
   a) the two people have just become engaged.
   b) the two people are not interested in each other.

Understanding Causes and Effects   141

_____ 3. From this picture, you can logically conclude that
   a) the young man is more interested in the young woman than she is in him.
   b) the young woman is more interested in the young man than he is in her.

_____ 4. From this picture, you can logically conclude that
   a) the couple disagrees about a subject.
   b) the couple agrees about a subject.

Practice

Read the following text paragraphs and check the conclusions that can be logically drawn.

In all types of jobs, many employees claim to be *alienated* from their work: They feel trapped, overwhelmed by meaninglessness, self-estrangement, isolation, and powerlessness. Alienation is usually regarded as an affliction of the blue-collar worker, but in recent years thousands of executives have abandoned their jobs for work that may pay less but promises to be more rewarding. For instance, they have become artists, craftworkers, or singers, or have established agricultural communes.

One of the effects of alienation is sheer escapism. Thousands of assembly line workers and an equal number of executives daydream through their work. More than half admit they are working at only half their potential. Others escape through drugs and alcohol: Workers in some factories stay high on drugs during their entire shift; and many executives rely on the three-martini lunch to get through the day (INSEL AND ROTH, 40).

_____ 1. Assembly line workers experience a great deal of alienation.

_____ 2. The majority of assembly line workers and executives are working at only half their potential.

_____ 3. Working on the production of an item, from start to finish, gives a person pride and a sense of achievement.

_____ 4. Alienation of workers costs companies a great deal.

_____ 5. Executives experience greater feelings of alienation than blue-collar workers do.

Applying Cause and Effect Skills in Selections

You now have the opportunity to practice the comprehension skills developed in this unit. First, preview the idioms and new vocabulary for each selection. Then, as you read, be aware of the development of causes and/or effects, the use of signal words and phrases, and the expression of points of view. You will also draw conclusions from the selections. Finally, you will use these skills as you complete a writing assignment.

Selection 1: "On the Pressures and Politics of Waiting in Line"
by Georgia Dullea

Vocabulary Preview

The following terms appear in the reading. Knowing their meanings will help you to understand the selection.

Idioms	Meanings
bump the line	move in front of others in a line
on hold	waiting on the phone until the other person is ready to speak to you
queue up	form a line
stacked up	being in one of a group of planes that are circling an airport waiting for permission to land
stake claims	declare possession of an area by placing a piece of personal property there
tied up	unable to move

Vocabulary	Meanings
accomplice	one who helps another in a wrongdoing
barging into	rudely pushing
consensus	general agreement
inanimate	lifeless
integrity	wholeness
penalized	placed at a disadvantage
persistent	continuous
ponder	consider something deeply
rational	based on reason
tedious	tiresome

The British **queue up** and the Americans wait in line, except for New Yorkers, who wait *on* line. No one seems to know the reason for this local idiom. It is something to **ponder** while waiting in/on line.

Another thing to ponder: It is estimated that Americans spend up to five years of their lives in that **tedious**, stressful but unavoidable process known as waiting. The estimate comes from Dr. Thomas Saaty, a University of Pittsburgh mathematician and systems analyst who is also an authority on waiting lines or queues, as scientists call them.

"Being forced to wait in long lines by faceless institutions is like being victimized by a monster," he remarked the other day in a telephone interview. . . . "Studies show that otherwise **rational** people act irrationally when forced to stand in line or wait in crowds, even becoming violent. Remember the gas lines a few years ago?"

Standing in line is not a necessary requisite to being part of a queue, as Dr. Saaty pointed out. One can be trapped **on "hold"** at the end of a phone line, **stacked up** over an airport, **tied up** in highway traffic, delayed in a doctor's crowded waiting room.

Of course, queues are more than a matter of academic interest to ordinary people. They are a grim reality of city life. While there seems to be no **consensus** on the city's worst line, the ones mentioned most often in talks here and there were lunchtime lines at banks and post offices and, among younger people, movie lines and college-registration lines.

"Bank lines," said Mark Sloane, an investor. "No matter what time of day you bank, the number of tellers is inadequate to the number of patrons. Even when the bank is open you see long lines in front of the money machines outside."

"Department stores," said Margot Albrecht, who resents missing a day's work as a systems engineer to wait for furniture deliveries, another queue of sorts. "They always tell you to expect delivery from 8 A.M. on. You sit home waiting and waiting, and they always arrive at 6 P.M. I don't know if anybody gets furniture delivered before 6 P.M."

"Supermarkets," said Ed Frantz, a graphic artist, who once abandoned a full shopping cart in the middle of a long checkout line. It was not a political act. "The line was filled with coupon clippers and check writers," he recalled. "And suddenly I had to walk away. Food no longer mattered."

Not all lines are deadly. "Some lines are actually fun," Doreen Schroeder insisted. She is a hair stylist, and she has met "some interesting men" in the Ray's Pizza line.

In any line the fundamental rule is first come, first served, or what social scientists call "distributive justice." Exceptions may be made, say, in fancy restaurants where the headwaiters have their favorites, but, in general, the rule prevails.

In theory, then, everyone should have an equal interest in keeping an orderly line. In practice, the interest varies depending on one's position in line. Researchers in one of Dr. Milgram's classes demonstrated this when they took turns **barging into** two kinds of lines—railroad ticket lines at Grand Central Terminal and theater ticket lines at Duffy Square.

In both cases the strongest protests came from the immediate victims or the people directly behind the line jumpers. People farther down the line complained less or not at all, even though they had been equally **penalized** by losing a place.

Similar findings were reported by Dr. Mary Harris, a University of New Mexico psychologist, in experiments at airports, theaters and supermarkets. She also found people less angered if the line jumper said, "Excuse me, please," or told a hard-luck story or if an **accomplice** in line agreed to admit the line jumper.

"People will put up with a lot of aggressive behavior as long as they don't feel it is directed at them personally," said Dr. Robert A. Baron, a specialist in human aggression at Purdue University. "Clearly, standing in line is an obnoxious activity for almost everybody. Realizing that you're not being singled out, that you're one of a large group of sufferers, seems to help."

If misery loves company, so do sports fans. Dr. Leon Mann documented this several years ago when, as a Harvard professor, he studied the long overnight queues for tickets to ball games in his native Australia.

"Outside the stadium something of a carnival atmosphere prevails," he wrote in The American Journal of Sociology. "The devotees sing, sip warm drinks, play cards and huddle together."

Like the teams they had come to watch, the fans in line took timeouts. Some worked in shifts, with certain members leaving to take naps or eat meals, while others saved their places in line. Some **staked claims** in line with items of personal property such as sleeping bags and folding chairs. "During the early hours of waiting," Dr. Mann noted, "the queues often consisted of one part people to two parts **inanimate** objects."

Nobody has ever seriously studied Helen Quinn's Saturday morning line for Metropolitan Opera tickets, but perhaps someone should.

Miss Quinn is not an official at the Met and she will be the first to tell you that. She is merely a **persistent** member of the line for standing-room tickets, one with a certain command presence and a certain philosophy: "Standing on line should not be a physical endurance contest. If the wait is long you should be able to report in and then leave to go to the washroom, go to church or have a bite to eat."

For 15 years standees at the opera have been doing just that, thanks to Miss Quinn's ticketing system, which functions like that of a busy bakery. She makes, dates and numbers her tickets—one for each of the 175 standing-room spots available—and dispenses them to early birds, who begin showing up about 6 A.M., two hours before the box office opens. Assured of a place, ticket holders then leave and return shortly before 8 A.M. to line up for the real tickets.

When Miss Quinn's authority as the self-appointed keeper of the line is questioned, she shrugs and says, "Somebody has to do it." When the **integrity** of her line is threatened she fights. "Last week we had some trouble with a man who tried to **bump the line**, but we caught him," she said firmly. "We almost always catch them."

Literal Comprehension

If the statement reflects information found in the selection, write TRUE (T). If it does not, write FALSE (F).

_____ 1. One "waits in line" in New York, but "queues up" in other parts of the country.

_____ 2. Being part of a queue always refers to standing in line.

_____ 3. Waiting in line is experienced by most people in this country.

_____ 4. Small numbers of customers are responsible for creating long bank lines.

_____ 5. Furniture is rarely delivered at the promised time.

_____ 6. Up to five years of the lifespan of every American is taken up with waiting in lines.

_____ 7. Everyone agrees that the worst type of line is the supermarket line.

_____ 8. Miss Quinn, an official of the Metropolitan Opera, is in charge of the Saturday morning line.

_____ 9. There is an almost carnival atmosphere at overnight queues in Australia.

_____ 10. Fans in Australia stake claims about who will win the ball game.

Cause and Effect

Complete the following statements based on your understanding of the causes and effects developed in the selection.

_____ 1. Waiting in line often leads one to
   a) have an equal interest in the composition of the line.
   b) protest when anyone steps into the front of the line.
   c) lose the feeling of being victimized.
   d) share a sense of belonging with a group of fellow sufferers.

_____ 2. Being part of a queue is frequently the result of
   a) encountering heavy air or highway traffic.
   b) being told that a college class has plenty of seats available.
   c) having reserved seats at a football game.
   d) staking a claim.

_____ 3. Standing in line often leads to
   a) waiting for a furniture delivery.
   b) seeing examples of unreasonable behavior.
   c) having favored customers at a fancy restaurant.
   d) giving up all one's possessions.

_____ 4. The theory of distributive justice should result in
   a) those at the end of a line protesting most vigorously.
   b) penalties for those who wait patiently.
   c) those who arrive first being served first.
   d) accomplices being welcomed into the line.

_____ 5. People stake claims or take numbers in order to
   a) relax, secure in the knowledge that their place is reserved.
   b) enjoy contests of physical endurance.
   c) avoid being victimized by monsters.
   d) have time to ponder their positions in the line.

Point of View

Check those statements the author would probably agree with.

_____ 1. Standing in line is stressful, yet unavoidable.

_____ 2. University researchers should not spend their time studying people who wait in line.

_____ 3. A study of the Saturday morning opera line would benefit others.

_____ 4. Lines are natural phenomena.

_____ 5. People should allow anyone to barge into a line.

Forming Conclusions

Check those conclusions you can logically draw from the selection.

_____ 1. There is an almost absolute system of equality in waiting in line.

_____ 2. Waiting in line is a common feature of modern society.

_____ 3. Nothing is important enough to force one to wait in line for hours.

_____ 4. Researchers who study queues can analyze group behavior.

_____ 5. The only people interested in lines or queues are research psychologists and sociologists.

_____ 6. Some people always take unfair advantage of others.

_____ 7. People who wait in line exhibit behavior that can range from aggressive to submissive.

_____ 8. Researchers rarely wait in line.

_____ 9. Most people can endure the demands of standing in lines.

_____ 10. Waiting in line involves acceptance of unstated rules about order and group behavior.

Vocabulary

A. Check each sentence in which the underlined term is used correctly.

_____ 1. Standing in line is so tedious that people look forward to doing it.

_____ 2. Queues usually form at sports arenas before championship games.

_____ 3. Only one person bumped the line as he left the theater.

_____ 4. The gardener staked his claim to the land by packing his belongings and leaving.

_____ 5. The salesperson's persistent efforts resulted in his making the sale.

B. Match each term with its meaning at the right.

_____ 1. tied up
_____ 2. barge into
_____ 3. ponder
_____ 4. consensus
_____ 5. rational
_____ 6. stacked up
_____ 7. inanimate
_____ 8. accomplice
_____ 9. on hold
_____ 10. penalize

a. lifeless
b. rudely push
c. put at a disadvantage
d. waiting for someone to speak to you on the telephone
e. based on reason
f. consider something carefully
g. unable to move
h. general agreement
i. one who helps another in a wrongdoing
j. waiting for airport clearance to land

Writing

Georgia Dullea wrote about the effects of waiting in lines and the reasons why people wait in lines. Consider how you feel waiting in line to register for a class or waiting in line for a parking spot in an overcrowded parking lot. Select either situation and develop a short essay of three or four paragraphs in which you describe the effects that the situation has on you.

Selection 2: "Cheating"
by Dena Kleiman

Vocabulary Preview

The following terms appear in the reading. Knowing their meanings will help you to understand the selection.

Idioms	Meanings
crib sheet	a list of correct answers used by students illegally during an exam
do something out of spite	do something in order to get revenge; in a vengeful way

Vocabulary	Meanings
attributed to	named as the cause of something
compromise	dishonor oneself; ignore one's principles
confronted with	faced with; having to deal with
disillusioned	disappointed
forge	illegally imitate someone's signature
integrity	ethical principles; honesty
pragmatic	practical
predecessors	forefathers
scandalous	disgraceful; improper
slackening	loosening; relaxing
synthesize	blend into a whole
trend	general tendency
vandalism	malicious or spiteful destruction or damage to property

Charlene, a sixteen-year-old sophomore at a high school in northern Connecticut, found herself **confronted with** an algebra test to which she knew none of the answers. Rather than fail, she smuggled the test out with her and, during lunch hour, filled in the answers with the help of her friends. During a break, she sneaked back into the classroom, crumpled the test with her shoe, and left it lying on the floor. The teacher assumed it had been dropped when the tests were collected; she corrected it, and Charlene received a B.

Paul, sixteen, who is president of the junior class at a New Jersey high school, recently turned in a book report written years before by his older brother. His brother had received an A minus on the report. Paul was luckier—he got an A.

Cheating is, of course, nothing new. But today, educators and administrators are finding that instances of academic dishonesty on the part of students have become more frequent—and are less likely to be punished—than in the past. Whether it is copying a friend's homework, using a **crib sheet** on an exam, stealing advance copies of a final, **forging** a teacher's recommendation, scribbling algebraic formulas on one's palm, or hiring someone else to write a term paper, cheating appears to have gained acceptance among a growing number of teen-agers.

In a 1978 study of cheating at twenty-two high schools in Georgia, Dr. Fred Schab, of the University of Georgia, in Athens, found that academic dishonesty was common among good and poor students alike—although both boys and girls said they thought boys cheated more. The four chief reasons students gave for **compromising** their **integrity**: "Too lazy to study," "Fear of failure," "Parental insistence on grades," and "It's easy to cheat."

Why is student cheating on the rise? No one really knows. Some blame the **trend** on a general **slackening** of moral values among today's youth. They point to statistics showing increased **vandalism** and school theft and claim that **scandalous** developments, such as Watergate and Abscam, have **disillusioned** youth about the moral integrity of people in positions of trust and power.

Others have **attributed** increased cheating to the fact that today's youth are far more **pragmatic** than their more idealistic **predecessors**. Whereas in the late sixties and early seventies, students were filled with visions about changing the world, today's students feel great pressure to conform and succeed.

In interviews with students at high schools and colleges around the country, both young men and women said that cheating had become easy. Some suggested they did it **out of spite** for teachers they did not respect. Others looked at it as a game. Only if they were caught, some said, would they feel guilty.

"A lot of what they expect you to learn, you'll never use anyway," said a seventeen-year-old junior from a Philadelphia high school. "I want to be a builder. What do I care about English and history? I cheat because I don't want to fail and have to take the whole thing over again."

"People are competitive," said a sixteen-year-old high school sophomore named Anna, from Chicago. "There's an underlying fear. If you don't do well on every single assignment, you're going to fail. Your life is going to be ruined. The pressure is not only from parents and friends but from yourself. To achieve. To succeed. It's almost as though we have to outdo other people to achieve our own goals."

"I decided I would do anything to get into college," said Stephen, a student at Dartmouth College, in Hanover, New Hampshire. When he was in high school, he and several friends always sat in the back of the room during exams and used finger signals to cheat. "Dishonesty is everywhere, and you have to do it to survive," he said.

Edward A. Wynne, editor of *Character,* a magazine that examines the policies that shape the character of American youth, blames the rise in academic dishonesty on the schools. He claims that administrators and teachers have been too hesitant to take action and specifically criticizes the University of Illinois at Urbana, where he teaches.

Under the current system at Illinois, students accused of cheating are entitled to three levels of appeal. "Teachers don't make cheating much of an issue," Dr. Wynne said, "because they don't want to get involved. And you know what happens when there is not a policeman on the highway: Everybody speeds. So it is with cheating."

Dwight Huber, chairman of the English department at Amarillo (Texas) High School, sees the matter differently, blaming the rise in cheating on the way students are evaluated.

"I would cheat if I felt I was being cheated," Mr. Huber said. He feels that as long as teachers give short-answer tests rather than essay questions and rate students by the number of facts they can memorize rather than by how well they can **synthesize** information, students will try to beat the system.

"The concept of cheating is based on the false assumption that the system is legitimate and there is something wrong with the individual who's doing it," he said. "That's too easy an answer. We've got to start looking at the system."

Literal Comprehension

Complete each statement with information found in the selection.

_____ 1. Educators are finding that students who cheat
   a) are more likely to be punished than before.
   b) have poor academic records.
   c) can be academically weak or strong.
   d) use the information in later years.

_____ 2. Each of the following is an example of cheating except for
   a) forging a teacher's recommendation.
   b) turning in a book report written by another student.
   c) speeding on a highway.
   d) memorizing algebraic equations.

_____ 3. Charges of weakness have been aimed at
   a) teachers who do not make an issue of cheating.
   b) patrolmen who are not assigned to highways.
   c) students of the sixties who had visions of changing the world.
   d) teachers who give essay exams rather than short-answer tests.

_____ 4. Students are characterized as
   a) lazy and poorly trained.
   b) pressured to succeed.
   c) visionary.
   d) having few or no values.

_____ 5. Educators have found that
   a) an increase in punishment leads to a decrease in cheating.
   b) a decrease in punishment leads to an increase in cheating.
   c) there is no relationship between punishment and cheating.
   d) none of the above.

Understanding Causes and Effects

Cause and Effect

Check those statements that reflect information in the selection.

_____ 1. The growth in national scandals relates to the increase in the number of disillusioned youth.

_____ 2. A major reason students cite for cheating is their fear of failure.

_____ 3. The 1960s vision of changing the world led students to conform.

_____ 4. Many students consider cheating a game that they are sure to win.

_____ 5. Parents blame students for trying to be successful.

_____ 6. Some people blame the educational system and its administrators for the rise in cheating.

_____ 7. Punishment for cheaters has always been severe in this country.

_____ 8. The student who cheats must be at fault because the system is correct.

_____ 9. The pressure to be accepted by a school is often cited as a factor in the rise in cheating.

_____ 10. Students are not the only ones who cheat.

Fact and Opinion

The following statements appear in the selection. Decide whether each is a FACT or an OPINION.

_____ 1. Cheating appears to have gained acceptance among a growing number of teen-agers.

_____ 2. Academic dishonesty is common among good students as well as among poor students.

_____ 3. Students state that "parental insistence on grades" is a chief reason for cheating.

_____ 4. Scandalous developments, such as Watergate and Abscam, have disillusioned youth about the moral integrity of people in positions of trust and power.

_____ 5. University of Illinois students accused of cheating are entitled to three levels of appeal.

Point of View

If the author would probably agree with the statement, write YES on the line. If she would not, write NO.

_____ 1. The educational system is sound, and students must follow every rule.

_____ 2. Parents alone must take responsibility for the rise in student cheating.

_____ 3. There is more than one cause for the rise in cheating.

_____ 4. The educational system in this country would benefit from a thorough evaluation.

_____ 5. Students who cheat should be expelled from school.

Forming Conclusions

Check those conclusions that can be logically drawn from the selection.

_____ 1. The problem of student cheating has its roots in deeper problems.

_____ 2. Testing procedures are not stressful to most people.

_____ 3. Competition is an external pressure applied to today's youth.

_____ 4. English majors should take only English courses.

_____ 5. Students do not cheat on essay tests.

_____ 6. A change in the educational system will eliminate the need to cheat.

_____ 7. Today's students are not pragmatists.

_____ 8. The behavior of elders affects the behavior of young people.

_____ 9. Most students cheat.

_____ 10. Punishment is an effective method of changing the negative values of a society.

Understanding Causes and Effects

Vocabulary

Check those sentences in which the underlined terms are used correctly.

_____ 1. Vandalism increased after security guards reduced the number of patrols in the building.

_____ 2. Ben hid a crib sheet in his jacket so that the teacher wouldn't see it.

_____ 3. The candidates confronted each other for the first time when they spoke in different cities.

_____ 4. My supervisor, like her two predecessors, usually holds Monday morning staff meetings.

_____ 5. Slacken the rope by carefully pulling it tighter.

_____ 6. She attributed her high grades to hours of studying.

_____ 7. Harry's behavior was so scandalous that everyone avoided him socially.

_____ 8. Stewart's pragmatic approach to the problem resulted in unrealistic ideas.

_____ 9. The winner of the marathon was disillusioned by the high standards and fairness displayed by all participants.

_____ 10. Forging a signature on government forms is unethical.

_____ 11. I gave you that gift out of spite and hope that you realize how fond I am of you.

_____ 12. Ellen placed herself in a compromising position when she did not report her best friend for cheating on the test.

_____ 13. How dare you question my integrity! I have held this trusted position for twelve years.

_____ 14. John synthesized his notes by separating class and lecture pages.

_____ 15. The trend toward having large families is decreasing.

Writing

Dena Kleiman took a position that student cheating is increasing. She supported that argument with the reasons why students cheat. Often situations involving the handling of money can lead to cheating. State a position on cheating in a money-handling situation, such as being a cashier. Support your position by illustrating the effects of cheating.

Selection 3: "America in Solitary"
by Kitty Hanson

Vocabulary Preview

The following terms appear in the reading. Knowing their meanings will help you to understand the selection.

Idioms	Meanings
Big Three-O	thirtieth birthday
close in	surround
coming of age	reaching adulthood; usually at eighteen or twenty-one years of age
cramp your style	limit your normal freedom
making sweeping changes	making great changes
post-war boom	period after World War II when a great number of babies were born
rattling around	wandering around without any purpose
tick off	list

Vocabulary	Meanings
booming	rapidly growing
cohabiting	living as a couple without marriage
communes	places where individuals live in a group, sharing all work and money
exotic	foreign and unusual
gentrifiers	middle-class people who move into a poor neighborhood, improving properties, but displacing the area's previous residents
hallmark	a distinguishing feature
household	the people of the house
opted	chose
phenomenon	an unusual and significant occurrence
syndrome	characteristics that distinguish a special situation
thriving	growing successfully
vie	compete

Four or five times a week, Helen Wahlgren, 38, executive secretary, sits down to a leisurely dinner in her Manhattan apartment at a table elegant with the sparkle of glasses, the gleam of silver and the glow of candlelight. The table is set for one. . . .

In a two-bedroom apartment in Forest Hills, John Ringer, a young attorney, spends most week nights studying and listening to classical music or experimenting with new and **exotic** recipes in his well-equipped kitchen. On weekends, he dates one of several girlfriends, or entertains at informal dinner parties at which he is both cook and host. . . .

Their names are fictitious, but these New Yorkers are very real. Alone in their own private worlds of pursuits and problems, triumphs and disappointments, each of them is a significant statistic. Together with millions of others like themselves, they make up a rapidly growing movement that is **making sweeping changes** in the way America lives.

Sociologists call it a profound sociological **phenomenon**. Most of us simply call it Living Alone. Some of us love it. Some of us hate it. All of us are affected by it.

From the let's-all-live-together **communes** of the '60s, through the **cohabiting-**couple **syndrome** of the '70s, America is moving with dramatic speed into the one-person/one-**household** life style. Once considered the unfortunate fate of old maids, confirmed bachelors and lonely widows and widowers, Living Alone is becoming increasingly common as an alternative to family living.

You can see it in the supermarkets, where the large economy sizes are being pushed aside by the staples of life in half-sizes, half-pints, mini-loaves, and servings-for-one.

You see it in **thriving** fast-food stores and busy restaurants. A study of spending patterns has found that the individual living alone spends almost as much on restaurant meals as a married couple.

You see it in the travel and entertainment industries, which thrive on live-aloners who spend their money on activities that provide companionship.

You see it in **booming** service and repair businesses. Without someone to share life's little chores, live-aloners buy more services.

And you see it in the appearance of new appliances as manufacturers **vie** for the one-person-household dollar with gadgets that will fry one egg, grill one sandwich, broil one steak.

It is a life style that experts say will be the **hallmark** of the '80s and will change American society for years to come. Its impact already is apparent in small towns, suburbs and city neighborhoods throughout the country. Sociologists and similar society-watchers **tick off** a number of reasons for the phenomenon:

- People are delaying marriage. Once it was customary for young adults to live with their parents until they got married. But when the babies of the **post-war boom** began **coming of age** at the rate of four million a year after 1965, many decided they weren't ready for marriage. They weren't ready to stay at home, either. To guarantee their independence, they **opted** to live alone.
- People are living longer. One result has been to create more widows. In 1900, a woman could expect to live two years after her husband's death. Today she'll probably live eight years longer. One out of every three live-alone householders is a widow.
- More people are being divorced and separated. Most of them live alone.
- People are more independent. The widowed mother or the divorced father, who once would have moved in with his children, today prefers

to remain independent. There are fewer children to depend on, anyway, and middle-aged kids can **cramp your style.**

Unlike the communes and cohabiting couples, the one-person household is a trend that is expected to continue for a long, long time.

This is the real "singles scene" in America today. It's more than the discos, more than the singles bars and senior citizens centers, more than adult education classes and cruises and self-improvement groups. It's the young law graduate in his first job.... It's the widowed grandmother in suburbia, **rattling around** in a house grown too big and too suddenly quiet.... It's the young artist in the low-rent neighborhood wondering where his next studio is going to be as **gentrifiers** and developers **close in**.... And it's the private secretary or woman executive wondering where her first baby will come from as she faces the **Big Three-O** still looking for the man who'll be the father.

Living alone in America today is a lot of people loving it and a lot of people hating it; a lot of people living for Friday, and a lot of people just trying to make it to Monday.

It's the '80s way of living, and it is affecting the way we live, the way we play, the way we love, the way we spend our time, and the way we spend our money.

More important, it can even affect how long we live and how healthy we are while we're doing it.

Literal Comprehension

Check those statements that reflect information found in the selection.

_____ 1. Most people hate to live alone.

_____ 2. Supermarkets carry products packaged in single-serving sizes.

_____ 3. Married couples and singles spend almost the same money dining out.

_____ 4. Living alone is a feature of American living that began during the post-war boom.

_____ 5. Older people today depend on their children more than in the past.

Cause and Effect

Decide whether each of the following is a reason why people live alone (CAUSE) or an effect of their living alone (EFFECT).

_____ 1. Food companies produce individually packaged single-servings of many items.

_____ 2. The repair business is booming.

_____ 3. Fewer people are getting married immediately after graduation.

_____ 4. The availability of apartments is decreasing.

_____ 5. Medical research has led to improved health-care products.

_____ 6. Peoples' attitudes toward divorce are changing.

_____ 7. Many city areas are undergoing renewal, and apartment buildings are being torn down.

_____ 8. Peoples' attitudes toward marriage are changing.

_____ 9. Many social labels, such as "old maid" and "confirmed bachelor," are disappearing.

_____ 10. Leisure activity industries are expanding their services.

Point of View

Check those statements the author would probably agree with.

_____ 1. People who live alone face many uncertainties.

_____ 2. In the 1990s, there will be no more communes or cohabiting couples.

_____ 3. Older people will continue to live with their children.

_____ 4. Large companies will respond to changes in American styles of living.

_____ 5. In the future, living alone will replace living with a family.

Forming Conclusions

Check those statements that are logical conclusions based on the information in the selection.

_____ 1. The majority of people living alone are young people.

_____ 2. People who lived in communes were rebelling against the idea of living alone.

_____ 3. Only older women can expect to live alone.

_____ 4. Some people do not look forward to weekends.

_____ 5. People who live alone do not need companionship.

_____ 6. People who live alone tend to buy houses in the suburbs.

_____ 7. Escort service companies are growing rapidly.

_____ 8. People who live alone earn high salaries.

_____ 9. The saying, "Two can live as cheaply as one," has some truth to it.

_____ 10. People who live alone have no one to share experiences with.

Vocabulary

A. Use one of the following idioms in each sentence.

make sweeping changes   close in
rattled around   cramp my style
post-war boom   tick off
Big Three-O   coming of age

1. We _____ from room to room in the mansion.

2. Students can _____ many reasons for not completing assignments.

3. The new administration is planning to _____ when it takes control of the company.

4. My bedroom is so small that at times I feel as if the walls are about to _____ on me.

5. _____ is often a requirement for being allowed to drink or vote.

6. I have found that working with a partner can often _____.

7. College enrollments soared with teenagers born during the _____.

8. Facing the _____ often produces anxiety for many people.

B. Combine the divided sentences that follow.

_____ 1. Joe wanted to change his lifestyle, and so he joined a

_____ 2. Communal living

_____ 3. Her food preferences range from the exotic

_____ 4. When students take exams,

_____ 5. Most of the class opted for

_____ 6. Even in poor economic times,

_____ 7. The stresses of married life affect even

_____ 8. A syndrome we could not correct

_____ 9. As gentrifiers have moved in

_____ 10. Census takers count the number of people in

a. the publishing industry thrives.

b. they vie for good grades.

c. a household.

d. some neighborhoods have changed dramatically.

e. was the lateness of staff members.

f. requires people to share what they earn.

g. farm commune in the country.

h. couples who cohabit.

i. to the ordinary.

j. an in-class test rather than a take-home quiz.

Writing

Kitty Hanson described the reasons why more people are living alone in the eighties. You will soon be faced with decisions about how you wish to live. Choose one lifestyle such as living alone, in a commune, or in a family, and, in a short essay of three or four paragraphs, develop the reasons why you prefer that way of living.

Selection 4: "Mind Over Matter"
by James V. McConnell

Vocabulary Preview

The following terms appear in the reading. Knowing their meanings will help you to understand the selection.

Idiom	Meaning
mind over matter	the ability of a person to overcome a mental, emotional, or physical situation by exercising mental powers

Vocabulary	Meanings
beset	attack
charlatan or quack	someone who pretends to have special training or skills, as in medicine
chronic	continuing for a long time or happening frequently
intoxication	the condition of being drunk
laced	mixed, usually by adding a slight amount of alcohol
potent	powerful

Mind Over Matter

The field of medicine has always attracted its share of **quacks** and **charlatans**—that is, disreputable women and men with little or no medical knowledge who promise quick cures at cheap prices. The reasons why quackery thrives even in modern times are not hard to find.

To begin with, pain seems to be a **chronic** human condition. A person whose body or mind "hurts" will often pay any amount of money for the promise of relief. Second, even the best medical treatment cannot cure all the ills that **beset** men and women. People who mistrust or dislike the truths that their physicians tell them often turn to more sympathetic ears.

Many people lack the training necessary to evaluate medical claims. Given the choice between (a) a reputable physician who says a cure for cancer will be long, difficult, expensive, and may not work at all, and (b) a salesperson who says that five bottles of a secret formula "snake oil" will cure not only cancer, but tuberculosis, syphilis, warts, and bad breath as well, some individuals will opt for the bottle of snake oil.

Many "snake oil" remedies are highly **laced** with alcohol or narcotic drugs. Anyone who drinks them may get so drunk or stoned that they drown their pains in the rising tide of pleasant **intoxication**. Little wonder that "snake oil" is a popular cure-all for minor aches and hurts! But let there be no misunderstandings. A very few "home remedies" actually work. However, most remedies sold by quacks are not only useless, but often can be harmful to the user as well.

The Placebo Effect

By far the most **potent** reason that quack medicines still are sold around the world has to do with the power of "**mind over matter**." Your brain is the master organ of your body: It regulates all the chemical processes that keep you alive and well. When you become depressed and lose hope, your **autonomic** (emotional) nervous system slows down these bodily processes and retards your chances of getting well. When you have hope and faith, these curative processes are speeded up. You are thus more likely to recover even from the most dreadful of diseases than when you are depressed.

The medical doctor who can *convince* her or his patients that they will recover typically cures more people than the physician whose behavior causes those patients to lose faith in themselves and in the medical profession.

If a sick person mistakenly believes that his or her condition can best be cured by taking a drug of some kind, most physicians are quite happy to give the patient a **placebo**, or pill made of sugar or ordinary flour. The placebo pill does no harm at all, but it may so help the patient *psychologically* that the person's *pain* diminishes and the patient may actually recover much faster than without taking the pill. Indeed, placebos may even have a *physiological* effect. In the late 1970's, several investigators reported that placebos cause the body to produce more of the natural pain-killers called **enkephalins**.

Many physicians estimate that at least half the patients they see suffer from psychological rather than physical ailments. For these patients, the "placebo effect" of taking a sugar pill is perhaps the best cure any medical doctor can offer. If sugar pills can be so helpful to physicians, little wonder that snake-oil remedies often appear to bring about miraculous cures.

Literal Comprehension

If a statement reflects information in the selection, write TRUE (T). If it does not, write FALSE (F).

_____ 1. Most home remedies are effective.

_____ 2. Snake-oil remedies are a popular cure-all for minor aches and pains.

_____ 3. A placebo can help a patient psychologically, but not physically.

_____ 4. If doctors can convince their patients that they will recover, they always do recover.

_____ 5. Physicians prescribe placebos for half the patients they see.

Cause and Effect

Complete each of the following statements.

_____ 1. All of the following are reasons why quacks continue to do business except which one?
   a) People who are in pain will often pay any amount of money for the promise of relief.
   b) The average person is not trained to evaluate medical claims and diagnoses.
   c) Although their remedies may not cure a disease, quacks nevertheless do not harm their patients.
   d) Quacks convince patients that they can help them.

_____ 2. The effect of becoming depressed about an illness is
   a) a slowing of the body's curative processes.
   b) a collapse of the autonomic nervous system.
   c) an emotional state that ranges from extremes of depression to happiness.
   d) a decrease in the physical symptoms of the disease.

_____ 3. Doctors who prescribe placebos are
   a) risking harm to their patients.
   b) prolonging their patients' agonies.
   c) curing over 50 percent of serious diseases.
   d) helping their patients psychologically.

_____ 4. The principal of "mind over matter" is seen in the
   a) speeding up of the autonomic nervous system.
   b) effectiveness of a placebo.
   c) relationship between being hopeful and the effectiveness of the body's curative system.
   d) all of the above.

Point of View

Check those statements the author would probably agree with.

_____ 1. Doctors should not lie to their patients.

_____ 2. States should jail those persons convicted of being quacks.

_____ 3. Medical boards of review should investigate any doctor who prescribes a placebo.

_____ 4. There will always be people who seek the help of charlatans.

_____ 5. Many who seek the help of a medical doctor should instead seek the help of a psychologist.

Forming Conclusions

Check those statements that can be logically drawn from the selection.

_____ 1. Quacks and charlatans are motivated by the desire to help mankind.

_____ 2. Only poorly educated people seek the advice of quacks.

_____ 3. Placebos have many of the same effects as snake-oil remedies.

_____ 4. The human brain is a powerful and mysterious organ.

_____ 5. A person's brain controls many aspects of the body's pain-tolerance level.

Vocabulary

Complete each sentence using one of the following terms:

potent   placebo   charlatan   beset   laced   chronic   intoxication

1. How can you talk to that _____ when I've recommended Dr. Evans, the best surgeon on the hospital staff?
2. The clinical test group was given a _____ instead of the prescription drug.
3. Have a cup of my special coffee; it's _____ with brandy.
4. Some people who are _____ by problems seek professional advice.
5. Quacks use _____ arguments to convince people to buy their remedies.
6. Is this a _____ condition or did you just notice the symptoms?
7. In your state of _____, you really shouldn't drive.

Writing

James V. McConnell discussed the reasons why quacks and charlatans are successful. Consider a situation in which a friend recommends an unorthodox remedy for symptoms you are experiencing. Take a position about the remedy and, in a paragraph, discuss the reasons why you took that position.

Role-playing

Consider the following story in which a young man is faced with a difficult situation that he must resolve. The activities that follow provide practice in speaking and in writing an argumentative essay.

The Situation

George is a young man living in the country of Zembla. He works as a machinist in a small factory. He is very good at his job and enjoys doing it, but he would like to go to college to study computer programming. He cannot do this in Zembla, where there is no computer industry to speak of. And so, even though he does not speak much English, he is thinking of taking his savings and coming to the United States on a student visa. He has saved about six thousand dollars which he believes will be enough to cover his tuition and living expenses for about a year. His parents are opposed to his plan, since they are both very old, and they fear that they won't see him again if he leaves. His father has offered to build George a home on some land the family owns in Zembla if he will only stay.

George does not know what to do. He is about to meet his friend, Rose, and Rose's cousin, Peter. Rose spent two years in the United States, but returned to make a life for herself in Zembla. She found the language problem difficult, the people unfriendly, and the pace of life in the United States far too hectic. Peter, on the other hand, has been living in the United States for the past seven years and has made a successful life for himself there. He speaks English well, has many American friends, and owns and manages an apartment complex in a large city. He is back in Zembla for a month's vacation. Rose will try to talk George out of emigrating to the United States, while Peter thinks that if George does just as he did, he too will be successful.

Directions

Choose three students who will play the roles of George, Rose, and Peter. The rest of the class will be divided into two groups of coaches, one to advise Peter and one to advise Rose. They must provide Peter and Rose with arguments to use in their upcoming discussion with George. When the coaches have finished advising the students who will play George, Rose, and Peter, these three may leave the classroom for a few minutes to plan how they will act out their roles. As soon as they return, the role-playing scene begins. It ends when George comes to a decision, one way or another. Afterward, the entire class can question George, Peter, or Rose, or participate in a general discussion: Did George make the right decision? Why or why not?

Topics for Discussion and Writing

1. Discuss your own decision to come to the United States (or to move to your area). Did you make it yourself, or was it made for you? Are you pleased with the decision? Why or why not?
2. Imagine that five years have gone by. George and Peter (or George and Rose) meet once again. How have things turned out for them? Complete this dialogue in which they discuss what has happened to them since George made his decision. Follow this form:

   Peter: George, how have you been?
   George: You won't believe what's happened to me!

3. Should George come to the United States? Write an essay of three or four paragraphs in which you describe George's situation, discuss the reasons for and against his coming to the United States, and present your own conclusions.
4. Peter managed to adapt to life in the United States while Rose did not. What personal qualities would cause one person to succeed? Write a short essay discussing these reasons.

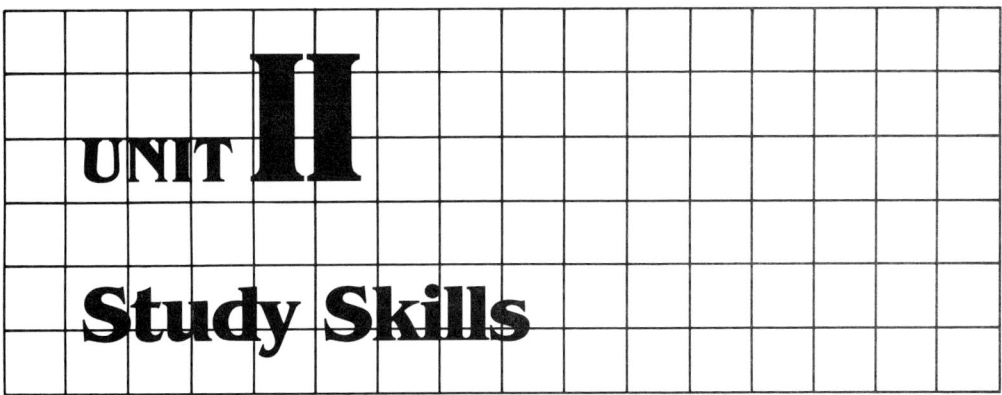

UNIT II

Study Skills

INTRODUCTION

In this text, you can develop reading skills essential to understanding different styles of writing: recognizing a sequence, listing, comparison-contrast, or cause-effect relationship between ideas; determining the use of fact, opinion, and point of view; and making predictions, assumptions, and forming conclusions. Here, you will focus on expository writing and will build upon your basic comprehension skills. For example, when you read a text chapter, you may need to understand a chronological sequence, a listing of descriptions, a comparison or contrast, or the causes or effects of an event. However, you must master still another skill component to achieve success with textbook work: study skills. You cannot succeed in text work if you simply comprehend the material. Your instructor expects you to demonstrate your mastery of it. You must, therefore, develop a system of locating the important ideas, organizing them for future recall, and studying them for a test. In the next part of this text, you will learn to develop those study skills that are necessary for demonstrating mastery of text material.

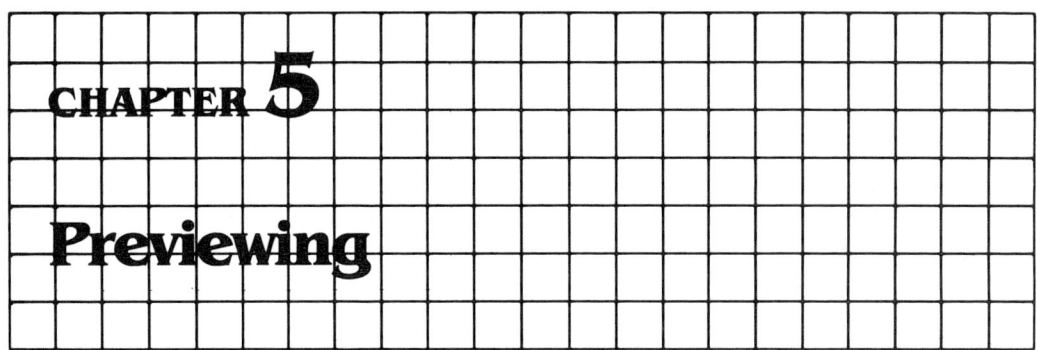

Understanding Text Organization

What do you do when you begin to read a newspaper or magazine? Do you turn the pages and glance at the headlines, titles, or pictures? Or, do you scan the table of contents and parts of the articles? How do you select a book from the library? Do you scan the titles of books on the shelves? Do you select a book and glance through the pages? Or, do you read its table of contents or preface to see what it is about?

What steps do you follow when you begin to read a textbook? Do you look at the number of pages in the assignment, the pictures or charts, and the size of the print? Do you ever glance at the table of contents, chapter titles, or pages before you begin your assignment?

If you do any of these, you are following steps students should take when they read a textbook. By *looking over* certain parts of an assigned chapter, you can have a better idea of what you are about to read and how you should approach reading it.

> You can **preview** or look over a text by examining specific parts of it before starting to read. Previewing provides you with an understanding of the content, the purpose, the level of difficulty, and the organization of a text.

Previewing The Textbook

Authors organize textbooks in a way that can help students to study. The following chart has three sections. The first, **Part of the Text**, provides the major sections of a textbook. The second, **Information Derived**, lists the information a reader can obtain in each part of the text. The third, **Location in the Text**, states where each section is usually found in a textbook.

Part of the Text	*Information Derived*	*Location in the Text*
Title Page	title name of author name of publisher	usually on the first or second page
Copyright Page	publication date names of copyright owners name and address of publisher	follows the title page
Preface or Introduction	author's message to the reader about the purpose of the text, the way to use the text, and acknowledgments by the author of the people who assisted in the preparation of the text	follows the copyright page
Table of Contents	outline, sometimes with a brief explanation, of the contents in page order	usually follows the preface
Chapter Titles	topics or subjects of each chapter	first page of each chapter
Chapter Introduction	specific information about the major ideas or general facts about the chapter topics	beginning of each chapter
Chapter Subtitles	major subject divisions in the chapter	throughout each chapter
Visual Aids; pictures, graphs, charts, italicized words	illustrations of portions of the written text; focus on important words and phrases	throughout each chapter

Part of the Text	Information Derived	Location in the Text
Chapter Summary	general, brief review of the important facts or the author's conclusions about information in the chapter	end of each chapter
Chapter Review or Questions	author's questions about important facts in the chapter	usually after the summary
Glossary	explanations of specific terms used in the text	end of the book; can be found before the index or at the end of chapters
Appendix	charts, graphs, and surveys that provide additional information on the material in the chapters	usually before the index
Index	alphabetical list of terms and subjects by page	last pages of the text

Practice

Use the preview chart to help you preview this book. Then answer the following questions.

1. Who are the authors? _____
2. What is the publication date? _____
3. What is one reason the authors wrote this text? _____
   _____
4. Where did you find the answer to Question 2? _____
5. Must you complete each Unit in sequence? _____
6. Does this text contain chapter summaries? _____
7. Does this text contain chapter introductions? _____
8. How do the authors focus your attention on each rule? _____
9. For what audience is this text intended? _____
10. Can you write answers in this book? _____
11. How many *New York Times* articles appear in this book? _____
12. Does each Unit contain a vocabulary drill? _____

13. Have the authors directed the Preface to the instructor, the student, or both? _____

14. Which Units contain outlining skills? _____
_____

15. Which Unit contains comparison and contrast selections? _____

16. Name the three major skill divisions in this text: _____
_____
_____
_____

17. Which Units contain instruction in recognizing signal words? _____
_____

18. Which Unit contains cause-and effect-instruction? _____

19. Which Unit contains fact- and opinion- instruction? _____

20. Name one textbook from which a reading selection was taken: _____
_____

21. Which Unit introduces idioms? _____

22. How many role-playing exercises appear in the book? _____

23. Does this text contain a glossary? _____

24. Name four types of context clues presented in this text: _____
_____
_____
_____
_____

25. Are photographs and illustrations presented in each Unit? _____

Previewing Chapters in Psychology and Sociology

Most instructors assign a chapter of the textbook as homework. Before you begin reading the assignment, preview the following parts of the chapter to gain an understanding of its contents: the introduction, the subtitles, the first sentences of several paragraphs, the visual aids, such as boldfaced terms, charts, and pictures, all review questions, and the summary or conclusion.

Texts may not contain all of these parts. However, most contain three or more of them. Here is a brief description of the information you can gain from each part of the chapter.

In an **Introduction**, the author usually gives a general idea of the material in the chapter and provides some background information relating to the subject of the chapter.

Through **Subtitles**, the author divides a chapter into topic sections. The subtitles appear in large, boldfaced print so that topic divisions can be easily seen. It is helpful to rephrase a subtitle as a question to gain an idea of what material may be presented in the section. For example, REM SLEEP, a subtitle from a psychology text, can be rephrased into the question: What is REM Sleep?

In the **First Sentence** of a paragraph, the author usually states the main idea. Previewing a few of the first sentences provides you with an understanding of some important ideas you will read about.

Through **Visual Aids** such as pictures, graphs, charts, boldfaced or italicized print, the author gives you a means of distinguishing special information from the rest of the text.

In **Summaries or Reviews**, the author generally restates the major ideas discussed in the chapter. Often, the author draws conclusions about the topics or draws several major ideas together in a single statement.

Finally, through **Review Questions**, the author focuses on the main ideas in the chapter.

The following exercises are designed to illustrate how much information you can gain by previewing a text chapter.

Practice

Preview the portions of the psychology chapter that follow. The important parts are highlighted so that they can be easily seen. When you have previewed them, answer the following.

A. When you have previewed the *introduction,*

1. List three topics that you will read about.

   _____

   _____

   _____

2. What is the length of time for nightly sleep cycles? _____

3. What is the relationship between nightmares and sleeping pills? _____

   _____

4. Which two types of sleepers will you read about?
   _____   _____

B. After you have previewed the *subtitle* and *the first sentence of the paragraphs,*

   1. Name two topics you will read about.
      _____   _____

   2. List three facts used to describe short sleepers.
      _____
      _____
      _____

   3. List three facts used to describe long sleepers.
      _____
      _____
      _____

C. After you have previewed the *boldfaced words* that are clearly defined,

   1. List the five words that are defined in the margin.
      _____   _____   _____
      _____   _____

   2. List seven words you will want to define as you read the chapter.
      _____   _____   _____
      _____   _____   _____
      _____

D. After you have previewed the *chapter summary,*

   1. What does state of consciousness mean? _____
      _____
   2. How many stages of sleep are there? _____
   3. During which stage of sleep do dreams occur? _____
   4. Name two types of nightmares and state when they will occur.
      _____
      _____

CHAPTER 3
Sleep, Drugs, and Altered States of Consciousness

> **Did You Know That...**
>
> "Consciousness" is a "primitive term" that is almost impossible to define?
>
> You can alter your normal state of consciousness by speeding up or slowing down your brain's activity level?
>
> Your body has regular physiological rhythms that vary according to the time of day?
>
> You go through several 90-minute sleep cycles nightly?
>
> You dream more just before you awaken?
>
> "Short sleepers" are often active, ambitious, and conformist, while "long sleepers" are often shy, passive, and sexually inhibited?
>
> Dreaming may help you store the day's experiences away in memory?
>
> Nightmares frequently occur a day or so after you've stopped taking sleeping pills?
>
> Drugs affect you chiefly by speeding up or slowing down your bodily processes?
>
> Your neurons can secrete both transmitters and inhibitors?
>
> "Uppers" act like neural transmitters, while "downers" act like neural inhibitors?
>
> Hallucinogens may have their odd effects because they disrupt the delicate functional balance between the two hemispheres?
>
> Marijuana apparently does less damage to the body than does alcohol?
>
> You can learn to control your brain waves using a biofeedback machine?

"Long" and "Short Sleepers"

"Short Sleepers" Baekeland and Hartmann report that the "short sleepers" had been more or less average in their sleep needs until the men were in their teens. But at about age 15 or so, the men voluntarily began cutting down their nightly sleep time because of pressures from school, work, and other activities. These men tended to view their nightly periods of unconsciousness as bothersome interruptions in their daily routines.

In general, these "short sleepers" appeared ambitious, active, energetic, cheerful, conformist in their opinions, and very sure about their career choices. They often held several jobs at once, or worked full- or part-time while going to school. And many of them had a strong urge to appear "normal" or "acceptable" to their friends and associates.

EEG machines. Electro-encephalo-graphs. These devices measure brain waves and other forms of electrical activity in the nervous system. The brain-wave pattern is usually displayed graphically on a sheet of paper, or flashed on a picture tube similar to the one used in television sets.

When asked to recall their dreams, the "short sleepers" did poorly. More than this, they seemed to prefer *not* remembering. In similar fashion, their usual way of dealing with psychological problems was to deny that the problem existed, and then to keep busy in the hope that the trouble would go away.

The sleep patterns of the "short sleepers" were similar to, but less extreme than, sleep patterns shown by many mental patients categorized as **manic**.

"Long Sleepers" The "long sleepers" were quite different indeed. Baekeland and Hartmann report that these young men had been lengthy sleepers since childhood. They seemed to enjoy their sleep, protected it, and were quite concerned when they were occasionally deprived of their desired 9 hours of nightly bed rest. They tended to recall their dreams much better than did the "short sleepers."

Many of the "long sleepers" were shy, anxious, **introverted**, inhibited, passive, mildly depressed, and unsure of themselves (particularly in social situations). A number of them, for instance were still virgins at age 25–30. Several openly stated that sleep was an escape from their daily problems.

Summary

1. Your ordinary state of mental functioning is defined as being your usual **state of consciousness**, or your usual state of awareness.

2. Certain experiences—such as falling asleep, dreaming, taking various drugs, achieving sexual orgasm, or concentrating intensely—can lead to unusual or **altered states of consciousness**.

3. When you relax, or fall asleep, most of your nerve cells fire at much slower rates than normal. Whenever you are extra-alert, or extremely excited, many of your neurons fire at much faster rates than normal.

4. The four stages of sleep run from light sleep (**Stage 1**) to deep sleep (**Stage 4**). Following Stage 4 sleep, you typically experience an **REM period** during which you will have one or more dreams.

5. Each sleep cycle is about 90 minutes long, including an REM period of about 10 minutes. Stage 4 (deep) sleep predominates during the first and second sleep cycles of the night. REM periods and **dreaming** increase during later cycles.

6. During REM sleep, most of the **voluntary muscles** in your body are inhibited—except for those that control eye movements.

7. There are two main types of nightmares: **anxiety dreams** and **incubus attacks**. Anxiety dreams take place during REM sleep and do not usually involve bodily movements. Incubus attacks take place during Stage 4 sleep and occasionally are followed by sleepwalking (McCONNELL, 59, 67, 89).

Manic (MANN-ick). From the Greek word mania, meaning "insanity." A manic person is someone terribly excited, almost to the point of madness. The opposite of depression.

Introverted (INN-trow-ver-ted). A term made famous by the Swiss psychiatrist, Carl Jung. Introverted people spend much of their time looking inward, inspecting their own thoughts, feelings, and values.

Psychological energizers. Drugs that speed up neural firing, that "turn on" the nerve cells by acting as super-transmitters, that make you use up your energy resources at a faster speed. Also called "stimulants" and "uppers," because they often elevate or "turn up" both your neural firing and your mood—at the price of using up more energy per minute.

Stimulants (STIM-you-lants). Another term for "psychological energizer" or "upper." Any drug that stimulates neural firing.

Practice

Preview the portions of the sociology chapter that follow. The important parts have been highlighted for you. When you have previewed them, answer the following.

A. After you have previewed the *introduction*,

1. List the four subjects you will read about.

   _____   _____

   _____   _____

2. Find the reason why we study disapproved behavior. _____

   _____

B. After you have previewed the *boldfaced words in the margins*, list the words you will need to know.

   _____   _____

   _____   _____

   _____   _____

C. After you have previewed the *subtitles*, name two major topics of "Structuring Conformity" that you will read about.

   _____   _____

D. After you have previewed the *first sentences of the selected paragraphs*,

   1. Is deviance necessary for a society's well-being? _____
   2. What does social control refer to? _____

   _____

   3. Name two types of social control.

   _____   _____

E. After you have previewed the *chapter summary*, answer these questions.

   1. Name four effects of deviant behavior.

   _____   _____

   _____   _____

2. Name three theories of the causes of deviance.

_____

_____

_____

3. How do norms function in society?

_____

_____

4. When does labeling occur? _____

_____

CHAPTER 6
Conformity and Deviance

Social order depends on most individuals doing what is expected of them by others. Yet, we are generally fascinated by tales of those who break the rules. *Deviants* are people who violate group norms, and we tend most often to think of criminals or the mentally ill. But deviance can also describe acts that are more industrious, more ambitious, more heroic, or more honest than that generally found or expected within the social system. For example, war heroes, self-made millionnaires, and Nobel prize winners are as deviant in terms of non-normative behavior as are skid row alcoholics or bank robbers.

> **Deviants** are people who violate group norms.
> **Deviance** refers to variations from the rules for usual, approved behavior.

The sociological study of deviant behavior, however, has been almost exclusively concerned with socially *disapproved* deviation from the norms of a society or group. Where there are rules of conduct, there are also definitions of deviance. To define **A** (acceptable behavior) is automatically to create another class of events, **non-A** (unacceptable behavior). Deviance and conformity thus are two sides of a coin; one cannot exist without the other.

By studying *disapproved* behaviors, we may learn what is valued in a society or subgroup, or at least what those who make the rules find threatening. Many theorists have proposed that people who violate norms must suffer from some sort of personal pathology; that is, they are immoral or sick. Yet, as we shall see in this chapter, deviant behavior differs in content, but not in essential nature, from what we call conformity. Indeed, the process whereby both deviant and nondeviant roles are constructed and performed is quite similar, flowing from group experiences and sanctions.

This chapter examines the types of norms members of groups and subgroups are expected to observe and how these are internalized, the social functions of deviance, the kinds of people and situations that are likely to be called deviant, and how norms are enforced and deviants punished.

Structuring Conformity

Whereas deviants were once thought to be possessed by devils, the deviant of today is viewed as in need of psychiatric help or punishment (or both). In either case, the deviant has disrupted ongoing relationships within a system by behaving in an unpredictable manner. But how is deviance possible given the powerful forces toward conformity?

Emergence of Norms

Norms are arrived at through social interaction and represent a kind of negotiated consensus, dominating individual perceptions and behaviors in diverse situations. Even in situations where no norms have been established, their emergence can be predicted.

What may one conclude about deviant behavior? Its common denominator obviously rests not in the particular behavior itself but upon the definitions by some social group, such as college students, middle-aged parents, or legislators. Deviance is signified by the **societal reaction** to an act or lifestyle that violates currently popular institutional or moral norms.

The insight that deviance does not reside in the act itself but rather in how the act is interpreted by others was noted by Emile Durkheim (1960) who further proposed that deviance, rather than being totally destructive or evil is necessary to societal well-being. To hope to eradicate all sin and waywardness is to neglect the very real functions that deviance plays in maintaining social order. Behavior that seems abnormal from a psychological or psychiatric viewpoint is not necessarily pathological from the perspective of the sociologist. Durkheim, for example, pointed out that crime is a necessary part of all societies. Paradoxical as this may sound, crime fulfills an important service to the extent that it generates **social cohesion** in opposition to such behavior. As members of a community or society come together to express outrage and to ventilate their anger about "criminal" acts, they develop closer ties to one another than previously existed. This coming together in shared moral indignation creates what Durkheim termed the "public temper," that is, a feeling shared by members of the group and belonging to no one individual in particular. Through creation of the public temper or, in more current terminology, group consensus, social organization is strengthened. This process is well illustrated by the public temper created in the United States by reports of mistreatment upon the release of the fifty-two persons held hostage in Iran for fourteen months in 1979–81. A wave of shared moral indignation swept the country, generating a sense of solidarity, and defining the Iranians as barbarians and outlaws with whom promises need not be kept. When deviants are identified and punished, members of the society are united in a common morality that strengthens their own belief system. Thus deviance has a dual function: **unification of the group** and **boundary setting**.

What do we mean by **boundary setting**? It is a process by which shared norms and values are established within a social collective such as the family, the school, the workplace, a professional group, one's hometown, or the entire society. Within these social collectives, boundaries are placed at the outer limits of

> Boundary setting is the process by which norms and values are established, setting limits on acceptable behavior.

acceptable and permissible behavior so that people's actions are limited in range, and made relatively stable and predictable. In other words, conduct is confined to legitimized forms; behavior outside the boundaries is clearly identified as unacceptable. Kai Erikson (1966) suggests that people learn boundaries through the process of **confrontation**. That is, the limits of acceptable behavior are constantly being tested to ascertain the boundary lines. Often, the nature of this confrontation is public, as are the demonstrations in support of gay rights or in the current controversy about hand-gun control.

> People learn where boundaries are set through the process of confrontation.

Social Control

Social control refers to planned or unplanned social processes by which people are taught, persuaded, or forced to conform to norms. It is the complement of deviance, for without deviant behavior there would be no need for social control and without social control there would be no way of recognizing the boundary between the acceptable and the unacceptable. In every society, some punishments or negative sanctions are established for deviant behavior, and the weight of the community is brought to bear on the deviant.

> Social control refers to processes by which normative behavior is enforced.

Social control may be either **formal** or **informal**. **Informal mechanisms** include expressions of disapproval by significant others, shunning, and withholding of positive rewards for the disapproved behavior. As discussed in Chapter 5, most people internalize norms in the course of socialization. This is any group's most powerful protection against deviance, in that the individual's own conscience operates as an agent of social control.

> Informal mechanisms of social control include disapproval by significant others and withholding of positive rewards.

When informal sanctions fail, **formal agents** of social control may be called upon. In contemporary society, such formal agents and agencies include psychiatry and other mental health professions; mental hospitals; police and the courts; prisons; and social welfare agencies. All these formal agents function to limit, correct, and control violation of norms. Conflict theorists would also point out that social control agents and systems tend, in any society, to serve the interests of powerful groups and to enforce the norms most beneficial to those who make the rules and who, therefore, define unacceptable behavior.

> Formal agents of social control include mental hospitals, police, courts, and prisons.

Social control, whether formal or informal, has a dual function. First, it punishes the wrongdoer and reaffirms the boundaries of acceptable behavior. Second, and less recognized, it regulates the flow and manner in which deviants are treated. Currie (1968) has suggested that there are two types of formal control systems: **repressive** and **restrained**. A **repressive** control system is characterized by unrestrained power to suppress deviance and by a high level of interest in ensuring conformity.

> Repressive control systems are characterized by unrestrained power to suppress deviance.

Summary

In every human group some behaviors become defined as appropriate standards of role performance. Once these **norms** are developed, conformity is encouraged and enforced through agents of social control. Norms set boundaries for acceptable behavior, and simultaneously define non-normative behavior that is beyond the boundary. **Deviance** refers to activities that violate the expectations of others and the rules of appropriateness. A **deviant** is one who others define as requiring attention by agents or agencies of social control.

In general, deviant behavior can be seen as a functional necessity in any society. Deviance **mobilizes the community** in support of its values and norms; it **clarifies the boundaries** between the accepted and the unacceptable; it **provides channels for the release of antisocial feelings**; and it can become the **cutting edge of long-term changes** that enhance the group's adaptability.

In the past, a great deal of research has focused on the individual causes of deviance. Theories based on **biological differences** have been particularly popular. Yet none of this research has demonstrated a direct link between a particular biological characteristic and a specific form of deviant behavior. Similarly, **psychological theories** have failed to establish any clear relationship between early childhood experience or mental states and a given act of nonconformity.

Sociological theories of deviance, by contrast, focus on the deviant act in its full **social context**: who does what, when, and where, and how do others respond. It is not the action that is central, but rather the response or effect the action has on others and society that defines the act. **Labeling** occurs when the behavior is judged to be outside normative boundaries, and when the individual is held responsible for that behavior (HESS, 135, 139, 140, 145, 158–159).

Chapter 6

Understanding Topics

Identifying Topics of Lists

Just as previewing helped you to understand the important ideas in a chapter, so identifying the topic of what you are reading helps you to understand its general subject. For example, a random list of words or phrases may appear meaningless unless there is a topic that identifies the items in the list. Consider the following example.

Example

Smith	Room 312	2 o'clock
Clark	Room 202	3:30 o'clock
Hotchkiss	Room 211	1 o'clock
Dugan	Room 308	12:30 o'clock
Kaufman	Room 320	11:00 o'clock

Questions

1. What is this list? _____
2. Try to name two possible subjects of this list: _____
_____

You probably experienced difficulty understanding the list because it has no title. Consider the following example to see how the addition of a topic or title immediately helps you to understand the subject of a list.

Example

Arrival Times

San Diego	12:00 A.M.
Chicago	10:00 A.M.
Miami	9:45 A.M.

Questions

1. What is the topic or subject of the list? _____
2. Do you know what the list is before you read the items? _____

Identifying the topic helps you to focus on the general subject of a reading. A **topic** is the general subject of the items in a list, the sentences in a paragraph, or the paragraphs in a selection. Identifying the topic of what you are reading is the first step toward understanding subject information.

Practice

Read the following lists. One item in each list is the title or topic, that is, the general subject of the items in the list. Highlight the topic in each list.

1. Supermarkets
   Retail Stores
   Discount Shops
   Department Stores
   Specialty Shops

2. Word Processors
   Business Machines
   Typewriters
   Computers
   Dictaphones

3. Horticultural Societies
   Hunting Societies
   Agricultural Societies
   Types of Societies
   Industrial Societies

4. Planning the Yearly Budget
   Directing Group Meetings
   Organizing New Departments
   Evaluating Staff Members
   Management Functions

Understanding Topics

Practice

Read the following lists of chapter subtitles. Decide what topic or chapter title is appropriate for each list and write it on the line.

1. *Job Benefits*
   Paid Vacation
   Bonus
   Commission
   Medical Insurance

2. _____
   Narrative
   Descriptive
   Argumentative
   Analytical

3. _____
   Microcomputers
   Minicomputers
   Hardware
   Software

4. _____
   Stimulants
   Sedatives
   Diet Pills

5. _____
   Tragedy
   Drama
   Melodrama

6. _____
   Meat Group
   Fruit and Vegetable Group
   Bread and Cereal Group
   Milk Group

7. _____
   Planets
   Comets
   Meteors
   Stars

8. _____
   Property Liability
   Fire and Theft Protection
   Automobile Coverage
   Health and Accident Benefits

9. _____
   Federal Reserve System
   Commercial Banks
   Savings and Loan Associations

10. _____
    Cohabitation
    Group Marriage
    The Single Life

Identifying Topics in Text Paragraphs

You practiced identifying the topic of a list of items. Consider the following paragraph to see how the topic is the general subject of the sentences in a paragraph and how it can be stated in one or two words.

Example

Yesterday, I received a copy of the registration and class schedule for the fall semester. I saw that Professor Smith's Biology class meets in Room 312 at 2:00, Dr. Clark's Physical Education class meets in Room 202 at 3:30, and that Professor Hotchkiss' English class meets in Room 211 at 1:00. In addition, Professor Dugan's Speech class, in Room 308 at 12:30, may be in conflict with Dr. Kaufman's Drama section in Room 320 at 11:00.

Question

What is the subject of this paragraph? _____

> Recognizing that the **topic of a paragraph** is the general subject of the ideas in that paragraph helps direct your attention to the most important ideas. The topic is much like a title for the paragraph and is stated in a few words. Knowing the paragraph topic builds a base of comprehension from which to move to further understandings about expository readings such as textbook chapters.

Practice

Read the following text paragraphs. Determine the topic of each by reading the entire paragraph carefully and then deciding what the general subject is. Write the topic in one or two words on the line.

1. _____

   No particular foods have special merit for a diet for athletes. Some coaches are under the impression that a high meat diet is essential and even recommend steak for breakfast. No additional protein is required except where there is an unusual development of muscle. Most athletes need only sufficient high-quality protein foods, such as eggs, meat, fish, and poultry, to meet the daily needs (FLECK, 334).

2. _____

   The importance of good parking facilities must not be overlooked in an evaluation of a location and a specific site within it. The vast majority of all retail stores built in the United States since the end of World War II include some provision for off-street parking. In several central business districts, parking facilities are provided by individual stores, cooperative arrangements among stores, and municipal governments. The number of parking spots, their distances from the store site, and the availability of employee parking should all be evaluated (BERMAN, 236).

3. _____

    Even a 15-minute walk, a University of Southern California study found, can be more relaxing than a tranquilizer for easing muscle tension and relieving anxiety. Exercise has also been found to increase energy, reduce free-floating hostility, improve concentration and alertness, and make people less self-conscious and better able to handle stress. Many runners and other athletes speak of experiencing a natural "high" during the course of exercise—an exhilarated and euphoric state that lasts for several hours afterwards. In fact, exercise has been used to treat mental disorders. University of Wisconsin researchers found that running three times a week for 30 to 45 minutes reduced symptoms of depression in a group of depressed patients (COMBS, 290).

4. _____

    The mass media are the various forms of communication that reach a large audience without any personal contact between the senders and the receivers of the messages: newspapers, magazines, books, television, radio, movies, and records. Although they are unquestionably a powerful socializing influence, the precise impact of the media is difficult to gauge. The most influential medium is probably television. There is a TV set in 95 percent of American homes, and the average American between the ages of three and sixteen spends more time in front of the TV set than in school (ROBERTSON, 119).

5. _____

    A distinguishing feature of the department store is indicated by its name. The entire store is organized around departments for the purpose of providing service, promotion, and control. A general merchandising manager is responsible for the store's product planning. Reporting to the manager are the buyers who manage each department. These buyers typically run the departments almost as independent businesses; they are given considerable discretion in merchandising and layout decisions. Acceptance of the retailing axiom that well-bought goods are already half-sold is indicated by the department manager's title of *buyer*. Buyers, particularly those in charge of high fashion departments, spend a considerable portion of their time deciding on the inventory to be carried in their departments (BOONE AND KURTZ, 242).

Practice

Read the following paragraphs from a health text. First, write the topic of each paragraph on the line marked Topic. Then, write the title or general topic for the entire passage on the line marked Title.

Title: _____

Topic: _____

In recent years there has been a movement toward fasting—that is, not eating for a given period of time. Advocates of fasting claim it to be a way not only of losing weight but also of getting rid of chemicals in the body, burning off old and diseased tissues, rejuvenating and revitalizing the body, and in general helping a person to feel better if he or she is feeling exhausted, depressed, and unenergetic. It is, they say, a form of "spring cleaning" of the body, a "burning of body rubbish."

Topic: _____

Fasting is supposedly diffferent from starving. In fasting the body uses its own tissue reserves, in inverse order of importance, with fat being used before muscle. Starving, on the other hand, deprives the body of essential nutrients, a process that can kill you. Fasting enthusiasts say that as long as you are not hungry it is generally safe to fast; but if you continue not to eat after your hunger returns, you are beginning to starve yourself. However, fasting produces a mild ketosis that interferes with hunger sensations, and it is common for people *not* to have a return of hunger during a fast.

Topic: _____

Although the body can tolerate fasts for up to 30 days (some people have gone longer, but that is pushing it), beginners are advised to fast no more than three to five days. During that time, it is essential to drink water, though some fasters also drink juice or other beverages, and many take vitamin supplements. Fasters must avoid all drugs and medicines, must not take long baths (since the blood pressure will drop, and prolonged bathing may lower it even further, causing dizziness or even blackout), and must keep warm, since their body temperature is apt to go down. Fasters continue to work and exercise at their normal levels. By the third day of the fast, the body will begin breaking down its own tissues. The longer people fast, the more gradually they must return to their normal diets, usually eating easily digestible foods in small quantities during the first few days (COMBS, 275).

Practice

Read the following paragraphs from a business text. First, write the topic of each paragraph on the line marked Topic. Then, write the title or general topic of the entire passage on the line marked Title.

Title: _____

Topic: _____

Mail order is a type of retailing where the company receives orders primarily by mail or telephone and offers its merchandise for sale in a catalog or through some other form of printed material. This type of retailing can be divided into three categories: general-merchandise catalog house, such as Sears and Montgomery Ward; stores offering telephone shopping; and firms, other than general-merchandise catalog houses, that sell goods over long distances by mail.

Topic: _____

Total 1976 mail-order sales have been estimated at $19.2 billion by Maxwell Sroge Company, a Chicago-based mail-order marketing consultant. Eight thousand businesses used mail order in selling their products. Among industries, ready-to-wear clothing was the mail-order leader with sales estimated at more than $2 billion. Insurance ($1.2 billion) was second; magazine subscriptions ($975 million) were third; and books ($966 million) were fourth. Total mail-order sales represented 18 per cent of U.S. general merchandise sales.

Topic: _____

Mail-order retailing has several strong points. First, costs are reduced: initial investment costs are low; a mail-order business can be operated out of a garage or basement; inventory levels are minimal; no fixtures or displays are needed; a prime location is unnecessary; store hours do not have to be maintained; and a personal sales force is not needed. Second, a large geographic area can be covered. Third, it is possible for a firm to offer lower prices because of its reduced costs relative to a store retailer. Fourth, the consumer is given a convenient method of shopping. Fifth, for a store retailer, mail-order trade supplements normal sales volume (BERMAN, 77).

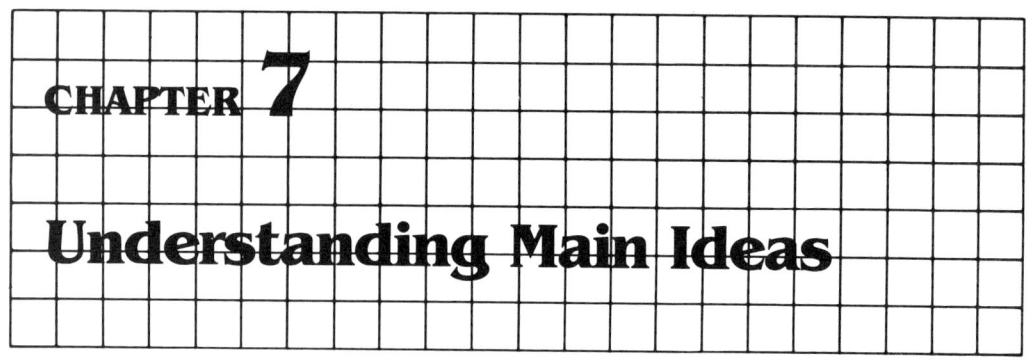

CHAPTER 7

Understanding Main Ideas

Relating Topics, Main Ideas, and Details

Reading text or expository material requires good comprehension and study skills. For example, recognizing the topic provides a frame of reference for the subject you are reading about. That understanding can be built upon by identifying the main idea of a paragraph. The main idea is the general statement the author makes about the topic. Consider the following two paragraphs to see how each has the same topic, "Foods for Athletes," yet each develops a different aspect of that topic.

Example

Paragraph A
No particular foods have special merit for a diet for athletes. Some coaches are under the impression that a high meat diet is essential and even recommend steak for breakfast. No additional protein is required except where there is an unusual development of muscle. Most athletes need only sufficient high-quality protein foods, such as eggs, meat, fish, and poultry, to meet the daily needs (FLECK, 334).

Paragraph B
The pre-game meal should consist of highly digestible foods and should be consumed not less than three hours before the athletic activity. Athletes frequently are under strain and stress prior to a game or contest and digestion may be prolonged. Replacing a solid pre-game meal with a calorie-rich meal of liquids has been tried and found to be sound from the practical and physiological points of view. Individual food preferences should be respected, for an athlete knows from experience the foods he tolerates best (FLECK, 334).

Questions

1. In the first paragraph, highlight the most general statement the author makes about a diet for athletes.

2. In the second paragraph, highlight the most general statement the author makes about a diet for athletes.

Even though the topic is the same for both paragraphs, the general statement or main idea is different in each paragraph.

3. Name three details that support the main idea in the first paragraph:

   _____

   _____

   _____

4. Name four details that support the main idea in the second paragraph:

   _____

   _____

   _____

   _____

> Identifying the topic and the main idea is the basis of understanding text paragraphs. A **main idea sentence** is the most general statement the author makes about the topic or subject of the paragraph. The main idea generally describes or "covers" the details in the paragraph.

Identifying the Main Idea in Various Locations in the Paragraph

It is important to understand the main idea of a paragraph. Consider the following example to see how an author can vary the placement, or location, of the main idea sentence.

Example

MAIN IDEA: **There are many reasons why people open their own businesses.**

_____. Independent retailers need a small initial investment. They can make all major decisions about business matters and general policy. Besides these, _____. In addition, they can limit their costs and increase their profits by carefully controlling expenditures for labor and merchandise. They are the primary recipients of financial returns from a well-run business. _____.

Question

Can you place the main idea sentence in any of the three blank spaces and still have a meaningful paragraph? _____

Another way that the author may write the same paragraph follows. Note that the main idea is not stated in this version.

Example

Independent retailers need a small initial investment. They can make all major decisions about business matters and general policy. In addition, they can limit their costs and increase their profits by carefully controlling expenditures for labor and merchandise. They are the primary recipients of financial returns from a well-run business.

Question

What is the main idea of the paragraph? _____

This last version has the same information as the previous paragraph, but the main idea is unstated. Textbook authors often write paragraphs in which there is no stated main idea. In that event, you must supply the main idea statement.

> **Locating the main idea** is essential for comprehension of expository material. Authors most frequently use the first sentence of the paragraph to state the main idea. However, they may place it in the middle, at the end, or leave it unstated. Comprehending subject matter depends on identifying the main idea.

Practice

Read each of the following paragraphs and decide what the subject or topic is. Then underline it. Next, decide on the general statement the author makes about the topic. Highlight the main idea sentence. If it is not stated, write it in the margin.

1. The vast majority of all retail stores built in the United States since the end of World War II includes some provision for off-street parking. In several central business districts, parking facilities are provided by individual stores, cooperative arrangements among stores, and municipal governments. The number of parking spots, their distances from the store site, and the availability of employee parking should all be evaluated. The importance of good parking facilities must not be overlooked in an evaluation of a location and a specific site within it (BERMAN, 236).

2. Even a 15-minute walk, a University of Southern California study found, can be more relaxing than a tranquilizer for easing muscle tension and relieving anxiety. Exercise has also been found to increase energy, reduce free-floating hostility, improve concentration and alertness, and make people less self-conscious and better able to handle stress. Many runners and other athletes speak of experiencing a natural "high" during the course of exercise—an exhilarated and euphoric state that lasts for several hours afterwards. In fact, exercise has been used to treat mental disorders. University of Wisconsin researchers found that running three times a week for 30 to 45 minutes reduced symptoms of depression in a group of depressed patients (COMBS, 290).

3. The mass media are the various forms of communication that reach a large audience without any personal contact between the senders and the receivers of the messages: newspapers, magazines, books, television, radio, movies, and records. Although they are unquestionably a powerful socializing influence, the precise impact of the media is difficult to gauge.
   The most influential medium is probably television. There is a TV set in 95 percent of American homes, and the average American between the ages of three and sixteen spends more time in front of the TV set than in school (ROBERTSON, 119).

4. The entire store is organized around departments for the purpose of providing service, promotion, and control. A general merchandising manager is responsible for the store's product planning. Reporting to the manager are the buyers who manage each department. These buyers typically run the departments almost as independent businesses; they are given considerable discretion in merchandising and layout decisions. Acceptance of the retailing axiom that well-bought goods are already half-sold is indicated by the department manager's title of buyer. Buyers, particularly those in charge of high fashion departments, spend a considerable portion of their time deciding on the inventory to be carried in their departments. A distinguishing feature of the department store is indicated by its name (BOONE AND KURTZ, 242).

Practice

Read each of the following paragraphs and highlight the main idea. Then choose the best restatement of the main idea from the choices after each paragraph.

1. It has been found that many obese persons eat food to derive certain types of satisfactions or to compensate for certain personality lacks. The overweight girl who is not socially acceptable may appease her discomfiture and ego by indulging in rich desserts or some other type of unwise eating. Persons who are undergoing tensions, such as fear, boredom, or frustration, may find that eating seems to relieve the situation. The individual who lacks affection, recognition, or the fulfillment of other emotional needs may turn to food as a solace. There is considerable evidence that psychological factors may play a role in obesity (FLECK, 118).

Check the best restatement of the main idea:

_____ a) Eating food satisfies some emotional needs.

_____ b) People who are overweight undergo tensions and frustrations.

_____ c) Psychological factors may have an influence on obesity.

2. Formal education in America is not merely freely available: it is actually compulsory. There are still many societies where this is not the case, or where schooling is compulsory for only the first few grades. American parents are legally obliged to send their children to school, although they may choose between public and private (including religious education—choices that are not offered in many other countries). Education in the United States is financed by taxing everyone, including people without children and people whose children attend private schools. The implication is that public education benefits the entire society, not merely those who happen to receive it. Every child is thus entitled to at least twelve years of schooling at public expense, and we even expect some skilled profes-

sionals to spend twenty years or more in school—a period equal to half the life expectancy in some of the less developed countries of the world (ROBERTSON, 380).

Check the best restatement of the main idea:

_____ a) In America, formal education is mandatory and free.

_____ b) Every child is entitled to twelve years of public education.

_____ c) By law, American parents must send their children to school.

3. The memory unit, or storage unit, is the heart of the total computer system. It is where information is stored. This element serves as the computer's filing cabinet. Both information for solving a problem and instructions on how to use the information are stored here. The memory storage unit can be both internal and external. Computer systems contain internal memory units for the storage of instructions and data. In addition, it is possible to increase the system's computer memory capacity through the use of external memory units that can be plugged into the system. The use of such external storage units provides added flexibility for the computer system (BOONE AND KURTZ, 367).

Check the best restatement of the main idea:

_____ a) The heart of the computer is the memory unit.

_____ b) There are internal and external memory units.

_____ c) Computers have memory units.

4. Good parents are not just born; they work at it. And it is hard work. Parenting well does not come automatically. Educating ourselves about the best methods of behavior and care during pregnancy and childbirth reduces pain and increases the safety and pleasure of those important events. The same careful preparation toward parenting will yield similar results. Parents can learn much about what to expect from children and from themselves as parents. Reading about childhood development and behavior, attending classes on parenting can all contribute to the joys of parenting and reduce the frustrations and anxieties (INSEL AND ROTH, 194, 195).

Check the best restatement of the main idea:

_____ a) Observing other children helps parents.

_____ b) Being a good parent involves great effort on the part of the parents.

_____ c) Good parenting is quickly achieved by most people.

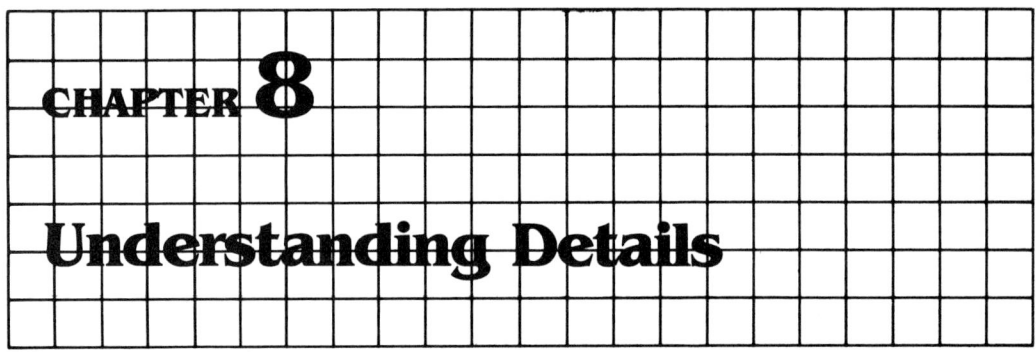

CHAPTER 8

Understanding Details

Relating Main Ideas and Details

You learned that the topic is the subject of what you are reading and that the main idea is the most general statement the author makes about the topic. Just as the main idea relates to the topic of the paragraph, it also relates to the details of the paragraph. Comprehension of important facts depends on your ability to understand the relationship between the main idea and the details. Consider the following paragraph to see how the details support the main idea.

Example

Finding a good job requires a great deal of work. Job seekers should tell as many people as possible that they are available for employment. For example, they can tell friends and relatives, inform college career placement officers, and call employment agencies. They can also send résumés to possible employers. In addition, they can read the job description ads in newspapers. All of these efforts usually require a fair amount of time. Remember that a good job is worth all the work that goes into finding it.

Questions

1. The topic of the paragraph is _____.
2. The main idea sentence is _____
   _____.

3. List five important details that support or relate to the main idea sentence: _____

_____

_____

_____

_____

> **Details** support the main idea sentence by illustrating or explaining it. Recognizing the main idea and details in text passages enables you to focus on the important ideas that you will want to remember.

Identifying Main Ideas and Details in Text Passages

In the following exercises you will practice locating the main idea sentence and identifying the supporting details. Remember to read each paragraph carefully before you decide what the topic and main idea sentence are. Then, determine which details explain or illustrate the main idea sentence.

Practice

Identify the main idea sentence and details in each of the following paragraphs by ==highlighting the main idea in one color== and the ==details in a second color.== Write the topic of the entire passage on the line.

1. _____

Physical availability depends upon the kinds of food attainable in a specific part of the United States or the world in which an individual or family lives. The productivity of the land, the climate, and agricultural technology are important factors. The seasons have a strong impact, for example, watermelon is not commonly eaten during the winter months in northern states. It may be imported but is usually too expensive for most families. Crises, such as freezes, floods, or crop failures may mean a shift to the consumption of other foods because certain items may not be available. Transportation of food to many parts of the nation compensates for the lack of foods that cannot be produced locally. The cost of producing food and the accessibility of adequate and competent labor are other considerations. Large urban centers such as New York and Chicago face critical problems if there is a strike that involves food such as milk or bread.

Cultural availability has a strong influence on food behavior. Beliefs and attitudes about food have considerable input. The emphasis on health and natural foods is an example. Another belief is associated with food and weight loss. Many women's magazines devote considerable space every month to recipes and weight loss diets. Eating in fast food restaurants is on the increase. Coffee breaks have become a cultural institution. Snacking is a national habit.

Religion and other movements sometimes emphasize the inclusion or the rejection of certain foods, such as a vegetarian diet. Fasting may be encouraged. The nutritive contributions of some of these diets bear scrutiny. The casualness of contemporary life styles has an effect on the way people eat. Age may determine how certain groups eat. This is especially true of teenagers whatever their ethnic background, who have common food preferences. Some elderly folks contend that certain food is best suited for their age and many are strong advocates of food supplementations, such as vitamins, minerals, and protein (FLECK, 36).

2. _____

Married partners tend to be of roughly the same age. Husbands are usually older than their wives, but this difference in age has been gradually declining throughout the century, from about 4 years in 1900 to about 2.5 years today.

Most people marry within their own social class. The reasons are obvious: we tend to live in class-segregated neighborhoods, to meet mostly people of the same class, and to share class-specific tastes and interests. Interclass marriages are relatively more common, however, among college students.

Most marriages are between people sharing the same religious faith, although Protestant interdenominational marriages are fairly common. Religious bodies generally oppose interfaith marriages, on the grounds that they may lead to personal conflicts, disagreements over the faith in which children should be raised, and an undermining of belief in a particular doctrine. Many people change their religion to that of their partner before marriage.

Husbands and wives generally have a similar educational level, and some degree of intellectual parity seems to be demanded by marital partners. The college campus is, of course, a marriage market in its own right, and college-educated people are especially likely to marry people of similar educational achievement.

Members of racial and ethnic groups are more likely to marry within their own group than outside it. In particular, interracial marriages are extremely rare. Until the sixties, several states had laws prohibiting interracial marriages, and such marriages still attract some social disapproval. Interracial marriages between blacks and whites are particularly unusual; in the majority of these cases, the husband is black and the wife white (ROBERTSON, 362–363).

3. _____

Young consumers seek more information than older consumers. They have little experience and are uncertain. Commercial, noncommercial, and social sources of information are sought by young customers to determine the products that are appropriate, the characteristics they possess, and the best choice. Older consumers are habitual and tend to repeat purchases. New information is less important for them, and the purchase process is completed quickly. Older consumers will usually not be persuaded to try a new product unless a social source has recommended it. Commercial and noncommercial sources do not have a strong effect on older consumers for new products.

The college-educated consumer uses the decision process more thoroughly than less-educated consumers. Noncommercial and social sources of information are especially sought by the college-educated consumer. This consumer is aware of the various types of information that are available and utilizes them. Advertising and selling that are honest and provide knowledge will attract the well-educated consumer, who conducts a complete search of alternatives and their characteristics before making a decision. New items, properly promoted, can be sold to the college-educated consumer. Less-educated consumers spend little time searching for or evaluating information. Commercial and social sources are used, noncommercial sources are not. New products or services are bought more infrequently by less-educated consumers.

The middle-income consumer uses the decision process more thoroughly than any other income group. Lower-income consumers frequently buy national (manufacturers') brands and do not look at the full range of alternatives. National brands provide consistency and security in product choice. Upper-income consumers do look at a variety of products or services before purchasing. The information search is not as intense as that of the middle-income consumer because price is not an important factor, and an unsatisfactory product can often be replaced. The middle-income consumer is concerned with price and uses a detailed search process for listing and evaluating alternatives. Noncommercial and social sources are very important to this group.

A consumer's occupation may be placed in one of two basic categories: white collar or blue collar. White-collar consumers (office workers or professionals) utilize the decision process more completely than blue-collar consumers (craftsmen, machine operators, and so on). The white-collar consumer knows of the available information sources and uses them more than the blue-collar consumer, who is not as aware of information and product or service alternatives. The white-collar consumer relies on noncommercial sources to a greater extent than the blue-collar consumer, who uses commercial sources.

The sex of the consumer has an impact on the purchase process. On the average, women are found to be more persuadable than men. Women are more apt to enjoy shopping than men. In a family setting, women are the decision makers for foods and beverages (nonalcoholic), health care items, housewares, and pet foods. Men are the decision makers for gasoline, alcoholic beverages, tobacco products, and automobiles. Both men and women are decision makers for appliances, cameras, and watches. Information sources should be directed toward the consumer making the decision, although it should be pointed out that married couples share decision making for expensive, important items even though one party may have the greater influence.

A consumer's marital status affects the decision process in much the same way as family size. A single person looks for and evaluates information independently. Commercial, noncommercial, and social sources of information are directed at one decision maker. A married couple may act independently or dependently, according to the importance of the product or service and the effect of the item on both parties. For important, expensive items, both spouses seek and evaluate information. The information source should be directed at both parties. When items are inexpensive and unimportant, one spouse will seek and evaluate information in the same manner as a single person. The process is usually longer and more thorough if two parties are involved (BERMAN, 137 –138).

CHAPTER 9

Taking Notes

You practiced the basic comprehension skills necessary for understanding expository writing: previewing a chapter, determining the topic of a paragraph, locating the main idea sentence in a paragraph, and determining which details support the main idea sentence. Next, you highlighted the important parts of a paragraph: its main idea and supporting details. You are at a stage where it can be assumed that you can locate and understand the important subject ideas.

This is a critical stage. You now need to move from the level of comprehending text material to the level of mastering ideas. At some time during the semester you will have to prove to the instructor that you have mastered the course content. This proof can take the form of a test, a report, or a term paper. To accomplish this, you need to move a step beyond comprehension: taking notes on the ideas you have selected as important. Your written notes serve as the basis of your study for quizzes and exams. It is important, therefore, that you take notes to help you study.

Understanding Outline Form and the Relationships Among Ideas in an Outline

Consider the following paragraph to see how a highlighted main idea and supporting details clearly illustrate the important facts.

Example

The ability of the body to adapt to its level of physical activity has a profound effect on its biological well-being. If a person is **chronically inactive**, then his or her body reflects the inactivity: the **heart** and **lungs have a lower capacity**; the **muscles, bones, and joints are weaker**; and the **metabolic capacity is impaired**. Research studies indicate that the **unfit person runs a higher risk** of a myriad **of health hazards** such as **heart disease, obesity, high blood pressure, backache, undernutrition**, and a **lower ability to cope with the effects of emotional stress**. Likewise, if a person is **chronically active, physiological function improves** and he or she tends to **become healthier** (INSEL/ROTH, 315).

> **Highlighting** the main idea in one color and the supporting details in a second color allows you to distinguish between the main idea and supporting details in text paragraphs.

You can now begin to organize the information in your own words. Consider the following paragraph and the accompanying outline to see how ideas are organized in written notes.

Example

Certain foods are also associated with each meal of the day. **Fruit juices, cereals, eggs, bacon,** and **sausage** belong to **breakfast**. Although **cereals** may be used in **preparing a dish for another meal**—in breading meats, in casseroles, or in desserts—they are **never served as cereal dishes at lunch or dinner**. And if a **luncheon dish—sandwiches or certain salads—is served as the main course at dinner**, a person may **feel cheated because the dinner** menu **should be more substantial and consist of meat, vegetables, and a dessert**. If **a food steps out** of its **assigned role, people can find it disturbing** (FLECK,2).

A. Certain foods are associated with each meal of the day.
 1. Breakfast: juice, eggs, cereal
 2. Cereals used in some dishes but not as lunch or dinner
 3. Lunch dish: sandwich, salad
 4. Sandwich and salad not served at dinner, a heartier meal
 5. Dinner: meat, vegetable, dessert
 6. Foods out of assigned roles are disturbing

Questions

1. Is the information in the outline the same as in the highlighted paragraph? _____

2. What are the differences between the highlighted and the outlined examples? _____

You should see that the outlined notes contain, in a shortened form, the same information as the highlighted paragraph. The outline is organized in a format that is easy to read.

An **outline** is a note-taking technique in which you organize text information in a clear and shortened form. The outline form requires using consistent and specific labels to place ideas:

Roman Numeral = chapter subtitle

⟶ Upper Case Letter = paragraph main idea

⟶ Number = paragraph detail

Chapter Title

I. First Subtitle
   A. Paragraph Main Idea
      1. Paragraph Detail
      2. Paragraph Detail
   B. Paragraph Main Idea
      1. Paragraph Detail
      2. Paragraph Detail
      3. Paragraph Detail
   C.
      1.
      2.
   D.
      1.
      2.

II. Second Subtitle
   A. Paragraph Main Idea
      1.
      2.
   B.
      1.
      2.

Outlining Lists

You see examples of items in outline form every day. Consider the following example. Can you recognize the important ideas in this modified outline?

Example

Menu

Salads

- House Salad
- Chef Salad
- Tuna Salad Platter
- Chicken Salad Platter

Soups

- Soup of the Day
- French Onion Soup
- Noodle Soup
- Mushroom Barley Soup

Meat Dishes

- Hamburger Platter
- Steak Special
- Lamb Chops
- Veal Chops

Questions

1. What are the three main categories of food in the sample menu?

   _____   _____   _____

2. How many items are in each category? _____

> Listed items can be organized into an **outline** in which the major items are shown in a consistent format and are easily distinguished from the supporting items.

Practice

Each of the following lists contains subtitles, main ideas, and details from a text chapter. The facts appear in their correct order, but they are not organized into an outline. Rewrite each list in outline form.

List 1

Travel Highlights
San Francisco
Golden Gate Bridge
Chinatown
Fisherman's Wharf
New York City
Chinatown
Yankee Stadium
Wall Street
World Trade Center
United Nations Building

Outline

I. Travel Highlights
   A. San Francisco
      1. Golden Gate Bridge
      2. Chinatown
      3. Fisherman's Wharf
   B.
_____
_____
_____
_____
_____

List 2

Types of Nonverbal Communication
Body Language
Facial Expressions
Hand Gestures
Posture
Physical Nearness
Intimate Distance
Personal Distance
Social Distance
Public Distance

Outline

_____
_____
_____
_____
_____
_____
_____
_____
_____
_____

List 3　　　　　　　　　　　　　　　　*Outline*

Television Productions

Soap Operas

"General Hospital"

"All My Children"

"The Young and the Restless"

Quiz Programs

"Family Feud"

"Wheel of Fortune"

"Tic Tac Dough"

Situation Comedies

"Three's Company"

"Alice"

"Diff'rent Strokes"

List 4　　　　　　　　　　　　　　　　*Outline*

Securities

Stocks

Common Stocks

Preferred Stocks

Cumulative Preferred Stocks

Convertible Preferred Stocks

Bonds

Secured Bonds

Debentures

Convertible Bonds

Serial Bonds

Sinking Fund Bonds

Redeemable Bonds

Outlining Text Passages

It is usually necessary to take notes on textbook chapters so that you will have a basis for studying. The following example contains many important facts. Read the example and the accompanying notes. Notice how the outline clearly emphasizes the important ideas.

Example

Studying

There are many steps to mastering a chapter. First, preview the selection to determine the important ideas. Next, read and understand the important facts, namely, the main ideas and details. Highlight these facts. Then, outline them in an organized and consistent way. In addition, recite the key ideas that aid in remembering facts. Finally, commit the facts to memory. When all these steps have been taken, you can feel confident that you have thoroughly read and studied the chapter.

Outline

I. Studying
  A. Six steps to mastering subject material
   1. Preview for important ideas
   2. Read to understand main ideas and details
   3. Highlight important facts
   4. Outline important facts
   5. Recite key ideas
   6. Memorize information

Practice

Highlight the following text passage. Then outline the information in the space provided.

Getting Started on an Exercise Program

The first step in exercising for most people is determining whether or not they should. This is particularly true with anyone over thirty-five, especially if they have been heavy smokers. Likewise, young adults who have been very inactive should proceed slowly and with caution. A physical evaluation from a physician is recommended, preferably one that includes an exercise-stress test. While a person is exercising, a stress test detects cardiovascular problems that might not show up when the body is at rest. This is done by monitoring blood pressure, pulse rate, oxygen consumption, and the heart's electrical activity while exercising.

Whatever exercise program is selected, it is important to start with warm-up periods. These should include stretching exercises, jumping jacks (jumping feet astride, bringing hands together overhead), or brisk walking. The idea is to increase heart rate and circulation slowly without placing a sudden strain on the heart or the muscles that are starting to work.

The next phase in developing an exercise program is to determine the amount of exercise that is enough to condition the muscles and cardiovascular system without overly straining the body. This involves taking one's pulse and finding one's target zone. This target zone, or safe-training pulse rate, is established by subtracting one's age from 220 and then taking 60 percent to 80 percent of that total. If you are just starting to exercise 60 percent is recommended; 80 percent is recommended if you are already in good condition (SINACORE, 136, 137, 140).

I. Getting Started on an Exercise Program

   A. _____
      1. _____
      2. _____
      3. _____
      4. _____
      5. _____

   B. _____
      1. _____
      2. _____

   C. _____
      1. _____
      2. _____
      3. _____
      4. _____

Practice

Highlight and outline the following text passage.

Changes in Department Store Strategies

Department stores have used innovative marketing strategies over the years. The first type of retailer to advertise prices was a department store. The first retailer to develop a one-price policy (all consumers pay the same price for a given quantity) was a department store. The use of the leased-department concept was begun by a department store. Totally automated checkout facilities have been readily adopted by department stores. Strong product guarantees have been given to customers. Decentralized management principles have been adopted. Finally, the department store has been quick to use suburban shopping center facilities while simultaneously altering its strategy to maintain central business district profitability. In 1976, department store branch units accounted for almost 78 per cent of total department store sales.

The second new change in department store strategy concerns lifestyle retailing. The stores are abandoning traditional merchandise groupings, such as price (budget, finer); fit (junior, misses'); and end use (gift, home improvement). These groupings are being replaced by departments that concentrate on life-styles. A men's clothing department may separately display and sell complete outfits for businessmen, students, and vacationers. A furniture department may concentrate on the concept of "casual living" and sell all types of furniture related to this concept within one group (BERMAN, 61, 68).

OUTLINE

Practice

Highlight and outline the following text passage.

The Private Enterprise System

Most U.S. businesses, large or small, belong to what is called the **private enterprise system**. This means simply that firms operate in a dynamic environment where success or failure is determined by how well they match and counter the offerings of competitors. **Competition** is the battle among businesses for consumer acceptance. Sales and profits are the yardsticks by which such acceptance is measured.

The business world has abundant examples of firms that were once successful but that failed to continue satisfying consumer demands. Competition assures that, over the long run, firms that satisfy consumer demands will be successful and those that do not will be replaced.

The private enterprise system requires that firms continually adjust their strategies, product offerings, service standards, operating procedures, and the like. Otherwise the competition will gain higher shares of an industry's sales and profits. Consider the following cases. A & P was long the largest supermarket chain. Now Safeway is the largest, and A & P is attempting a recovery. Ford once was the dominant automaker. Today, it is second to General Motors, among domestic producers. These events suggest the dynamic environment of the private enterprise system.

Competition is a critical mechanism for guaranteeing that the private enterprise system will continue to provide the goods and services that make for high living standards and sophisticated life styles. Few organizations that offer a product or service can escape the influence of competition. The American Cancer Society competes for contributions with the American Heart Association, your own college, and other nonprofit enterprises. The armed forces compete in the labor market with private employers. Even the U.S. Postal Service faces competition. United Parcel Service competes for package shipments. Express Mail faces competition from Western Union's mailgrams. And firms like The Mailbox, which rents post office boxes in the Seattle area, compete for the post-office-box business. (BOONE AND KURTZ 9–10).

Private enterprise system. The system under which firms operate in a dynamic environment where success or failure is determined by how well they match and counter the offerings of competitors.

Competition. The battle among businesses for consumer acceptance.

OUTLINE

Practice

Highlight and outline the following text passage.

Agents of Socialization

If culture is learned, there must be channels of transmission. This is the task of **agents of socialization**—people and organizations charged with conveying the rules. Chief among these are parents, peers, teachers, the media, and religious authorities.

> **Agents of socialization** are individuals and organizations responsible for the transmission of culture.

The first and most important agents of socialization are the people who care for infants. In the earliest months, messages from nurturers constitute the child's basic understanding of the world around it. This is the infant's first introduction to the **language** that shapes perception and elicits emotions. What the child learns is the culture as mediated through others. A desire for continued interaction with the nurturers, combined with a fear of losing these sources of pleasure, motivates the infant to become sensitive to the cues of those entrusted with its care.

> The child's first understanding of the surrounding culture is mediated through nurturing adults.

Another powerful source of information and socialization is the friendship group of **age peers**. Peers are equals, whereas parents are superiors in relation to the child. The greater power of parents makes some kinds of learning difficult. A distance and formality must be observed even in the most indulgent homes. Peers, on the other hand, are those one can deal with on the same level as oneself: tease, insult, let imagination loose upon, share dreadful mistakes with, and so on, but without the heavy emotional overlay of family relationships.

> **Peers** are equals, and age peers are important sources of information and socialization.

Much formal socialization is placed in the hands of professionals. Teachers from kindergarten on are specifically designated agents of socialization, and are paid for the task. Ideally, a teacher is one who has both knowledge and the skills to present it. During the course of teaching their subjects, classroom instructors provide role models and attempt to convey the excitement of learning itself.

> **Teachers** are professional agents of socialization who convey knowledge and skills to their students.

In an earlier time, parents, friends, and teachers would comprise the list of primary childhood socializers. Children's books, comics, and magazines might also have been mentioned as sources of information on norms and role models. Today one must add three powerful indirect (nonpersonal) socialization agents: radio, movies, and television. Many people learn about politics, form a vision of the good life, and develop attitudes toward others from what they see on the screen and hear through loudspeakers (HESS, 116–120).

> **The media**, especially radio, television, and movies, are powerful agents of socialization in modern societies.

OUTLINE

Practice

Highlight and outline the following text passage.

What Are the Functions of Money?

Money serves primarily as a **medium of exchange**—the function performed by money in facilitating exchange and eliminating the need for a barter system. Rather than follow the complicated process of trading wheat directly for gasoline or clothing (the barter system), a farmer can sell the wheat and use the money from the sale to make other purchases.

Money also functions as a **unit of account**—the common denominator for measuring the value of all products and services. A new car is worth, say, $9,500, a certain cut of beef $4, and a 40-yard-line ticket to a football game $20. Using money as a common denominator aids in comparing widely different products and services.

Finally, money acts as a temporary **store of value**—a way of keeping accumulated wealth until it is needed to make new purchases. Wealth can also be held in the form of stocks and bonds, real estate, antiques, works of art, houses, precious gems, or any other kind of valuable goods. The advantage of storing value in goods other than money is that they often produce additional income in the form of dividends, interest payments, rent, or increases in value. For example, paintings by Renoir, Monet, and van Gogh have greatly increased in value over the past 20 years. But money offers one substantial advantage as a store of value: It is highly liquid. An asset is said to be liquid if it can be obtained and disposed of quickly and easily (BOONE AND KURTZ, 446).

OUTLINE

CHAPTER 10

Taking Tests

Studying for Exams

You have practiced previewing a chapter, reading and understanding text passages, highlighting important ideas, and taking notes in outline form. These skills are all effective methods for reading text material. You have a solid foundation for studying the important ideas in text passages. When an instructor announces an exam, you have additional preparation to do. The following suggestions will help you to study for your exams.

- When your instructor announces an exam, he or she may or may not discuss the specifics of the test. Ask the instructor about the exam. Determine whether the test will include an essay or whether the questions will be of the short answer type. Find out which chapters, lectures, and labs you will be tested on. Ask whether you will be allowed to use extra materials, such as a dictionary or a calculator.
- Get an overview of your text and class notes. Skim the text and your notes to determine the important topics.
- Use 3" by 5" index cards to help you study. Note important topics on one side of a card and supporting details on the other side.

Example

(Side 1)	(Side 2)
Studying Six steps to mastering subject material	1. preview important ideas 2. read for main ideas and details 3. highlight 4. outline 5. recite 6. memorize

- Create your own test questions based on the main ideas and details. Use your outline as you create the questions. Then attempt to answer the questions.
- Recite the information. Some information may require that you commit a list to memory. Try to compose a <u>mnemonic device</u>, such as a sentence made up from the first letters of other words.

Here is a typical mnemonic that music students often use to remember the notes of the staff:

<u>E</u>very <u>G</u>ood <u>B</u>oy <u>D</u>oes <u>F</u>ine = EGBDF

Here is a mnemonic that is a word made up from the first letters of the names of the Great Lakes:

HOMES = Lakes <u>H</u>uron, <u>O</u>ntario, <u>M</u>ichigan, <u>E</u>rie, and <u>S</u>uperior

Be careful to create meaningful mnemonics and to be selective in your use of this study aid.

- Allow yourself comfortable time study periods. Don't overstudy or try to cram all your studying into one or two evenings. Short study sessions spread over regular intervals are usually more beneficial. After studying alone, you may find it helpful to meet with a classmate to discuss and review the important ideas.
- Understanding that textbook authors use different writing styles to present information gives you an effective approach to studying.

  In <u>narrative passages</u>, the author emphasizes a chronological order of ideas. Your notes should reflect this logical sequence of information. When you study these notes, create questions that emphasize that sequence. For example, you might set up a question such as "Trace the six steps to mastering subject material."

In descriptive passages, the author emphasizes a detailed listing of information. Your notes should contain enough details to describe the main ideas. When you study these notes, create questions that emphasize knowing the types of descriptions and the listing of characteristics. For example, you might set up a question such as "Name the four basic types of context clues and describe the features of each."

In argumentative passages, the author emphasizes the causes and/or the effects of events or ideas. Your notes should reflect the cause-effect relationships in the text. When you study these notes, create questions that emphasize that relationship. For example, you might set up a question such as "Why is it important to take notes?"

In analytical passages, the author emphasizes a comparison or contrast of two subjects by showing their similarities or differences. Your notes should contain those comparisons and contrasts. When you study these notes, create questions that emphasize the differences or similarities of subjects. For example, you might set up a question such as "What are the similarities between highlighted and outlined notes?"

When you are aware of an author's style of writing, you become sensitive to the types of questions instructors create for tests. Your awareness of writing styles helps you to create your own questions as you study. Then, as you answer your questions, you are preparing to answer the instructor's questions.

Learning Approaches to Taking Tests

Exams are a regular part of college coursework. Teachers give tests to determine what students have learned. Many students have difficulty taking an exam. Some of the reasons for this follow:

- Some students do not read the text.
- Some students are excessively late or absent.
- Some students attempt to read all the assignments several days before the exam.
- Some students confuse reading and understanding the material with having studied it.
- Some students glance at the text or at their notes and believe they have thoroughly studied the material.
- Some students read, understand, take notes, and study the material, yet they have trouble answering questions.

Many students start to answer test questions immediately after receiving the paper. Actually, this is not advisable. Rather, other steps should be taken before you begin to answer the questions. First, glance over the test. When you do this, notice how many questions there are and the point value of each question. Also estimate how much time you can spend on each item. For example, a ten-point True or False question should be given less time than a twenty-point essay question. If some questions appear easier than others, spend less time with them so that you will have additional time for the more difficult questions.

Many students either do not read test directions or read and ignore them. Read the directions carefully and then remember to follow them. Directions provide specific information about what you are required to answer and how you are required to respond. Unless the directions state that points will be deducted for guessing, it is advisable to answer every question on a test. Your final grade is usually determined by the number of correct answers. If you omit answers because you are not sure of the response, your grade will suffer. Don't leave blank spaces.

When you begin the exam, answer the easy questions first. These will usually take the least time to answer. Also, these questions may help you to remember and answer the more difficult questions. Do not stay with a difficult item too long; skip it. Answer the questions you do know and return to the more difficult items later.

Leave a few minutes at the end of the exam to reread your answers and to complete the questions you skipped. Check to see that you responded to all of the questions, placed your answers on the answer sheet in the correct way, and followed all directions carefully. Only change an answer if you are sure of the correction.

In addition to following these general rules, some students have difficulty answering specific types of test questions. You will now look more closely at the specific features of objective and essay test questions.

Taking Objective Tests

Objective tests are also called short answer tests; they include multiple-choice, true-false, completion, fill-in, and matching items. Instructors use these types of questions to determine how much students know about the course content. Although the questions vary in form, each requires an instant recall of facts.

Answering Multiple-choice Items and Following Directional Words on Tests

Multiple-choice questions contain one correct and several incorrect answers. You must read directions carefully to see if you must choose only one answer or if you can select more than one choice. You must also read all the choices carefully. Often, some of the choices are very close in meaning to the correct answer. For example, consider the following question.

Example

_____ 1. Working with toxic chemicals can be a health hazard often associated with
    a) heart disease.
    b) lung disease.
    c) diabetes.
    d) circulatory and respiratory ailments.

Although answers a) and b) appear to be correct, each is included in d), the most complete answer.

> If there are several choices that seem correct on a multiple-choice question, select the **most complete answer**, that is, the one that includes the other choices.

Often, students fail to see that "all of the above" is one of the choices. Read and consider all of the choices carefully. If you are certain that at least two of the answers are correct, you can select "all of the above." Consider the following question.

Example

_____ 2. The risk of having a heart attack is greater for persons who
    a) have high blood pressure.
    b) smoke cigarettes.
    c) have a family history of heart disease.
    d) all of the above.

> When you are certain that at least two choices are correct on a multiple-choice item, select the **"all of the above"** answer. Be sure to read each choice carefully.

Some students do not notice that a test item contains a word or phrase that changes the usual way of stating a question. Pay attention to words that can alter the meaning of the question: "except," "but," "incorrect," and "false" are examples of such words. Underline these words in the test item so that you notice them as you consider your answer.

Example

_____ 3. All of the following require that a person wear a protective helmet <u>except</u>
   a) jumping rope.
   b) playing football.
   c) racing a bicycle.
   d) riding a motorcycle.

> Words such as "except," "but," "incorrect," "false," and "however" change the meaning of test questions. Consider these words carefully when you answer test items.

Some students do not notice the appearance of a specific determiner, that is, a word or phrase that affects the meaning of the statement and determines how you answer the question.

Example

_____ 4. <u>Every</u> hurricane causes
   a) widespread destruction.
   b) flooding.
   c) heavy rain.
   d) none of the above.

_____ 5. College basketball games <u>usually</u> attract
   a) enthusiastic audiences.
   b) disinterested audiences.
   c) only college freshmen.
   d) baseball fans.

> **Specific determiners** qualify a statement. Some leave no possible alternatives: "all," "none," "every," "always," "never," and "invariably" are typical examples. Others offer the possibility of alternatives and are frequently better choices on tests: "most," "few," "many," "some," "several," and "generally" are examples of this type of determiner. Recognizing the inclusion of a specific determiner helps you to answer objective test items.

You will now practice answering multiple-choice test items. Be aware of specific determiners, words that change the usual way of stating a question, "all of the above" choices, and general answers that include information from other answers. Read each question and the choices carefully and completely before you answer the item.

Practice

Place the letter of the correct answer on the line.

_____ 1. The large United States oil corporations include all of the following except
   a) Mobil.
   b) Texaco.
   c) Ford.
   d) Exxon.

_____ 2. The type of product that is most appealing to children is
   a) soap.
   b) toys.
   c) clothing.
   d) liquor.

_____ 3. The type of business which does not offer its employees lower prices on its product is
   a) manufacturing.
   b) banking.
   c) retailing.
   d) air travel.

_____ 4. Crimes against victims include all of the following except
   a) prostitution.
   b) robbery.
   c) murder.
   d) child abuse.

_____ 5. Television advertising is least frequently used to sell
   a) cigarettes.
   b) home owner insurance.
   c) magazine subscriptions.
   d) cars.

Practice

Answer the following by writing the letter of the correct choice on the line.

_____ 1. The career that does not require a college degree is
   a) repairing watches.
   b) teaching.
   c) figure-skating.
   d) both a) and c).

_____ 2. All of the following are specialists in the medical profession except
   a) a cardiologist.
   b) a general practitioner.
   c) a surgeon.
   d) an orthopedist.

_____ 3. Studying under poor conditions can result in
   a) a backache.
   b) eye strain.
   c) fatigue.
   d) all of the above.

_____ 4. Current trends in American family lifestyles include
   a) an increase in the number of working wives.
   b) a decrease in family size.
   c) an increase in the number of one-parent families.
   d) all of the above.

_____ 5. Students who do well on final exams always
   a) highlight their textbooks.
   b) attend every class.
   c) get grades of A in their courses.
   d) none of the above.

Practice

Answer the following items by writing the letter of the correct response on the line.

_____ 1. In their bargaining maneuvers, union officials always
   a) threaten a strike.
   b) start with a boycott.
   c) hold an election.
   d) none of the above.

_____ 2. A characteristic of the American health care system is
   a) the existence of too many medical laboratories.
   b) poorly trained doctors and nurses.
   c) the high cost of a hospital room.
   d) its expensiveness.

_____ 3. A department store that appeals to teen-age buyers usually carries
   a) jeans.
   b) swimwear.
   c) boots and sneakers.
   d) sports and outdoor-type clothing.

_____ 4. Video game centers usually attract
   a) high school students.
   b) babies.
   c) the elderly.
   d) teenagers.

_____ 5. A major advantage of the suburban lifestyle is
   a) the overpopulation of communities.
   b) long-distance commutation to businesses.
   c) the availability of land.
   d) the lack of cultural activities.

Answering True-False Items

Some students have difficulty answering True-False questions. These questions may appear difficult if you do not read them carefully. When you attempt a True-False item, read each statement carefully and apply your understanding of the subject to the question. In addition, consider the following guides to answering True-False questions. The following examples indicate specific features of some True-False items that may, indeed, make them difficult. Try to answer each example by marking it T or F.

Example

_____ 1. Large cars usually give poor gas mileage and poor passenger comfort.

_____ 2. There must be adequate snow on the ground for both downhill and cross-country skiing.

Statement one is only partially true. Therefore, you must answer it FALSE. Statement two is entirely true. Therefore, you must answer it TRUE.

> In order to mark a statement TRUE, read it carefully to determine that **the entire statement is true**. If you know that any part of the statement is wrong, you must mark it FALSE.

Some True-False statements contain specific determiners. Pay particular attention to the wording of these test items.

Example

_____ 3. All college students are required to enroll in a foreign language course.

_____ 4. College students must always take a foreign language course.

> Carefully read statements that have **specific determiners** such as "all," "never," and "always." These words or phrases can determine whether or not a statement is TRUE or FALSE.

Practice

Decide whether each statement is TRUE (T) or FALSE (F).

_____ 1. Most college instructors require their students to attend weekly labs and to purchase a textbook.

_____ 2. Street vendors often sell their merchandise at more reasonable prices than department stores.

_____ 3. Courses in finance, marketing, and law are offered by all business departments.

_____ 4. Advertisers often convince customers to buy a product for emotional rather than rational reasons.

_____ 5. The sports of tennis, racquet ball, and badminton all require the use of a racquet and a ball.

Practice

Answer the following items TRUE (T) or FALSE (F).

_____ 1. All senior citizens retire with pensions.

_____ 2. If one shops for groceries when one is hungry, one will usually purchase more items.

_____ 3. Slot machines in Las Vegas never pay off.

_____ 4. It is always difficult to distinguish between twins.

_____ 5. Most American schools begin their year in September and end their year in May.

_____ 6. An urban area is characterized by great numbers of people and considerable amounts of uninhabited land.

_____ 7. Welfare recipients receive funds through illegal means.

_____ 8. Most American parents are upset by their children's behavior.

_____ 9. Two-income families earn more than single-income families.

_____ 10. The suburbs are generally less crowded than the major cities.

Practice

Decide whether each of the following is TRUE (T) or FALSE (F).

_____ 1. A single-parent household always refers to a mother and one child.

_____ 2. Most American workers retire when they reach their sixties.

_____ 3. Fear of crime is great in most American cities, but is minimal in small towns.

_____ 4. There are only two alternatives to traditional marriage in America.

_____ 5. Taking drugs causes juvenile delinquency.

_____ 6. If found guilty, a defendant must serve a jail sentence.

_____ 7. Many American college officials must raise tuition rates yearly.

_____ 8. All three-story buildings must have elevators.

_____ 9. Vegetarians avoid eating meat, but some eat fish.

_____ 10. The selection of merchandise by store buyers usually depends on regional tastes and styles.

Practice

Answer five of the following items TRUE (T) or FALSE (F).

_____ 1. Boutiques and department stores are retail businesses that attract the same types of customers.

_____ 2. The sale of new cars and fur coats usually decreases in a recession.

_____ 3. Writing an essay and writing a lab report require different writing styles.

_____ 4. Boxing and wrestling are both contact sports.

_____ 5. Some colleges require that students have an interview, but all colleges require that students take a placement test.

_____ 6. Most people prefer to use cash when paying bills.

_____ 7. Exercising three times a week is beneficial, while exercising once a week provides no benefits.

_____ 8. Electrically heated homes always cost more to heat than solar-heated homes.

_____ 9. Cosmetics sold in department stores are never available in pharmacies.

_____ 10. Many more men than women are involved in contact sports.

Taking Essay Tests and Following Directional Words

Instructors use essay tests to determine how students demonstrate their understanding of major ideas and supporting facts as they interpret, evaluate, and organize information in essay form. For this type of exam, you must demonstrate an ability to recall facts, organize ideas, and write well. You must also read directions carefully and follow them completely.

Some students do not follow the instructor's directions on essay tests. In order to demonstrate your understanding, you must be aware of some frequently-used terms.

- The terms "describe," "discuss," "explain," and "illustrate" require that you write in detail about the characteristics of a person, place, event, or idea. Generally, you can write a full explanation and use examples to illustrate your understanding.
- The terms "enumerate," "list," "define," "state," and "summarize" require that you write about the parts or features of something. You can include brief remarks about each feature.

- The terms "develop," "diagram," "trace," and "discuss the steps or stages" require that you write about the facts in a chronological order. You may have to draw and label parts or steps in a diagram.
- The terms "compare," "contrast," "show the differences," and "show the similarities" require that you show how two or more subjects are different or similar with respect to selected features.
- The terms "give the reasons," "show the results," and "discuss the causes" require that you discuss the reasons for an act or the result of an action.

Once you have read and understood what the instructor requires, you can begin to organize your answer. Write a brief outline of your essay. The outline will help in several ways. First, you can be sure that you have included all the ideas you wish to write about. In addition, you can use the outline as you write the essay. You will not risk forgetting an important idea.

As you begin the essay, write a brief introduction in the form of a restatement of the essay question. Then, follow your outline, and include the facts and explanations you already noted. When you are ready to end the essay, include a statement that briefly summarizes what you have written. Finally, allow time to reread your essay.

The following practice will give you a chance to consider the type of essay required and to list briefly the ideas you would include in your answer.

Practice

Read each essay test question and be aware of the directional word or phrase that signals the type of response required. Then, write a brief outline of the way you would answer each question.

1. Discuss three of the problems foreign students have when they enroll in American colleges.

   _____
   _____
   _____
   _____
   _____
   _____
   _____
   _____

2. Compare or contrast the schools in America with the schools in another country.

_____
_____
_____
_____
_____
_____
_____
_____
_____
_____

3. Trace the steps you can follow to prepare for a final exam.

_____
_____
_____
_____
_____
_____
_____
_____
_____
_____

4. Discuss the reasons why people claim that milk products are an important part of every diet.

_____
_____
_____
_____
_____
_____
_____
_____
_____

5. Briefly discuss the steps you followed when you registered for classes this term.

_____
_____
_____
_____
_____
_____
_____
_____
_____
_____

6. Define and illustrate the four types of context clues you can use to learn the meanings of new words.

7. Contrast urban and suburban lifestyles. Include four features.

8. Summarize your reasons for choosing a career curriculum.

9. Develop at least three reasons why computers are becoming a necessity in business and in home management.

10. Compare or contrast teen-agers who live in the city and teen-agers who live in the suburbs.

_____
_____
_____
_____
_____
_____
_____
_____
_____
_____

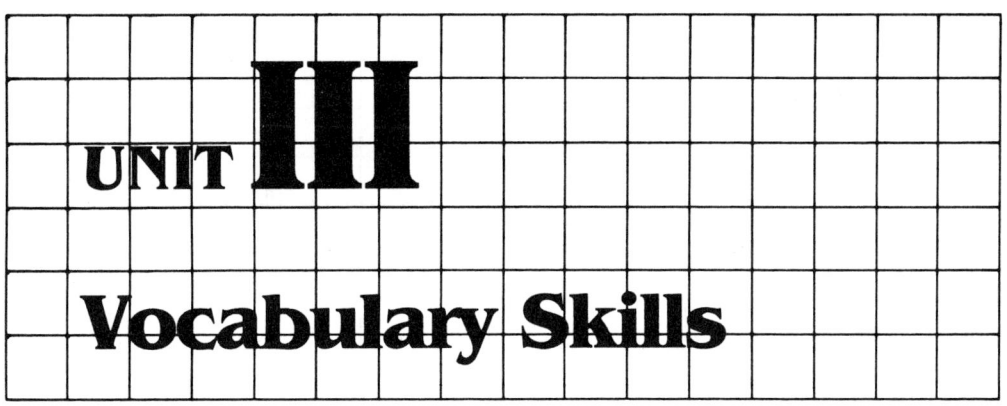

UNIT III
Vocabulary Skills

Drawing by Brian Schatell from an idea by Ray Forest.

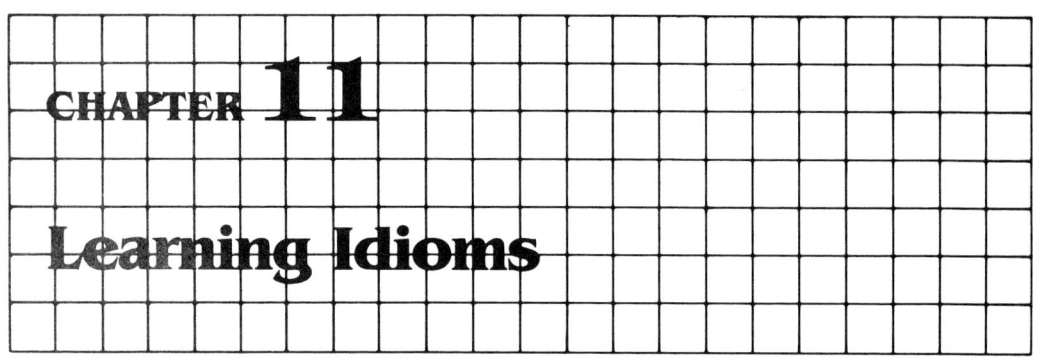

CHAPTER 11

Learning Idioms

Drawing by Brian Schatell from an idea by Ray Forest.

Preview

The following idioms appear in this chapter. Look at them briefly and place a check next to each idiom that you know.

_____ all in all	_____ it's not the end of the world
_____ are you with me	_____ keep at it
_____ at length	_____ leaf through
_____ at one's fingertips	_____ look up
_____ back it up	_____ lose track of
_____ bear in mind	_____ make up
_____ by all means	_____ on the tip of one's tongue
_____ child's play	_____ plan on
_____ come around to see me	_____ point out
_____ deal with	_____ put up with
_____ face the music	_____ rack one's brains
_____ fall behind	_____ scratch the surface
_____ far-fetched	_____ skip
_____ fill me in	_____ stick to the topic
_____ fill out	_____ take a dim view
_____ first hand	_____ take a seat
_____ get around it	_____ take it for granted
_____ get to the point	_____ take this down
_____ give it your best shot	_____ talk in circles
_____ go over	_____ the bottom line
_____ have an edge on	_____ think it over
_____ hit the nail on the head	_____ turn in
_____ how come	_____ within reason
_____ in the long run	_____ work it out

Vocabulary Skills

Comprehension of a passage is built upon understanding the vocabulary in that passage. Authors select words and phrases to express special moods, ideas, and images. Sometimes those words and phrases are difficult for the reader. One special type of phrase that presents difficulty for the reader is the idiom. This is because the word-by-word or literal definition of an idiom usually does not make sense.

Example

Whenever Professor English wants his students to remember an important grammar rule, he begins by saying, "Class, take this down."

Questions

1. If you define each of the underlined words literally, what is Professor English asking his students to do? _____

2. What in fact does Professor English want his students to do? _____

To understand the phrase, it is useless to define "take," "this," and "down" separately. The phrase "take this down" is an idiom that means "copy on paper what I am about to tell you."

> **Idioms** are groups of words that have a special meaning as a phrase and should not be defined in a word-by-word or literal manner. Although some idioms are listed in dictionary entries and many are found in idiom books, they are often difficult to locate.

People use idioms in a variety of daily situations. In each of the following exercises, idioms are grouped according to school and job situations.

Practice

Here are several idioms that instructors often use when giving directions and explanations. Study the meanings and use the idioms in the paragraph that follows. Then write your own sentences using the idioms.

Idioms	Meanings
at length	in considerable detail
get to the point	say what you mean directly
take a seat	sit down
talk in circles	talk in a confusing manner; talk around the topic
work it out	go step by step through the problem or exercise until you have the answer

As the class entered the lecture hall, the instructor said, "Will everyone please _____." He then began his talk. One student found the lecture difficult to understand and asked the instructor to repeat what he had said. After the instructor explained, he then decided to allow the students time to work on some problems. He told them to listen carefully. "Turn to page twelve and look at the example. Consider it carefully and then _____." One student was confused and talked _____ about the problem. The instructor said, "_____. I can only help if you are specific. Till now all you've done is _____."

Sentences

1. _____

2. _____

3. _____

4. _____

5. _____

Practice

Here are idioms that instructors frequently use in class. Study their meanings and write the idiom that best completes each sentence. Then use each idiom in your own sentence.

Idioms	Meanings
are you with me	do you understand what I've said
how come	why
skip	not to do something; ignore it
think it over	consider all possibilities before you make a decision
the bottom line	the basic consideration; the end result

1. Be sure to study Chapters One and Two. You can _____ Chapters Three and Four which contain unimportant material, and continue your studies with Chapter Five.

2. My explanation of the new theory has been complex. _____. Should I repeat what I've said?

3. _____ your instructor takes attendance and mine doesn't?

4. Don't write about every argument for and against the sale; just get to _____.

5. Voting for this tax bill requires that you understand every aspect of the new law. _____ before you vote.

Sentences

1. _____

2. _____

3. _____

4. _____

5. _____

Practice

Consider each classroom situation and select the letter of the idiom that best describes it. Then, based on your understanding of the idioms, write a sentence for each.

Idioms
a. come around to see me
b. fill me in
c. fill out
d. take it for granted
e. turn in (hand in)

Meanings
visit or see someone
tell me everything that happened
write all the information requested on an application or form
assume as true
bring or deliver completed work

Situations

__b__ 1. "I missed the first half of the lecture," said Anna to Raphael. "Please *let me know what the professor has been talking about.*"

____ 2. Bob earned a poor grade on his paper and asked for a conference with Professor Smith. The instructor told Bob that *she is available for an office conference* at noon.

____ 3. The instructor announced the date of the final exam and asked if anyone had a question. Since no one raised a hand, the instructor *was certain* that everyone understood the work and would do well on the test.

____ 4. The school administrators need academic and personal information about all entering college freshman. They send forms to each applicant and include instructions *to answer all questions on the survey.*

____ 5. "As each of you finishes the exam, I want you *to place the answer booklet on my desk,*" announced Professor Dale.

Sentences

1. _____

2. _____

3. _____

4. _____

5. _____

Idioms	Meanings
a. all in all	in general
b. at one's fingertips	close by; easily available
c. I'm going to cover	introduce what one will talk about
d. it's not the end of the world	not as bad as the situation appears to be
e. take a stab at	try or attempt; guess the answer

Situations

_____ 1. The history teacher wants his class to understand the topics they will discuss this term. And so he *briefly introduces the topics, explains the importance of each, and notes how much time they will spend with each.*

_____ 2. In order to work successfully through this scientific experiment, one must have every piece of equipment *ready for immediate use.* It is foolish to stop midway through the procedure because a necessary tool is not *available.*

_____ 3. You have no idea what the answer to a test question is. *You must, however, write something,* or you will certainly lose ten points on the test.

_____ 4. Bob and his teacher meet for a final conference. They discuss the progress Bob has made this term: his ability to express himself more clearly, his growth in the use of vocabulary, and his growth in the use of correct punctuation. They agree that Bob *has shown considerable improvement this term.*

_____ 5. Jay is very upset when he learns he has failed the first quiz. Ronny explains that there will be four more quizzes, two papers, an oral report, and the final exam. *Ronny assures Jay that he can improve his average and that the first quiz is only a small part of the work.*

Sentences

1. _____

2. _____

3. _____

4. _____

_____

5. _____

_____

Practice

Two idioms and their meanings accompany each of the following short situations. Use each idiom in its correct place in the situation. When you have completed all five situations, write a sentence using each idiom.

Situation 1
face the music (accept any penalty)
bear in mind (remember)

Lester: Steve, you've been with the company for two years. How could you make such a terrible mistake? Because of your error, the entire shipment may be defective.

Steve: You're absolutely right. But, _____, I've been doing the same job day after day, and thought I had the entire routine memorized.

Lester: You'd better tell the boss before the shipment is sent.

Steve: Why? Maybe it won't be too bad.

Lester: It's better to _____ now so that we can correct the problem. If we don't, we'll be in real trouble later.

Situation 2
child's play (something easy to do)
get around it (avoid doing something)

Sandy: Can you believe that all freshmen must enroll in a basic swimming course?

Larry: Actually, you can _____ by taking a swim test. If you pass, you are excused from the course.

Sandy: Great! A swim test will be _____ . In high school, I was captain of the swim team and earned an advanced swimmer's certificate.

Situation 3
on the tip of my tongue (not being able to state something that you know)
hit the nail on the head (be correct)

Teacher: Barbara, can you name the seven continents?

Barbara: Sure. There's Africa, Asia, North America, South America, and . . . .

Teacher: Yes. So far you've _____.
Now, try to name the final three.

Barbara: Let me think for a moment. I knew them a minute ago. They're
_____.
Give me another minute to remember.

Situation 4
far-fetched (unbelievable; exaggerated)
first hand (from personal experience)

A patrolman arrived at the crash scene within minutes of the accident. After making sure that no one was injured, he began to take notes for his report. Several witnesses offered reasonable accounts of the accident. The driver at fault, however, made wild statements and accusations that the officer knew were too _____ to be true. He recognized that _____ accounts by witnesses at the scene would prove more reliable in court.

Situation 5
in the long run (eventually; later)
make-up (substitute)

Because of the snowstorm, half the class missed the first quiz. "Would it be better," asked the teacher, "to assign each student a short paper or to schedule an extra session with a _____ exam?" She decided that _____, it would be easier to write a new quiz than to grade twenty papers.

Sentences

1.
2.
3.
4.
5.
6.
7.
8.
9.
10.

Practice

The following idioms are presented with their meanings. Place a check (√) next to those idioms that are used correctly and an X next to those that are not used correctly.

Idioms	Meanings
by all means	definitely; in any possible way
fall behind	not to be current in one's work
go over	review; examine ideas
have an edge on	have a slight advantage
leaf through	turn the pages and look at briefly
lose track of	lose contact with
put up with	tolerate
rack one's brain	try hard to remember or think of something
scratch the surface	not go deeply into a subject
take a dim view of	have a low opinion of

__√__ 1. Let me <u>go over</u> your essay before you type it.

__X__ 2. You have done thorough and extensive research and have <u>scratched the surface</u>.

_____ 3. I'll <u>leaf through</u> these notes and return them in five minutes.

_____ 4. Having a father who coaches tennis <u>gives me an edge on</u> the other players.

_____ 5. Having been raised by strict parents, I <u>take a dim view of</u> wild parties.

_____ 6. <u>By all means</u>, we'd love to attend your graduation.

_____ 7. I am the top student in my class because I have <u>fallen behind</u>.

_____ 8. When Patti forgot her locker combination, she <u>racked her brain</u> for hours in an attempt to remember.

_____ 9. I have a terrible headache and can easily <u>put up with</u> that noise.

_____ 10. The lecture ended five minutes late because the teacher <u>lost track of</u> the time.

Use the idioms in your own sentences.

1. _____

2. _____

3. _____

4. _____

5. _____

6. _____

7. _____

8. _____

9. _____

10. _____

Practice

The following idioms express instructions a teacher might want you to follow. Note how each is used in the paragraph and answer the questions that follow.

Idioms	*Meanings*
back it up	support an idea with appropriate examples
deal with	discuss
give it your best shot	try to do the best you can
keep at it	continue to do something
look up	search for in a reference book
plan on	depend on; assume that something will happen
point out	emphasize (an idea)
stick to the topic	stay with one idea
within reason	sensibly

Lewis presented his first assignment, an informative speech. He began by telling the class that he would <u>point out</u> the important study habits necessary for success in school. Next, he told the class to <u>plan on</u> noting the three major study techniques he would develop. The first technique he <u>dealt with</u> was the ability <u>to keep at it</u>. Lewis related several amusing stories about his experiences as a beginning jogger. He used many technical terms and repeatedly told the group that the terms were unimportant. Because he was enjoying himself, he did not realize how little time remained. Before he could talk about the second technique, he realized the class was nearly over. Lewis hurriedly told the class to <u>look up</u> the other techniques.

1. In your opinion, did Lewis <u>give it his best shot</u>? _____

2. Did Lewis <u>stick to the topic</u>? _____

3. Did he <u>back up</u> the major ideas? _____

4. Did he plan his time <u>within reason</u>? _____

5. Did he adequately <u>deal with</u> his topic? _____

Preview

The following idioms appear in the next series of exercises. Look at them briefly and place a check next to each idiom that you know.

_____ a square deal _____ in black and white

_____ a standing order _____ keep an eye on

_____ a tall order _____ keep track of

_____ back out _____ knowhow

_____ break even _____ let slide

_____ broke _____ level best

_____ burned out _____ look into

_____ call it a day _____ play with fire

_____ carry the ball _____ pull oneself together

_____ change hands _____ pull one's weight

_____ chip in _____ pull strings

_____ cream of the crop _____ run out of

_____ drawback _____ run the risk

_____ draw the line _____ run through

_____ fall short _____ save face

_____ fill the bill _____ step on it

_____ follow-up _____ suited for

_____ fringe benefit _____ swamped

_____ get one's act together _____ take a break

_____ get one wrong _____ the works

_____ get the ax _____ to wire

_____ get with it _____ turn out

_____ go through channels _____ up-and-coming

_____ have an in with _____ up for grabs

_____ in a pinch _____ weed out

Practice

Read each of the following job-related sentences carefully. Determine the meaning of each idiom and write its letter on the line.

1. Mr. Stevens, you've been working at your desk for three hours without even drinking a cup of coffee. Don't you think it's time to take a break?

    Take a break means _____

    a) relax for several minutes.

    b) continue working.

2. "Bruce, I have to leave my desk for ten minutes in order to check on the sales reports. Can you keep an eye on things while I'm gone?"

    Keep an eye on means _____

    a) leave the room.

    b) take care of.

3. Ever since we advertised the special discount sale on stereo equipment, we've been swamped with customers. We had to hire four extra salespeople to help.

    Swamped means _____

    a) overloaded.

    b) in need of.

4. I don't think this engine design will ever work properly. We've tested it for more than six months and have never been successful. This project is hopeless; why don't we just call it a day?

    Call it a day means _____

    a) stop work completely.

    b) work even harder.

5. Marilyn and Janet are the two who have worked for months on this presentation. It's too bad that Marilyn is ill. Still, the presentation must be made today. Janet will have to carry the ball for both of them.

    Carry the ball means _____

    a) work as a team member.

    b) not be responsible for.

Practice

Study the ten idioms and their meanings. Then complete the sentences.

Idioms	Meanings
a tall order	a difficult request to follow or accomplish
chip in	contribute
get one wrong	misunderstand
go through channels	follow a set procedure to get something done
have an in with	have special influence
let slide	be careless in doing work
pull one's weight	do what one is responsible for
run through	review or rehearse
(to) wire	telegraph
up for grabs	available to many people

1. Since you <u>have an in with</u> the personnel department, you will probably _____.

2. If you <u>let</u> your work <u>slide</u>, you'll _____.

3. _____ is <u>a tall order</u> even for an experienced mechanic.

4. Doctor, can we <u>run through</u> this procedure before _____?

5. Mr. Davis decided <u>to wire</u> the Chicago office that _____.

6. In order to _____, you'll have to <u>go through channels</u>.

7. If the account is still <u>up for grabs</u>, we have _____.

8. In this office, everyone <u>pulls his own weight</u> or else _____.

9. Let's all <u>chip in</u> and get _____.

10. Don't <u>get me wrong</u>: I enjoy working here even though _____.

Practice

Each of the following situations contains an idiom. Determine the meaning of each idiom and write its letter on the line.

1. I have been with this company for six years. During that time I have been called upon to leave my family to take extended business trips, to work late hours, and to do the work others cannot complete. I <u>draw the line at</u> cancelling my vacation plans so that the owner's son can have an extended holiday.

   Draw the line means _____

   a) set a limit. b) be happy.

2. Billy recently completed a course in photography. When he read an advertisement for work as a photographer's assistant, he immediately decided that he was <u>suited for</u> that position.

   Suited for means _____

   a) well-dressed. b) qualified.

3. "We have twelve applicants for this position," stated Mr. Baker. "We must read all the résumés and <u>weed out</u> those with the least experience."

   Weed out means _____

   a) congratulate. b) eliminate the least desirable.

4. Joan decided to apply for the position of store manager. Although she had little experience, she believed that she could work hard and learn the duties quickly. Certainly, she would <u>do her level best</u> in the job.

   Level best means _____

   a) a fine effort. b) making no attempt to improve.

5. Tony very much needed this job and was anxious to do well at the interview. Up till now, however, nothing was going right: he had overslept, had missed his bus, and had gotten caught in traffic. By the time he arrived at the office, he knew he would have <u>to get his act together</u> in order to impress the interviewer.

Get his act together means _____

a) remain calm and concentrate on the situation.

b) make excuses for being late for an appointment.

Practice

Study the meanings of the following idioms. Then, consider the divided sentences. Show your understanding of the idioms by combining the parts into meaningful sentences.

Idioms	Meanings
break even	have no losses or profits in business
change hands	pass from one owner to another
play with fire	risk danger or penalty
run out of	totally use one's supply of an item
step on it	hurry

__2__ If you continue to cheat on your exams,

____ We'll probably break even this month

____ The company has been through three different ownerships and

____ We've run out of paper,

____ If you don't step on it,

1. is changing hands again.
2. you know you're playing with fire.
3. since our costs equal our cash income.
4. we'll be late for the theater.
5. so please order ten packages immediately.

Write your own sentence for each idiom.

1. _____

2. _____

3. _____

4. _____

5. _____

Practice

Study the meanings of the following idioms. Then, consider the divided sentences. Show your understanding of the idioms by combining the parts into meaningful sentences.

Idioms   *Meanings*
in a pinch   in an emergency
in black and white   in writing
look into   investigate
run the risk   take a chance of a loss
save face   keep one's dignity

_____ The only way to save face in this awful situation is to

_____ If you allow everyone to use the materials,

_____ This executive is a very sly businessperson, so I suggest you

_____ We can always rely on Carole in a pinch since she

_____ Since the company has no reason to send a bill for the cancelled order,

1. you run the risk of not having enough for yourself.

2. I would appreciate your looking into the matter.

3. has studied the role and only needs a day's notice to prepare her part.

4. get every part of the agreement in black and white.

5. admit your mistake and do superior work from now on.

Write your own sentence for each idiom.

1. _____

2. _____

3. _____

4. _____

5. _____

Practice

Study the following idioms and their meanings. Then, check those sentences in which the idioms are used correctly and place an X next to those sentences in which the idioms are used incorrectly.

Idioms	Meanings
a standing order	an order that does not change
back out	withdraw from; fail to fulfill an obligation
fall short of	fail to measure up to
fill the bill	satisfy the requirements
fringe benefit	something given in addition to salary
get with it	become more efficient; do what you are supposed to be doing
keep track of	maintain a record of
the works	everything
turn out	produce
up-and-coming	ambitious; promising

Sentences

_____ 1. The up-and-coming artist won critical approval for his new paintings.

_____ 2. After signing the contract and shaking hands, the two lawyers happily backed out of the agreement.

_____ 3. Having fallen short of the daily production rate, the factory workers doubled their efforts the next day.

_____ 4. The new secretary found it difficult to keep track of the many phone messages.

_____ 5. An important fringe benefit of many jobs is a good medical plan paid for by the company.

_____ 6. A good copying machine can turn out thirty-five copies a minute.

_____ 7. Since I am on a diet, I'll order a plate of ice cream with the works on it.

_____ 8. A standing order of most hospitals is not to allow any children inside.

_____ 9. Since you've broken every sales record and have become the number one salesperson, I believe it's time for you to get with it.

_____ 10. You cannot type, do not know how to take dictation, and have no experience; I believe you will fill the bill perfectly.

Practice

Complete each of the dialogues with the idioms that are defined. Then write a sentence using each idiom.

1. square deal (an honest arrangement)
   drawback (limitation or obstacle)

   Mark: This car is one year old and has been driven 20,000 miles. The only problem I've had is with the starter. Sometimes it takes a minute or two to start the engine. Other than that _____, everything is perfect.

   Dick: It seems as if you're offering me a _____. I'll give you a deposit now and will pay the rest later.

Sentences

_____
_____
_____
_____

2. pull oneself together (gain control of one's emotions)
   know-how (knowledge of how to do something)

   Amy: Bea, you are the best candidate for this job. You have the _____ to get the work done, and you have ten years of experience with the company. No one else can do the job as well as you can.

   Bea: I know you are right. Still, I can't help being nervous. The other applicants are probably equally deserving. Why should the boss choose me? Maybe I shouldn't waste my time and hers.

Amy: Bea, _____. You know you want the job. Right now you may be nervous, but don't let that stop you.

Sentences

_____
_____
_____
_____

3. pull strings (use influence)
   follow-up (further action)

   Guy: Now that we have the initial lab test results, we need a _____ that will provide more information.

   Ira: That won't be easy. Those secondary tests require additional money, extra personnel, and more subjects. You know that we have a limited budget.

   Guy: I don't care. You'll have to _____ to get the money, supplies, and subjects. It's vital that these tests are conducted properly and promptly.

Sentences

_____
_____
_____
_____

4. broke (without money)
   cream of the crop (the best)
   burned out (exhausted and lacking in new ideas)
   get the ax (be discharged from one's job)

   Mabel: Just think! Only five years ago we were chosen from more than fifty applicants. We had the best qualifications and were considered the _____. No one was better than we were.

   Henry: Yeah! Now look at us. We haven't had any new ideas for a project in months. They've begun to think that we're _____. They think we've lost the enthusiasm and creativity we once had.

   Mabel: Do you think we'll _____? Maybe they'll let us have some extra time to draw up plans. If we lose this job, we'll be totally _____.

   Henry: You're right. We'll have to come up with something. I have no savings and don't know what I'll do if I lose this job.

   Mabel: Let's get with it.

Sentences

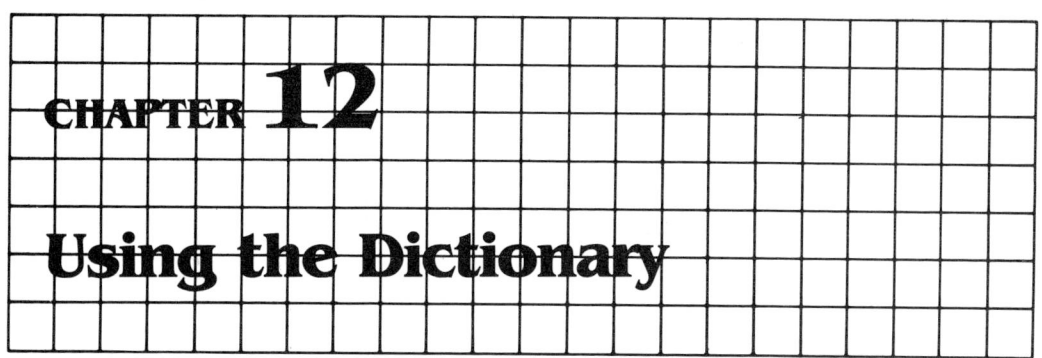

CHAPTER 12
Using the Dictionary

Preview

You will learn that the meaning of each of the following words can change according to the word's function in a sentence. Read the list and check those words for which you know one or two meanings.

_____ accord	_____ heat	_____ revolutionary
_____ arch	_____ interest	_____ scour
_____ barge	_____ intermediary	_____ sheer
_____ briefs	_____ kindred	_____ shingle
_____ buckle	_____ last	_____ singled
_____ cache	_____ live	_____ start
_____ cash	_____ mine	_____ stop
_____ chance	_____ model	_____ tap
_____ copy	_____ motive	_____ tether
_____ crown	_____ official	_____ truly
_____ deduct	_____ one	_____ upstage
_____ elevated	_____ pay	_____ veil
_____ entrée	_____ perpetrators	_____ void
_____ essential	_____ pile	_____ walk
_____ fake	_____ principal	_____ warrant
_____ fast	_____ private	_____ yarn
_____ grant	_____ range	

Using a Word's Part of Speech to Determine Meaning

Understanding the meanings of new words is important. This skill is essential to reading and comprehending the many kinds of printed matter you see every day, such as newspapers, texts, magazines, and job-related materials. One way you can find the meanings of new words is to find and read definitions in a dictionary. Consider the sample entry that follows. Then, read the sentences and answer the questions.

Example

a·ban·don¹ (ə ban′dən), *v.t.* **1.** to leave or forsake completely and finally: *to abandon a sinking ship; to abandon a child.* **2.** to give up; discontinue; withdraw from: *to abandon a research project.* **3.** to give up the possession or control of: *to abandon a city to a conqueror.* **4.** to yield (oneself) utterly to one's emotions or to an impulse. **5.** *Law.* to cast away, leave, or desert, as property or a child. **6.** *Insurance.* to relinquish (insured property) to the underwriter in case of partial loss, thus enabling the insured to claim a total loss. **7.** *Obs.* to banish. [ME *abando(u)ne* < MF *abandon(er)* for OF (*mettre*) *a bandon* (put) under ban = *a* at, to (< L *ad*; see AD-) + *bandon* < LL *bandum*, var. of *bannum* interdict < Gmc; see BAN²] —**a·ban′don·a·ble,** *adj.* —**a·ban′don·er,** *n.* —**a·ban′don·ment,** *n.*
a·ban·don² (ə ban′dən), *n.* a complete surrender to natural impulses without restraint or moderation; freedom from constraint or conventionality: *to dance with reckless abandon.* [< F, back formation from *abandonner* to ABANDON¹]
a·ban·doned (ə ban′dənd), *adj.* **1.** forsaken; deserted: *an abandoned child; an abandoned cabin.* **2.** unrestrained; uncontrolled. **3.** utterly lacking in moral restraints; shameless. [ME] —**a·ban′doned·ly,** *adv.* —Syn. 3. See **immoral.**

1. You may have to <u>abandon</u> all your possessions if the floodwaters rise higher.
2. As the music grew louder, the crowd began to dance with <u>abandon</u>.
3. The <u>abandoned</u> child cried out for help.

Questions

1. In which sentence is "abandon" a verb? _____

2. In which sentence is "abandon" a noun? _____

3. In which sentence is "abandon" an adjective? _____

The word "abandon" has a different function in each sentence. Its function, or part of speech, is as a verb in the infinitive form in Sentence One, as a noun in Sentence Two, and as an adjective in Sentence Three.

4. Find the verb meaning for "abandon" in the entry: _____

5. Find the noun meaning for "abandon" in the entry: _____

6. Find the adjective meaning for "abandon" in the entry: _____

The verb meaning is "to leave completely"; the noun meaning is "complete freedom"; and the adjective meaning is "deserted." You can check the meanings you found by substituting each into its sentence. Often, in order to do this, you must shorten the dictionary meaning or use your own words to sum up that meaning. If you have chosen the correct meaning, the definition will make sense in the sentence.

Example

1. You may have to completely leave all your possessions if the floodwaters rise higher.
2. As the music grew louder, the crowd began to dance with total freedom.
3. The deserted child cried out for help.

Dictionaries provide much **information about the entry word.** Here is the labelled and complete information for the entry word "abandon."

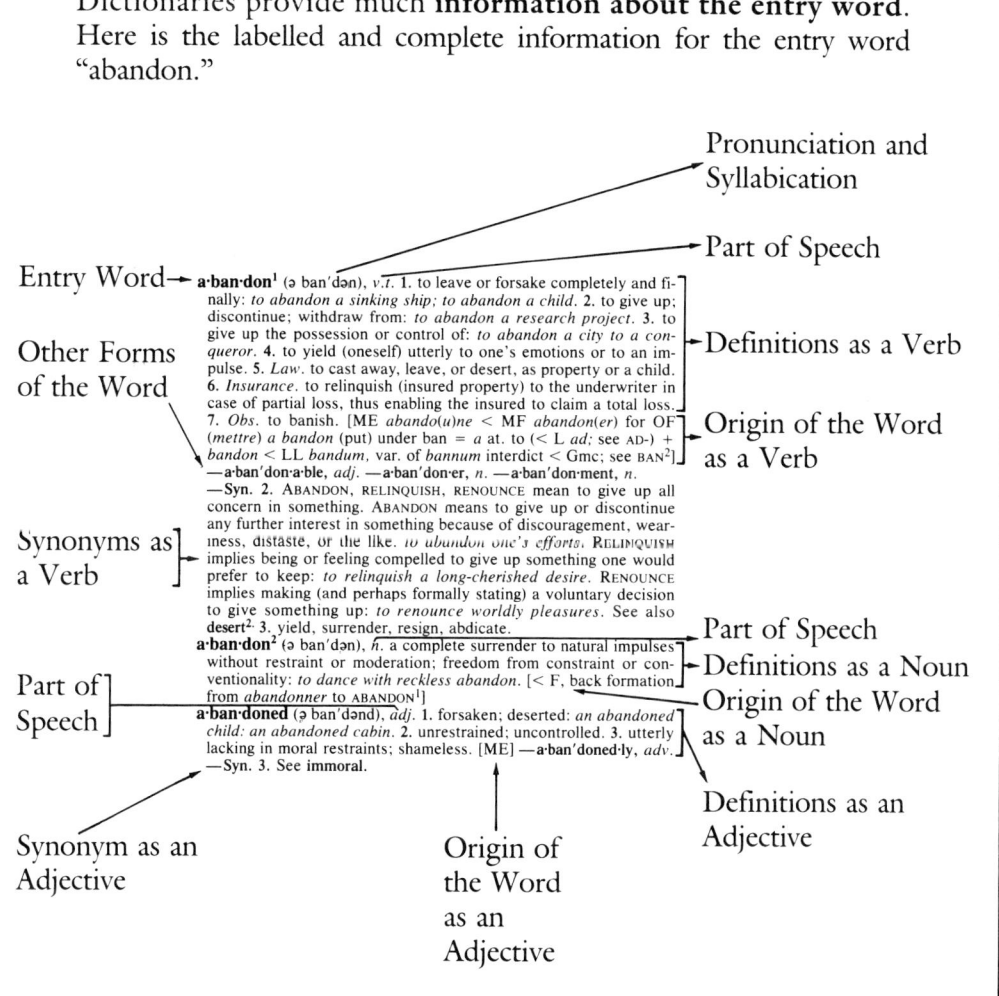

More than one dictionary entry is given for words that are spelled the same but have different origins.

Knowing how a word is used in its sentence, that is, its function or part of speech, can help you to locate the appropriate meaning in the dictionary. Here are the basic **parts of speech** you will be using. A complete list of parts of speech is located at the front of most dictionaries.

Part of Speech	Dictionary Abbreviation	Function in a Sentence
Adjective	adj.	A word that modifies or describes a noun
Adverb	adv.	A word that modifies a verb, adjective, or adverb
Noun	n.	A word that names a person, place, thing, or quality
Pronoun	pron.	A word that substitutes for a noun
Verb	v.	A word that expresses an action or state

Practice

For each of the following words, use the entries given to locate the required meanings. Simplify the definition into a key word or phrase.

Entry

1. **cop·y** (kop′ē), *n., pl.* **cop·ies** for 1, 4–6, *v.,* **cop·ied, cop·y·ing.** —*n.* **1.** an imitation, reproduction, or transcript of an original. **2.** written matter or artwork to be reproduced in printed form. **3.** text to be read or heard, as distinguished from pictures to be seen, in newspapers, magazines, television commercials, etc. **4.** one of the various examples or specimens of the same book, engraving, or the like. **5.** *Brit. Informal.* (in schools) a composition; a written assignment. **6.** *Archaic.* something that is to be reproduced; an example or pattern. —*v.t.* **7.** to make a copy of; transcribe; reproduce. **8.** to follow as a pattern or model. —*v.i.* **9.** to make a copy or copies. **10.** to make or do something in imitation of something else. [ME *copie* < ML *cōpia* abundance, something written, L: wealth, abundance; see COPIOUS] —**Syn. 1.** duplicate, carbon, facsimile. **8.** See **imitate.**

Meaning

noun _____

verb _____

Using the Dictionary 263

2. **pay**[1] (pā), *v.*, **paid** or (*Obs. except for def. 10*) **payed; paying;** *n.; adj.* —*v.t.* **1.** to satisfy (a demand or obligation) by giving over money or the like, as in a business transaction: *to pay the rent.* **2.** to give over (money or the like), as in a business transaction: *to pay $100 a month for an apartment.* **3.** to give over money or the like to (a person or organization), as in order to do business or fulfill an obligation: *to pay the landlord.* **4.** to reward or give compensation for. **5.** to be profitable to. **6.** to yield as a return: *The stock pays four percent.* **7.** to retaliate upon or punish (usually fol. by *back, off,* or *out*): *He paid me back by not coming.* **8.** to give or render (attention, compliments, etc.) as if due or fitting. **9.** to make (a call, visit, etc.). **10.** *Naut.* **a.** to let (a vessel) fall off to leeward. **b.** to let out (a rope) by slackening.
—*v.i.* **11.** to give over money or the like to acquire something or settle an obligation. **12.** to yield a return, profit, or advantage; be worthwhile: *It pays to be honest.* **13.** to undergo revenge or retribution. **14. pay off, a.** to pay someone everything that is due him, esp. as final wages. **b.** to pay a debt in full. **c.** *Slang.* to bribe. **d.** to retaliate upon or punish. **e.** *Naut.* to fall off to leeward. **15. pay one's way,** to pay one's portion of shared expenses. **16. pay up, a.** to pay fully. **b.** to pay upon demand.
—*n.* **17.** wages, salary, or a stipend. **18.** paid employ: *in the pay of the enemy.*

noun _____

verb _____

3. **of·fi·cial** (ə fish′əl), *n.* **1.** a person charged with certain duties in an organization, esp. in the government. —*adj.* **2.** of or pertaining to an office of duty or authority. **3.** appointed, authorized, or approved by a government or organization. **4.** formal and public, as a ceremony. **5.** holding office. **6.** *Pharm.* noting drugs or drug preparations that are recognized by and that conform to the standards of the *United States Pharmacopoeia* or the *National Formulary.* [< LL *officiāl(is)* of duty. See OFFICE, -AL[1]] —**of·fi′cial·ly,** *adv.*

noun _____

adjective _____

4. **stop** (stop), *v.*, **stopped** or (*Archaic*) **stopt; stop·ping;** *n.* —*v.t.* **1.** to cease from, leave off, or discontinue. **2.** to cause to cease; put an end to. **3.** to interrupt, arrest, or check (a course, proceeding, process, etc.). **4.** to cut off, intercept, or withhold. **5.** to restrain, hinder, or prevent (usually fol. by *from*). **6.** to prevent from proceeding, operating, etc. **7.** to block, obstruct, or close (a passageway, channel, etc.) (usually fol. by *up*): *She stopped up the sink with a paper towel. He stopped the hole in the tire with a patch.* **8.** to fill the hole or holes in (a wall, a decayed tooth, etc.). **9.** to close (a container, tube, etc.) with a cork, plug, or the like. **10.** to close the external orifice of (the ears, nose, etc.). **11.** *Sports.* **a.** to check (a stroke, blow, etc.); parry; ward off. **b.** to defeat (an opposing player or team). **c.** *Boxing.* to defeat by a knockout or technical knockout: *Louis stopped Conn in the 13th round.* **12.** *Banking.* to notify a bank to refuse payment of (a check). **13.** *Bridge.* to have an honor card and a sufficient number of protecting cards to keep an opponent from continuing to win in (a suit). **14.** *Music.* **a.** to close (a finger hole) in order to produce a particular note from a wind instrument. **b.** to press down (a string of a violin, viola, etc.) to alter the pitch of the tone produced from it.
—*v.i.* **15.** to come to a stand, as in a course or journey; halt. **16.** to cease moving, proceeding, speaking, etc.; pause; desist. **17.** to cease; come to an end. **18.** to halt for a brief visit (often fol. by *at, in,* or *by*). **19. stop down,** *Photog.* to reduce the diaphragm opening of (a camera). **20. stop off,** to halt for a brief stay at some point on the way elsewhere. **21. stop out,** to mask (certain areas of an etching plate, photographic negative, etc.) with varnish, paper, or the like, to prevent their being etched, printed, etc. **22. stop over,** to stop in the course of a journey, as for the night.
—*n.* **23.** the act of stopping. **24.** a cessation or arrest of movement, action, operation, etc.; end. **25.** a stay or sojourn made at a place, as in the course of a journey. **26.** a place where buses or other vehicles halt to load or unload passengers. **27.** a closing or filling up. **28.** a blocking or obstructing.

noun _____

verb _____

5. **walk** (wôk), *v.i.* **1.** to advance on foot at a moderate pace; proceed by steps; move by a coordinated activity of the feet. **2.** to move about in this way for exercise or pleasure. **3.** to move about in visible form, as a ghost. **4.** (of things) to move in a manner suggestive of walking: *He typed so hard that the lamp walked right off the desk.* **5.** to follow a particular way or pattern of life: *He walked in sorrow.* **6.** *Baseball.* to receive a base on balls. —*v.t.* **7.** to move through, over, or upon by walking: *to walk the floor.* **8.** to cause or help to walk. **9.** to conduct or accompany on a walk: *He walked them about the park.* **10.** to move (a box, trunk, or other object) in a manner suggestive of walking, as by a rocking motion. **11.** *Baseball.* (of a pitcher) to give a base on balls to (a batter). **12.** to examine, measure, etc., by walking. **13. walk off**, to get rid of by walking: *to walk off a headache.* **14. walk off** or **away with, a.** to remove illegally; steal. **b.** to win or attain, as in a competition: *to walk off with the first prize; to walk away with all the honors.* **15. walk out,** *Informal.* **a.** to go on strike. **b.** to leave in protest: *to walk out of a committee meeting.* **16. walk out on,** *Informal.* to leave unceremoniously; desert; forsake: *to walk out on one's family.* **17. walk out with,** *Brit.* to court or be courted by. **18. walk over,** *Informal.* to treat inconsiderately or contemptuously. **19. walk the plank.** See **plank** (def. 5). **20.** *Theat.* **walk through,** to give a perfunctory performance, as at a first rehearsal. —*n.* **21.** the act or an instance of walking. **22.** a distance walked or to be walked, often in terms of the time required: *not more than ten minutes' walk from town.* **23.** a characteristic or individual manner of walking. **24.** a particular form of activity, occupation, status, etc.: *in every walk of life.* **25.** a place or path for walking.

noun _____
verb _____

6. **pri·vate** (prī′vit), *adj.* **1.** belonging to some particular person or persons. **2.** concerning or restricted to only one person or specific persons. **3.** not intended to be made publicly known. **4.** intimate; most personal. **5.** having nothing to do with public life. **6.** of one of the lowest military ranks: *a private soldier.* —*n.* **7.** a soldier of one of the three lowest enlisted ranks. **8. privates.** Also called **pri′vate parts′.** the external genitals. **9. in private,** away from public notice; privately. [ME *pryvat* < L *prīvāt(us)* private, lit., taken away (from public affairs), special use of ptp. of *prīvāre* to rob. See DEPRIVE, -ATE¹] —**pri′vate·ly,** *adv.* —**pri′vateness,** *n.* —**Syn. 1, 2.** particular. **5.** sequestered, retired. —**Ant. 1–4.** general, public.

noun _____
adjective _____

7. **one** (wun), *adj.* **1.** being or amounting to a single unit or individual or entire thing, item, or object. **2.** being unique in kind for a particular reason: *You're the one man I can trust.* **3.** noting some indefinite time: *one evening this week.* **4.** shared by or common to all or everywhere within understood limits: *one nation, indivisible.* **5.** a certain: *One John Smith was chosen.* —*n.* **6.** the first and lowest whole number, being a cardinal number; unity. **7.** a symbol of this number, as 1 or I. **8.** a single person or thing: *one at a time.* **9.** something, as a domino face, that signifies one unit. **10.** *Informal.* a one-dollar bill. **11.** (*cap.*) *Neoplatonism.* the ultimate reality, seen as a central source of being by whose emanations all entities have their existence. **12. at one,** in a state of unity or harmony. —*pron.* **13.** a person or thing of a number or kind: *one of the poets.* **14.** a person: *He's a quiet one.* **15.** some indefinite person, taken as a typical example: *In time, one just gets fed up.* **16. all one, a.** all the same. **b.** insignificant. **17. one with,** in agreement with. [ME *oon,* OE *ān;* c. D *een,* G *ein,* Goth *ains,* L *ūnus* (OL *oinos*); akin to Gk *oínē* ace on a die]

noun _____
pronoun _____

8. **pile**¹ (pīl), *n., v.,* **piled, pil·ing.** —*n.* **1.** an assemblage of things laid or lying one upon the other. **2.** a heap of wood on which something is burned. **3.** a lofty or large building or mass of buildings. **4.** *Informal.* a large accumulation of money. **5.** a bundle of pieces of iron ready to be welded and drawn out into bars; fagot. **6.** reactor (def. 4). —*v.t.* **7.** to lay or dispose in a pile (often fol. by *up*): *to pile up leaves.* **8.** to accumulate or store (often fol. by *up*): *to pile up money.* **9.** to cover or load with a pile or piles. —*v.i.* **10.** to accumulate, as money, debts, evidence, etc. (usually fol. by *up*): *The bills keep piling up.* **11.** *Informal.* to get somewhere in a more or less disorderly group. **12.** to gather or rise in a pile or piles (often fol. by *up*). [late ME < MF < L *pīla* pillar, mole of stone] —**Syn. 1.** collection, heap, mass, accumulation. **2.** pyre. **3.** edifice. **8.** amass, collect.

noun _____
verb _____

9. **cash**¹ (kash), *n.* **1.** money in the form of coin or of negotiable paper, esp. that of a government. **2.** money or an equivalent, as a check, paid at the time of making a purchase. —*v.t.* **3.** to give or obtain cash for (a check, money order, etc.).

noun _____

verb _____

10. **mine**¹ (mīn), *pron.* **1.** a form of the possessive case of *I* used as a predicate adjective: *The yellow sweater is mine.* **2.** that which belongs to me: *Mine is the car with the flat tire.* **3.** *Archaic.* my (used before a word beginning with a vowel or a silent *h*, or following a noun): *mine eyes; lady mine.* [ME, OE *mīn;* c. Icel *mīn*, G *mein*, Goth *meina;* see ME] **mine**² (mīn), *n., v.,* **mined, min·ing.** —*n.* **1.** an excavation made in the earth for the purpose of extracting ores, precious stones, coal, etc. **2.** a natural deposit of such minerals. **3.** an abundant source; store: *a mine of information.* **4.** *Mil.* **a.** a subterranean passage beneath the enemy's fortifications. **b.** an enclosed explosive charge for destroying ships, land vehicles, or personnel. **5.** a passageway in the parenchyma of a leaf, made by certain insects. —*v.i.* **6.** to dig in the earth for the purpose of extracting ores, coal, etc.; make a mine. **7.** to extract ores, etc., from a mine. **8.** to make subterranean passages. **9.** to dig or lay mines, as in military operations. —*v.t.* **10.** to dig in (earth, rock, etc.) in order to obtain ores, coal, etc. **11.** to extract (ore, coal, etc.) from a mine. **12.** to make subterranean passages in or under; burrow. **13.** to make (passages, tunnels, etc.) by digging or burrowing. **14.** to dig away or remove the foundations of. **15.** to attack, ruin, or destroy by secret or slow methods. **16.** to dig or lay military mines under. [ME < MF, perh. < OF *miniere* mine] —**min′a·ble, mine′a·ble,** *adj.*

noun _____

pronoun _____

Practice

In each sentence, identify the part of speech (noun, pronoun, verb, adjective, or adverb) of the underlined word.

_____ 1. The dentist replaced my broken tooth with a <u>crown</u>.

_____ 2. Books can <u>range</u> in price from inexpensive to expensive.

_____ 3. The space shuttle <u>heats</u> up on reentry but is protected by special tile shields.

_____ 4. Both lawyers submitted <u>briefs</u> to the judge.

_____ 5. Law enforcement agents placed a <u>tap</u> on all phones in the suspect's office.

_____ 6. "You have <u>truly</u> beautiful hair," said the stylist.

_____ 7. <u>Revolutionary</u> ideas often lead to discoveries of scientific value.

_____ 8. Four officers arrested the <u>perpetrators</u>.

_____ 9. Max was <u>singled</u> out for his role in the movie.

_____ 10. Paul's chief <u>interest</u> is collecting stamps.

Practice

In each sentence, identify the part of speech for the underlined word.

_____ 1. The judge will now crown the winner with a jeweled tiara.

_____ 2. The scout looked out on the range for signs of a storm.

_____ 3. The first heat of the race ended in a tie.

_____ 4. As soon as Joan briefs the committee on the new amendment, she will call for a vote.

_____ 5. If you tap gently on the jar, you can remove the lid easily.

_____ 6. I truly believe your story.

_____ 7. The revolutionary was taken before a military court.

_____ 8. Don't perpetrate this hoax on unsuspecting customers.

_____ 9. Only a single was needed to score the winning run.

_____ 10. Can I interest you in a subscription to our magazine?

Practice

Identify the part of speech of each underlined word. Then use the dictionary entry to locate the appropriate meaning for that word. You may need to restate or simplify the dictionary meaning.

mod·el (mod/əl), *n., adj., v.,* **-eled, -el·ing** or (*esp. Brit.*) **-elled, -el·ling.** —*n.* **1.** a standard or example for imitation or comparison. **2.** a representation, generally in miniature, to show the structure or serve as a copy of something. **3.** an image in clay, wax, or the like, to be reproduced in more durable material. **4.** a person or thing that serves as a subject for an artist, sculptor, writer, etc. **5.** a person, esp. an attractive young woman, whose profession is posing with, wearing, using, or demonstrating a product for purposes of display or advertising. **6.** a pattern or mode of structure or formation. **7.** a typical form or style. —*adj.* **8.** serving as a model: *a model apartment.* **9.** worthy of serving as a model; exemplary: *a model student.* —*v.t.* **10.** to form or plan according to a model. **11.** to give shape or form to; fashion. **12.** to make a representation of. **13.** to display, esp. by wearing: *to model dresses.* —*v.i.* **14.** to construct models. **15.** to produce designs in some plastic material. **16.** to serve or be employed as a model. [earlier *modell* < It *modell(o),* dim. of *modo* MODE¹] —**mod′el·er;** *esp. Brit.,* **mod′el·ler,** *n.* —**Syn. 1.** prototype, archetype, mold. See **ideal.**

Using the Dictionary   267

1. Charles is a model student.

   In this sentence, model is a(an) ___adjective___.
   (part of speech)

   Model means ___worthy of serving as an example___.

2. Andy began to model clay in her art class.

   In this sentence, model is a(an) _____.

   Model means _____.

> **chance** (chans, chäns), *n., v.,* **chanced, chanc·ing,** *adj.*
> —*n.* **1.** the unpredictable and unwilled element in an occurrence. **2.** luck or fortune: *a game of chance.* **3.** a possibility or probability of anything happening: *a fifty-percent chance of success.* **4.** an opportunity: *Now is your chance.* **5.** *Baseball.* an opportunity to field the ball and make a put-out or assist. **6.** a risk or hazard: *Take a chance.* **7. chances,** probability: *The chances are that the train hasn't left yet.* **8.** *Archaic.* an unfortunate event; mishap. **9. by chance,** without plan or intent; accidentally. **10. on the chance,** in the mild hope or against the possibility. **11. on the off chance,** in the very slight hope or against the very slight possibility. —*v.i.* **12.** to happen or occur by chance: *It chanced that our arrivals coincided.* —*v.t.* **13.** *Informal.* to take the chances or risks of; risk (often fol. by impersonal *it*): *I'll have to chance it, whatever the outcome.* **14. chance on** or **upon,** to come upon by chance. —*adj.* **15.** occurring by chance: *a chance encounter.* [ME < OF, var. of *cheance* < VL *cadentia* a befalling, happening; see CADENZA] —**chance′ful,** *adj.* —**Syn. 2.** accident, fortuity. **3.** contingency. **4.** opening. **12.** befall. See **happen. 15.** casual, accidental, fortuitous. —**Ant. 1.** necessity.

3. We were given one chance to answer the questions.

   In this sentence, chance is a(an) _____.

   Chance means _____.

4. The chance meeting led to a solid friendship.

   In this sentence, chance is a(an) _____.

   Chance means _____.

Vocabulary Skills

last[1] (last, läst), *adj.*, *a superl. of* **late** *with* **later** *as compar.* **1.** occurring or coming after all others, as in time, order, or place. **2.** the most recent; next before the present; latest: *last week.* **3.** being the only remaining. **4.** final: *in his last hours.* **5.** conclusive; definitive. **6.** utmost; extreme. **7.** coming after all others in one's expectations, consideration, etc. **8.** individual; single: *I want every last man here.* —*adv.* **9.** after all others. **10.** most recently: *He was alone when last seen.* **11.** in the end; in conclusion; lastly. —*n.* **12.** a person or thing that is last. **13.** a final appearance or mention: *We haven't heard the last of this.* **14.** the end or conclusion. **15. at last,** after a lengthy pause or delay. **16. at long last,** after much annoying or troublesome delay. **17. breathe one's last,** to die. [ME *last, latst,* syncopated var. of *latest,* OE *latest, lætest,* superl. of *læt,* LATE] —Syn. **1.** LAST, FINAL, ULTIMATE refer to what comes as an ending. That which is LAST comes or stands after all others in a stated series or succession; LAST may refer to objects or activities: *a seat in the last row.* That which is FINAL comes at the end, or serves to end or terminate, admitting of nothing further; FINAL is rarely used of objects: *to make a final attempt.* That which is ULTIMATE (literally, most remote) is the last that can be reached, as in progression or regression, experience, or a course of investigation: *ultimate truths.* —Ant. **1, 2, 4, 7, 9, 11, 12, 14.** first. —Usage. LAST is properly a superlative form of LATE, with LATER and, formerly, LATTER as comparatives. Therefore, English speakers who insist on precision maintain that LATTER should be used only to refer to the second of two items, with LAST being confined to the final item in a list of three or more. (LATER is not used in this sense in modern English.) *Of the two choices, I prefer the latter. John, George, and James were her sons, and she obviously favored the last.*
last[2] (last, läst), *v.i.* **1.** to go on or continue in time. **2.** to remain unexhausted; be enough: *Will our money last long?* **3.** to continue in force, vigor, effectiveness, etc. —*v.t.* **4.** to continue to survive for the duration of. [ME *last(en),* OE *læstan* to follow, (lit., go in the tracks of), perform, continue, last; c. G *laisten* to follow, Goth *laistjan.* See LAST[3]] —**last′er,** *n.* —Syn. **1.** See **continue.**

5. Sandy worked on her paper up to the <u>last</u> minute.

   In this sentence, last is a(an) _____.

   Last means _____.

6. Professor Smith's lectures usually <u>last</u> two hours.

   In this sentence, last is a(an) _____.

   Last means _____.

grant (grant, gränt), *v.t.* **1.** to bestow or confer, esp. by a formal act: *to grant a charter.* **2.** to give or accord: *to grant permission.* **3.** to agree or accede to: *to grant a request.* **4.** to admit or concede; accept for the sake of argument: *I grant that point.* **5.** to transfer or convey, esp. by deed or writing: *to grant property.* —*n.* **6.** something granted, as a privilege or right, a sum of money, or a tract of land. **7.** the act of granting. **8.** *Law.* a transfer of property. **9.** a geographical unit in Vermont, Maine, and New Hampshire, originally a grant of land to a person or group of people. [ME *gra(u)nt(en)* < OF *graunt(er),* var. of *crëanter* < VL **creantare* < L *crëdent-* (s. of *crëdens,* prp. of *crëdere* to believe) + *-äre* inf. suffix] —**grant′a·ble,** *adj.* —**grant′er,** *n.* —Syn. **1.** award, vouchsafe; give. **2.** See **give. 6, 7.** concession. —Ant. **1, 2.** receive; take.

7. Joan's tuition <u>grant</u> was renewed for next year.

   In this sentence, grant is a(an) _____.

   Grant means _____.

8. The dean agreed to <u>grant</u> money for the program.

   In this sentence, grant is a(an) _____.

   Grant means _____.

fast¹ (fast, fäst), *adj.* **1.** moving or able to move, operate, function, or take effect quickly; quick; swift; rapid: *a fast horse; a fast pain reliever.* **2.** done in or taking comparatively little time: *a fast race.* **3.** (of time) indicating a time in advance of the correct time, as a clock. **4.** adapted to, allowing, productive of, or imparting rapid movement: *a hull with fast lines.* **5.** characterized by unrestrained conduct or lack of moral conventions. **6.** characterized by extreme energy or activity, esp. in the pursuit of pleasure. **7.** resistant: *acid-fast.* **8.** firmly fixed in place; not easily moved. **9.** held or caught firmly, so as to be unable to escape or be extricated. **10.** firmly tied, as a knot. **11.** closed and made secure. **12.** such as to hold securely: *to lay fast hold on a thing.* **13.** firm in adherence; loyal: *fast friends.* **14.** permanent, lasting, or unfading: *a fast color.* **15.** deep or sound, as sleep. **16.** *Photog.* **a.** (of a lens) able to transmit a relatively large amount of light in a relatively short time. **b.** (of a film) requiring relatively little exposure to attain a given density. **17.** *Horse Racing.* **a.** (of a track condition) completely dry. **b.** (of a track surface) very hard. **18. pull a fast one,** *Slang.* to play an unfair or unscrupulous trick; practice deceit. —*adv.* **19.** tightly; firmly: *to hold fast.* **20.** soundly: *fast asleep.* **21.** quickly, swiftly, or rapidly. **22.** in quick succession. **23.** in a wild or dissipated way. **24.** ahead of the correct or announced time. **25.** *Archaic.* close; near: *fast by.* **26. play fast and loose.** See **play** (def. 56). [ME; OE *fæst;* c. D *vast,* Icel *fastr* firm, G *fest;* akin to FAST²] —**Syn. 1, 2.** fleet, speedy. See **quick. 5.** dissolute, immoral; wild. **8.** secure, tight, firm. **9.** inextricable. **13.** faithful, steadfast. **14.** enduring. **19.** securely, tenaciously. **23.** recklessly, wildly. —**Ant. 1, 2.** slow. **8.** loose.

fast² (fast, fäst), *v.i.* **1.** to abstain from all food. **2.** to eat only sparingly or of certain kinds of food, esp. as a religious observance. —*n.* **3.** an abstinence from food, or a limiting of one's food, esp. as a religious observance; fasting. **4.** a day or period of fasting. [ME *faste(n),* OE *fæstan;* c. G *fasten.* Goth *fastan,* Icel *fasta*]

9. Mary Ann ended her <u>fast</u> by drinking orange juice.

   In this sentence, fast is a(an) _____.

   Fast means _____.

10. <u>Fast</u> boats can be exciting to ride in.

    In this sentence, fast is a(an) _____.

    Fast means _____.

Vocabulary Skills

Practice

Read each sentence and determine the part of speech for each underlined word. Use the dictionary entry to locate its meaning and rewrite the sentence using that definition or a shorter phrase.

> **start** (stärt), *v.i.* **1.** to begin, as on a journey or activity. **2.** to appear or come suddenly into action, life, view, etc. **3.** to spring, move, or dart suddenly from a position or place. **4.** to give a sudden, involuntary jerk, jump, or twitch, as from a shock of surprise, or pain. **5.** to protrude or emerge: *eyes seeming to start from their sockets.* **6.** (of an object) to spring, slip, or work loose from a place where it has been fastened. **7.** to be among the entrants in a race or the initial participants in a game or contest. —*v.t.* **8.** to set moving, going, or acting. **9.** to bring into existence, operation, or effect: *to start a new business.* **10.** to begin work upon: *to start a book.* **11.** to enable or help (someone) in beginning a journey, career, etc. **12.** to cause or choose to be an entrant in a game or contest. **13.** to cause (an object) to work loose from a place where it has been fastened. **14.** to rouse (game) from its lair or covert; flush. **15.** *Archaic.* to startle. —*n.* **16.** the beginning of an action, journey, etc. **17.** a signal to move, proceed, or begin, as on a course or in a race. **18.** a place or time at which something begins. **19.** the first or beginning part of anything. **20.** a sudden, springing movement from a position. **21.** a sudden, involuntary jerking movement of the body, as from surprise or pain. **22.** a lead or advance of specified amount, as over competitors or pursuers. **23.** the position or advantage of one who starts first. **24.** a chance, opportunity, aid, or encouragement given to a person starting on a course or career. **25.** the action of parts that work loose from their fastenings. **26.** the resulting break or opening. **27.** *Archaic.* an outburst or sally, as of emotion, wit, or fancy. [ME *sterten* (c. MHG *sterzen*); r. OE *styrtan*, c. G *stürzen*] —**Syn. 10.** See **begin**. **16.** commencement, onset.

1. The <u>start</u> of every college year includes an orientation.

   In this sentence, start is a(an) *noun*.
   Start means *the beginning*.
   The beginning of every college year includes an orientation.

2. How can you <u>start</u> to apply for a job when you have no experience?

   In this sentence, start is a(an) _____.

   Start means _____.

   _____

> **de·duct** (di dukt′), *v.t.* **1.** to take away, as from a sum or amount. **2.** detract; abate (usually fol. by *from*). [< L *dēduct(us)* brought down, withdrawn, ptp. of *dēdūcere*]
> **de·duct·i·ble** (di duk′tə bəl), *adj.* **1.** that can be deducted. **2.** *U.S.* allowable as a tax deduction. —*n.* **3.** an insurance policy having a deductible clause. —**de·duct′i·bil′i·ty,** *n.*
> **de·duc·tion** (di duk′shən), *n.* **1.** the act or process of deducting; subtraction. **2.** something that is deducted. **3.** the act or process of deducing: *His deduction led him to the correct conclusion.* **4.** something that is deduced. **5.** *Logic.* **a.** a process of reasoning in which a conclusion follows necessarily from the premises presented. **b.** a conclusion reached by this process. Cf. **induction** (def. 2). [ME < L *dēductiōn-* (s. of *dēductiō*) a leading away]

Using the Dictionary 271

3. Unions may take <u>deductions</u> for dues from members' salaries.

   In this sentence, deductions is a(an) _____.

   Deductions means _____.

   _____

4. <u>Deduct</u> the cost of books from your weekly allowance.

   In this sentence, deduct is a(an) _____.

   Deduct means _____.

   _____

> **el·e·vate** (el′ə vāt′), v., **-vat·ed, -vat·ing,** adj. —v.t. **1.** to move or raise to a higher place or position; lift up. **2.** to raise to a higher state, rank, or office; exalt; promote: *to elevate an archbishop to cardinal.* **3.** to raise to a higher intellectual or spiritual level: *to elevate the mind.* **4.** to raise the spirits; put in high spirits. —adj. **5.** Archaic. raised; elevated. [< L *ēlevāt(us)* lightened, lifted up (ptp. of *ēlevāre*) = ē- E- + *lev(is)* light + -*ātus* -ATE¹] —**el′e·vat′ing·ly,** adv.
> —**Syn. 1.** lift, hoist. **2.** promote, advance, dignify. ELEVATE, ENHANCE, EXALT mean to raise or make higher in some respect. To ELEVATE is to raise something up to a relatively higher level, position, or state: *to elevate the living standards of a group.* To ENHANCE is to add to the attractions or desirability of something: *Landscaping enhances the beauty of the grounds. Paved streets enhance the value of real estate.* To EXALT is to raise very high in rank, character, estimation, mood, etc.: *A king is exalted above his subjects.*
> **el·e·vat·ed** (el′ə vā′tid), adj. **1.** raised up, esp. above the ground: *an elevated platform.* **2.** exalted or noble: *elevated thoughts.* **3.** elated; joyful. —n. **4.** an elevated railroad.

5. The <u>elevated</u> trains shook our windows every hour.

   In this sentence, elevated is a(an) _____.

   Elevated means _____.

   _____

6. <u>Elevate</u> your leg until the pain goes away.

   In this sentence, elevate is a(an) _____.

   Elevate means _____.

   _____

fake¹ (fāk), *v.*, **faked, fak·ing,** *n., adj.* —*v.t.* **1.** to prepare or make (something specious, deceptive, or fraudulent). **2.** to pretend; simulate: *to fake illness.* —*v.i.* **3.** to fake something; pretend. —*n.* **4.** anything made to appear other than it actually is; counterfeit. **5.** a person who fakes; faker. **6.** a spurious report or story. —*adj.* **7.** designed to deceive or cheat; not real; counterfeit. [orig. vagrants' slang: to do for, rob, kill (someone), shape (something); ? var. of obs. *feak, feague* to beat, akin to D *veeg* a slap, *vegen* to sweep, wipe] —**Syn. 5.** fraud, impostor, charlatan.

7. The museum staff was shocked to discover the <u>fake</u> statue.

   In this sentence, fake is a(an) _____.

   Fake means _____.

   _____

8. You can't <u>fake</u> illness in order to miss the quiz.

   In this sentence, fake is a(an) _____.

   Fake means _____.

   _____

cache (kash), *n., v.*, **cached, cach·ing.** —*n.* **1.** a hiding place, esp. one in the ground, for provisions, treasures, etc. **2.** anything hidden or stored. —*v.t.* **3.** to put in a cache; conceal; hide. [< F < *cacher* to hide, press < VL *coacticāre* to stow away, orig. to pack together = L *coact(us)* collected (ptp. of *cōgere*) + *-icā-* formative v. suffix + *-re* inf. ending]

9. The thieves' <u>cache</u> grew with each robbery.

   In this sentence, cache is a(an) _____.

   Cache means _____.

   _____

10. The young girl <u>cached</u> her diary in the closet every night.

    In this sentence, cached is a(an) _____.

    Cached means _____.

    _____

Practice

Read each sentence and determine the part of speech of the underlined word. Then, choose the dictionary meaning that best defines the word and write its part of speech and number on the line.

1. _____

    mo·tive (mō′tiv), *n., adj., v.,* -tived, -tiv·ing. —*n.* 1. something that prompts a person to act in a certain way or that determines volition; incentive. 2. the goal or object of one's actions. 3. (in art, literature, and music) a motif. —*adj.* 4. causing or tending to cause motion. 5. pertaining to motion. 6. prompting to action. 7. constituting a motive or motives. —*v.t.* 8. to motivate. 9. *Obs.* to relate to a motif in a work of art. [ME < ML *mōtīv(um)* that which moves someone to do something, n. use of neut. of *mōtīvus* serving to move = L *mōt(us)* moved (ptp. of *movēre*) + -*īvus* -IVE] —**mo′tive·less**, *adj.* —**mo′tive·less·ly**, *adv.* —**mo′tive·less·ness**, *n.*

    The <u>motive</u> force behind the senator's re-election was his campaign manager.

2. _____

    shin·gle¹ (shing′gəl), *n., v.,* -gled, -gling. —*n.* 1. a thin piece of wood, slate, metal, asbestos, or the like, usually oblong, laid in overlapping rows to cover the roofs and walls of buildings. 2. a close-cropped haircut. 3. *Informal.* a small signboard, esp. as hung before a doctor's or lawyer's office. —*v.t.* 4. to cover with shingles, as a roof. 5. to cut (hair) close to the head. [ME, var. of *shindle* < LL *scindula* alter. of L *scandula* = *scand-* split, scatter, c. Gk *skedánnynai*, E SCATTER, SHATTER + *-ula* -ULE] —**shin′gler**, *n.*

    The workers can begin to <u>shingle</u> your roof tomorrow.

3. _____

    es·sen·tial (ə sen′shəl), *adj.* 1. absolutely necessary; indispensable: *Discipline is essential in an army.* 2. pertaining to or constituting the essence of a thing. 3. noting or containing an essence of a plant, drug, etc. 4. being such by its very nature or in the highest sense; natural; spontaneous: *essential happiness.* —*n.* 5. a basic, indispensable, or necessary element; chief point. [ME *essencial* < ML *essenciāl(is)* for LL *essentiālis.* See ESSENCE, -AL¹] —**es·sen′tial·ly**, *adv.* —**es·sen′tial·ness**, *n.* —**Syn.** 1. fundamental, basic, inherent, intrinsic, vital. See **necessary.** —**Ant.** 2. accidental, extrinsic.

    When Charles proposed the new piece of legislation, he made every attempt to discuss only the <u>essentials</u>.

4. _____

    kin·dred (kin′drid), *n.* 1. a body of persons related to another; family, tribe, or race. 2. a person's relatives collectively; kinfolk; kin. 3. relationship by birth or descent, or sometimes by marriage; kinship. 4. natural relationship; affinity. —*adj.* 5. associated by origin, nature, qualities, etc. 6. having the same belief, attitude, or feeling. 7. related by birth or descent; having kinship. 8. belonging to kin or relatives. [ME, var. (with epenthetic *d*) of *kinred(en).* See KIN, -RED] —**kin′dred·ly**, *adv.* —**kin′dred·ness**, **kin′dred·ship′**, *n.*

    Mike and I are <u>kindred</u> spirits in our appreciation of fine foods.

5. _____

    sheer¹ (shēr), *adj.* 1. transparently thin, as some fabrics; diaphanous: *sheer stockings.* 2. unmixed with anything else: *We drilled a hundred feet through sheer rock.* 3. unqualified; utter: *sheer nonsense.* 4. very steep; almost completely vertical: *a sheer descent of rock.* —*adv.* 5. clear; completely; quite: *ran sheer into the thick of battle.* 6. perpendicularly; vertically; very steeply. —*n.* 7. a thin, diaphanous material, as chiffon or voile. [ME *scere*; OE *scēr* clear, undisputed (in legal context); c. Icel *skærr*; akin to OE *scīr*, Icel *skīr*, G *schier*, Goth *skeirs* clear] —**sheer′ly**, *adv.* —**sheer′ness**, *n.* —**Syn.** 2. unadulterated. 3. absolute. 4. abrupt, precipitous. —**Ant.** 1. opaque.
    sheer² (shēr), *v.i.* 1. to deviate from a course, as a ship; swerve. —*v.t.* 2. to cause to sheer. —*n.* 3. a deviation, or divergence, as of a ship from her course; swerve. 4. the fore-and-aft upward curve of the hull of a vessel at the main deck or bulwarks. 5. the position in which a ship at anchor is placed to keep her clear of the anchor. [from SHEER¹; cf. sense development of CLEAR]

    The construction crew worked for hours drilling through <u>sheer</u> rock.

6. **void** (void), *adj.* 1. *Law.* having no legal force or effect; not legally binding or enforceable. 2. useless; ineffectual; vain. 3. devoid; destitute (usually fol. by *of*): *a life void of meaning.* 4. without contents; empty. 5. without an incumbent, as an office. —*n.* 6. an empty space; emptiness. 7. a gap or opening, as in a wall. 8. *Typography.* counter³ (def. 8). —*v.t.* 9. to make ineffectual; invalidate; nullify: *to void a check.* 10. to empty; discharge; evacuate: *to void excrement.* 11. to clear or empty (often fol. by *of*): *to void a chamber of occupants.* 12. *Archaic.* to depart from; vacate. 13. *Obs.* **a.** to avoid. **b.** to send away; dismiss; expel. [ME *void(e)* < AF, OF < VL *vocita*, fem. of *vocĭtus*, dissimilated var. of L *vocĭvus*, var. of *vac(ĭ)vus* empty; see VACUUM] —**void′er,** *n.* —**void′ness,** *n.* —**Syn. 5.** vacant.

Your excuses are void of meaning, and you should reconsider your actions.

7. **war·rant** (wôr′ənt, wor′-), *n.* 1. authorization, sanction, or justification. 2. something that serves as a guarantee, pledge, or security. 3. a writing or document certifying or authorizing something. 4. *Law.* an instrument, issued by a magistrate, authorizing an officer to make an arrest, seize property, make a search, or execute a judgment. 5. the certificate of authority or appointment issued to an officer of the armed forces below the rank of a commissioned officer. 6. a written authorization for the payment or receipt of money. —*v.t.* 7. to give authority to; authorize. 8. to give adequate reason or justification for. 9. to declare with conviction: *You'll be glad for a rest, I'll warrant!* 10. to give a formal assurance or guarantee of: *to warrant safe delivery.* 11. to guarantee (something sold) to be as represented. 12. to guarantee (a purchase) against loss. 13. *Law.* to guarantee title of an estate (to a grantee). [ME *warant* < AF (var. of OF *guarant*) < Gmc; cf. MLG *warend*, *-ent* warranty, n. use of prp. of *waren* to warrant; see GUARANTY] —**war′rant·less,** *adj.* —**Syn. 2.** warranty, surety. 3. permit, voucher, writ, order, chit.

Do you think your overtime work warrants another salary increase?

8. **ac·cord** (ə kôrd′), *n.* 1. proper relationship or proportion; harmony. 2. a harmonious union of sounds. 3. consent or concurrence of opinions or wills; agreement. 4. an international agreement. —*v.t.* 5. to make to agree or correspond; adapt. 6. to grant; bestow: *to accord due praise.* —*v.i.* 7. to be in agreement or correspondence; agree. [late OE *ācordian* < VL *acordāre* = L *ac-* AC- + *cord-* heart, mind + *-āre* inf. suffix (translated *-ian* in OE)] —**ac·cord′a·ble,** *adj.* —**ac·cord′er,** *n.* —**Syn. 5.** reconcile. 7. concur. See **correspond.**

The accord was short-lived since new arguments began immediately.

9. **barge** (bärj), *n., v.,* **barged, barg·ing.** —*n.* 1. a flat-bottomed vessel, usually without power and intended to be pushed or towed, for transporting freight or passengers. 2. a vessel of state used in pageants: *elegant barges on the Grand Canal in Venice.* 3. *Navy.* a boat reserved for a flag officer. —*v.t.* 4. to carry or transport by barge. —*v.i.* 5. *Informal.* to move clumsily; bump into things; collide: *to barge through a crowd.* 6. **barge in** or **into,** *Informal.* to intrude, interrupt, or interfere, esp. rudely or clumsily: *I hated to barge in without an invitation. He barged into the conversation.* [ME < MF = ML *barga*, ? var. of LL *barca* BARK³]

I often barge into things when I am in a hurry.

10. **en·trée** (än′trā), *n.* 1. the act of entering; entrance. 2. the privilege of entering; access. 3. a means of obtaining entry, as into a particular social or professional world. 4. *U.S.* See **main course** (def. 1). 5. a dish served at dinner before the main course or between the regular courses. Also, **en′tree.** [< F, n. use of fem. ptp. of *entrer* to enter; see ENTRY]

The entrée was served cold and had to be returned to the kitchen.

Using the Dictionary

Practice

Read each sentence and determine the part of speech of the underlined word. Then, choose the dictionary meaning that best defines the word and write its part of speech and number on the line.

Entry

1. _____

prin·ci·pal (prin′sə pəl), *adj.* **1.** first or highest, as in rank, importance, or value. **2.** of or constituting principal or capital: *a principal investment.* —*n.* **3.** a chief or head. **4.** the head or director of a school or, esp. in England, a college. **5.** a person who takes a leading part in any activity, as a play; chief actor or doer. **6.** the first player of a division of instruments in an orchestra, excepting the leader of the first violins. **7.** something of principal or chief importance. **8.** *Law.* **a.** a person who authorizes another, as an agent, to represent him. **b.** a person directly responsible for a crime, either as an actual perpetrator or as an abettor present at its commission. **9.** a person primarily liable for an obligation. **10.** the main body of an estate or the like, as distinguished from income. **11.** *Finance.* a capital sum, as distinguished from interest or profit. **12.** a principal framing member, as a major roof truss. **13.** each of the combatants in a duel, as distinguished from the seconds. [ME < L *prīncipāl(is)* first, chief] —**prin′ci·pal·ship′**, *n.*

When we closed the account, we realized that the principal had nearly doubled in ten years.

2. _____

up·stage (up′stāj′), *adv., adj., v.,* **-staged, -stag·ing,** *n.* —*adv.* **1.** on or toward the back of the stage. —*adj.* **2.** of or pertaining to the back of the stage. —*v.t.* **3.** to move upstage of (another actor), forcing him to act with back to the audience and thereby overshadowing his performance. **4.** to outdo professionally, socially, etc. —*n.* **5.** the rear half of the stage. **6.** any stage position to the rear of another.

The star was particularly skilled at upstaging inexperienced performers.

3. _____

veil (vāl), *n.* **1.** a piece of opaque or transparent material worn over the face. **2.** a piece of material worn so as to fall over the head and shoulders on each side of the face, forming a part of the headdress of a nun. **3.** something that covers, separates, screens, or conceals. **4.** *Bot., Anat., Zool.* a velum. **5.** *Dial.* a caul. **6. take the veil,** to become a nun. **7. the veil,** the life or vows of a nun. —*v.t.* **8.** to cover or conceal with or as with a veil. —*v.t.* **9.** to don or wear a veil.

How can she veil her emotions when she obviously cares greatly?

4. _____

yarn (yärn), *n.* **1.** thread made of natural or synthetic fibers and used for knitting or weaving. **2.** a continuous strand or thread made from glass, metal, plastic, etc. **3.** the thread, in the form of a loosely twisted aggregate of fibers, as of hemp, of which rope is made. **4.** *Informal.* a tale, esp. a long story of adventure or incredible happenings. **5.** *Informal.* to spin a yarn; tell stories. [ME; OE *gearn;* c. G *Garn;* akin to Icel *görn* gut, Gk *chordḗ* intestine, chord, Lith *žarnà* entrails, L *hernia* a rupture, Skt *hirā* vein]

The old cowboy told yarns about the early West and kept us fascinated all evening.

5. _____

arch¹ (ärch), *n.* **1.** *Archit.* a curved masonry construction for spanning an opening, consisting of a number of wedgelike stones, bricks, or the like, set with the narrower side toward the opening. **2.** a doorway, gateway, etc., having a curved head; archway. **3.** any curvature in the form of an arch: *the arch of the heavens.* **4.** something bowed or curved; any bowlike part: *the arch of the foot.* **5.** a device in shoes for supporting the arch of the foot. —*v.t.* **6.** to cover with a vault, or span with an arch. **7.** to throw or make into the shape of an arch; curve: *A horse arches its neck.* —*v.i.* **8.** to form an arch. [ME *arch(e)* < OF *arche* < VL **arca,* fem. var. of L *arcus* ARC]
Arch
A, Abutment; S, Springer; V, Voussoir; K, Keystone Ex., Extrados; P, Pier; I, Impost; In, Intrados
arch² (ärch), *adj.* **1.** chief; most important; principal: *the arch rebel.* **2.** cunning, roguish, or mischievous: *an arch smile.* [see ARCH-] —**arch′ly,** *adv.* —**arch′ness,** *n.*
arch-, a learned borrowing from Greek meaning "chief," used in the formation of compound words: *archbishop; archfiend.* Also, **-arch, archi-, -archy.** [ME; OE *arce-, erce-* < L *arch(e)-, archi-* < Gk *arch-* (s. of *archḗ* beginning)]

The annual football game brought together two arch-rivals in a tremendous contest.

276 Vocabulary Skills

6. _____

buck·le (buk/əl), n., v., **-led, -ling.** —n. **1.** a device for fastening two loose ends, as of a belt or strap, usually attached to one end and grasping a hole in the other by a prong or tongue. **2.** an ornament resembling such a device. **3.** a bend, bulge, or kink, as in a board or saw blade. —v.t. **4.** to fasten with a buckle or buckles. **5.** to prepare (oneself) for action; apply (oneself) vigorously to something. **6.** to bend, warp, or cause to give way suddenly, as with heat or pressure. —v.i. **7.** to be closed or fastened with a buckle: *His boot wouldn't buckle.* **8.** to prepare oneself or apply oneself (often fol. by *down*). **9.** to bend, warp, bulge, or collapse: *The bridge buckled in the storm.* **10.** to yield, surrender, or give way to another (often fol. by *under*). [ME *bocle* < MF < L *buccula* beaver (of a helmet), boss (of a shield) = *bucc(a)* cheek + *-ula* -ULE] —**buck/le·less,** adj.

Feeling faint, the old man tried to find a seat before his legs <u>buckled</u>.

7. _____

scour¹ (skour, skou/ər), v.t. **1.** to cleanse or polish by hard rubbing. **2.** to remove (dirt, grease, etc.) from something by hard rubbing. **3.** to clear or dig out (a channel, drain, etc.), as by the force of water, by removing debris, etc. **4.** to purge thoroughly, as an animal. **5.** to clear or rid of what is undesirable. **6.** to remove by or as by cleansing; get rid of. —v.i. **7.** to polish or clean a surface. **8.** to become clean when scoured. —n. **9.** the act of scouring. **10.** the place scoured. **11.** something that scours. **12.** the erosive force of moving water. **13.** Usually, **scours.** *Vet. Pathol.* diarrhea in horses and cattle caused by intestinal infection. [ME *scour(en)* < Scand; cf. Dan *skure* to rub, scour, Icel *skora* to rub]
scour² (skour, skou/ər), v.i. **1.** to move rapidly or energetically. **2.** to range about, as in search of something. —v.t. **3.** to run or pass quickly over or along. **4.** to range over, as in search: *They scoured the countryside for the lost child.* [ME *scour(en)* < obs. *scour* speed, ? < Scand; cf. Icel *skúr* storm (of wind, rain, battle); c. SHOWER]

The scouts <u>scoured</u> the deserted town for signs of the enemy.

8. _____

teth·er (teth/ər), n. **1.** a cord, chain, or the like, by which a movable or moving object is fastened to a fixed object. **2.** the utmost length to which one can go in action; the utmost extent or limit of ability or resources. **3. at the end of one's tether,** at the end of one's resources, patience, or strength. —v.t. **4.** to fasten or confine with or as with a tether. [ME *tethir* < Scand; cf. Icel *tjōthr*, c. D *tuier*]

Since we know how playful our new puppy is, we will put him on a <u>tether</u> in the yard before the guests arrive.

9. _____

live¹ (liv), v., **lived** (livd), **liv·ing.** —v.i. **1.** to have life, as an animal or plant; be capable of vital functions. **2.** to remain alive: *to live to a ripe old age.* **3.** to continue in existence, operation, memory, etc. **4.** to rely for one's maintenance (usually fol. by *on* or *upon*): *to live on one's income.* **5.** to feed or subsist (usually fol. by *on* or *upon*): *to live on rice.* **6.** to dwell or reside: *to live in a cottage.* **7.** to pass life in a specified manner: *They lived happily ever after.* **8.** to direct or regulate one's life. **9.** to experience or enjoy life to the full. **10.** to cohabit (usually fol. by *with*). —v.t. **11.** to pass (one's life). **12.** to represent or exhibit in one's life: *to live a lie.* **13. live down,** to live so as to allow (a scandal, disgrace, etc.) to be forgotten or forgiven. **14. live high off the hog.** See *hog* (def. 6). **15. live in** or **out,** to reside at or away from the place of one's employment. **16. live it up,** *Informal.* to live in an extravagant, wild, or carefree manner. **17. live up to,** to live in accordance with some ideal or standard. [ME *live(n),* OE *lifian, libban*; c. D *leven,* G *leben,* Icel *lifa,* Goth *liban*]
live² (liv), adj., **liv·er, liv·est** for 4–9, adv. —adj. **1.** having life; alive. **2.** of, pertaining to, or during the life of a living being. **3.** characterized by or indicating the presence of living creatures. **4.** full of spirits, energy, or activity. **5.** *Informal.* (of a person) energetic; alert; up-to-date. **6.** *Chiefly U.S.* of current interest or importance, as a question or issue. **7.** burning or glowing, as a coal. **8.** vivid or bright, as color. **9.** having resilience or bounce: *a live tennis ball.* **10.** being in play, as a baseball or football. **11.** loaded or unexploded, as a cartridge or shell. **12.** *Elect.* electrically connected to a source of potential difference, or electrically charged so as to have a potential different from that of earth: *a live wire.* **13.** moving or imparting motion; powered. **14.** still in use, or to be used, as type set up or copy for printing. **15.** (of a radio or television program) broadcast or televised at the moment it is being presented at the studio. **16.** made up of actual persons: *a live audience.* **17. live one,** *U.S. Slang.* **a.** a person who spends money readily. **b.** a person easily imposed upon or made the dupe of others. —adv. **18.** (of a radio or television program) at the moment of occurrence or performance: *brought to you live from New York.* [aph. var. of ALIVE, used attributively] —**live/ness,** n.

The President's news conference was broadcast <u>live</u> from the White House.

10.

in·ter·me·di·ar·y (in/tər mē/dē er/ē), *adj., n., pl.* **-ar·ies.**
—*adj.* **1.** being between; intermediate. **2.** acting between persons, parties, etc.; serving as an intermediate agent or agency: *an intermediary power.* —*n.* **3.** an intermediate agent or agency; a go-between or mediator. **4.** a medium or means. **5.** an intermediate form or stage. [< LL *intermedi(um)* (n.) + -ARY; see INTERMEDIATE¹]

The <u>intermediary</u> phase between infection and the appearance of symptoms is called incubation.

Preview

You will learn that each of the following words can have more than one meaning. Read the words and check those for which you know one or two meanings.

_____ arrested	_____ hatch	_____ peep
_____ before	_____ hazard	_____ pet
_____ camper	_____ hook	_____ pluck
_____ chum	_____ humble	_____ plump
_____ claw	_____ import	_____ revolve
_____ conserve	_____ impression	_____ sap
_____ copy	_____ lie	_____ scoop
_____ detached	_____ mock	_____ scramble
_____ dispute	_____ mum	_____ stage
_____ drive	_____ must	_____ standard
_____ enjoin	_____ paddle	_____ tidbit
_____ errant	_____ page	_____ trim
_____ essence	_____ panel	_____ valet
_____ even	_____ parrot	_____ wash

Understanding Multiple Meanings of Words

You have identified a word's part of speech, or function in a sentence, and have located the appropriate group of definitions in a dictionary entry. For example, you looked directly at the noun meanings in the entry when you understood that the word functioned as a noun in its sentence.

Many nouns in the English language have more than one meaning. This is also true of verbs, adjectives, and some adverbs. How can you decide which dictionary meaning is correct, and how can you locate that meaning quickly? Read the following sentences carefully and use the dictionary entry to help you answer the questions that follow.

Example

ar·rest (ə rest'), *v.t.* 1. to seize (a person) by legal authority or warrant. 2. to attract and hold: *to arrest the attention*. 3. *Disease.* to check the course of; stop or slow down: *to arrest progress.*—*n.* 4. the act of taking a person into legal custody, as by officers of the law. 5. the state of being taken into legal custody (sometimes prec. by *under*). 6. any act of taking by force. 7. the act of stopping or slowing. 8. the state of being stopped or slowed. [ME *areste*(n) < MF *areste*(r) = a- A-⁵ + *rester* to REST; ME *arest*(e) (n.) < OF (v.)] —**ar·rest'a·ble**, *adj.* —**ar·rest'er**, *n.* —**ar·rest'ment**, *n.* —Syn. 1. apprehend. 2. secure, occupy. 3. stay. See **stop**. 4. detention, apprehension. 7. stoppage, stay, check. —Ant. 1–4. release.

1. The doctors disagreed with us and said that the patient's disease had not been cured; it had only been <u>arrested</u>.

2. The thieves were <u>arrested</u> as they attempted to leave the scene of the robbery.

Questions

1. What part of speech is "arrested" in Sentence 1? _____

2. What part of speech is "arrested" in Sentence 2? _____

3. Which sentence talks about crime? _____ About disease? _____

4. Write the dictionary meaning for "arrested" that refers to crime: _____

5. Write the dictionary meaning for "arrested" that refers to disease: _____

Although "arrested" is a verb in both sentences, it has a different meaning in each. Sentence One clearly talks about disease, and Sentence Two talks about crime. The dictionary meaning that refers to disease is "to check the course of; stop or slow down," and the meaning that refers to crime is "to seize a person by legal authority or warrant." Although both meanings refer to stopping, each has a different reference because of the sense of the sentence.

> A word's meaning can change completely or vary slightly according to the sentence or paragraph, that is, the **context** in which it appears. In order to **locate the correct dictionary meaning**, first consider the word's part of speech. Next, consider what the sentence or paragraph talks about. Then, read the dictionary entry for that part of speech and locate the definition that matches what the sentence talks about.

Practice

Notice that two separate entries for "page" are given in this exercise. The dictionary offers separate entries for words that are spelled identically but have different derivations or origins. Consider the way "page" functions in each sentence and complete the chart that follows.

page[1] (pāj), *n., v.,* **paged, pag·ing.**—*n.* 1. one side of a leaf of something printed or written, as a book. 2. the entire leaf. 3. a noteworthy event or period: *a bright page in English history.* —*v.t.* 4. to put in order. —*v.i.* 5. to turn pages (usually fol. by *through*). [< MF < L *pāgina,* akin to *pangere* to fix, make fast]
page[2] (pāj), *n., v.,* **paged, pag·ing.**—*n.* 1. a boy servant or attendant. 2. a youth in attendance on a person of rank or, in medieval times, a youth being trained for knighthood. 3. a young male attendant or employee, who carries messages, ushers guests, runs errands, etc. —*v.t.* 4. to summon formally by calling out the name of repeatedly. [ME < OF < ?]

1. The page hurried the people along in the darkened movie house.
2. The nurse paged Dr. Emory over the public address system.
3. I quickly paged through the book to see how difficult it would be.
4. The signing of the treaty opened a new page in the history of the two nations.
5. This text has four hundred pages.
6. The editor paged the manuscript so that she could read it in the correct order.

Sentence	Part of Speech For "Page"	The Sentence Talks About	Dictionary Meaning for "Page"
#1	noun	the movies	an employee who ushers guests
#2			
#3			
#4			
#5			
#6			

Using the Dictionary 281

Practice

Each dictionary entry is accompanied by sentences in which the entry word is underlined. Consider the context of each sentence: the word's part of speech and what the sentence talks about. Then, write the number of the best meaning found in the entry.

> **pad·dle**¹ (pad′l), n., v., -dled, -dling. —n. 1. a short, flat-bladed oar for propelling and steering a canoe, usually held in both hands and moved through a vertical arc. 2. any of various similar implements used for mixing, stirring, or beating. 3. an implement with a short handle and a wide, rounded blade, used as a racket in table tennis. 4. a similar instrument used for spanking a child or in hazing freshmen, initiates to a fraternity, etc. 5. Also called **float**. a blade of a paddle wheel. 6. See **paddle wheel**. 7. a flipper or limb of a penguin, turtle, whale, etc. 8. an act of paddling. —v.i. 9. to propel or travel in a canoe or the like by using a paddle. 10. to row lightly or gently with oars. 11. to move by means of paddle wheels, as a steamer. —v.t. 12. to propel with a paddle. 13. to spank with or as with a paddle. 14. to stir, mix, or beat with or as with a paddle. 15. to convey by paddling, as in a canoe. 16. to hit (a table-tennis ball or the like) with a paddle. [late ME *padell*]
> —pad′dler, n.

1. We picked up our ping-pong <u>paddles</u> and went to the gameroom.

   part of speech _noun_

   sentence talks about _a game_

   meaning number _#3_

2. The teacher <u>paddled</u> the child for being the trouble-maker in class.

   part of speech _____

   sentence talks about _____

   meaning number _____

3. The rowing coach decided to use both <u>paddles</u> in the swift-moving stream.

   part of speech _____

   sentence talks about _____

   meaning number _____

haz·ard (haz/ərd), *n.* **1.** danger; risk; peril. **2.** something causing danger, peril, risk, or difficulty: *the many hazards of the big city.* **3.** the absence or lack of predictability in an event; chance; uncertainty. **4.** an unexpected or unpredictable event; accident. **5.** *Golf.* a bunker, sand trap, or the like, constituting an obstacle. **6.** a game played with two dice, an earlier and more complicated form of craps. **7.** something risked or staked. **8.** *Court Tennis.* any of the winning openings. **9.** (in English billiards) a stroke by which the player pockets the object ball (**winning hazard**) or his own ball after contact with another ball (**losing hazard**). —*v.t.* **10.** to offer (a statement, conjecture, etc.) at the risk of criticism, disapproval, etc.; venture: *to hazard a guess.* **11.** to put to the risk of being lost; expose to risk; gamble: *In making the investment, he hazarded all his savings.* **12.** to take or run the risk of (a misfortune, penalty, etc.): *Thieves hazard arrest.* **13.** to venture upon (anything of doubtful issue). [ME *hasard* < OF; cf. Ar *az-zahr* the die] —**Syn. 1.** See **danger. 3.** accident, fortuity, fortuitousness. **11.** stake, imperil. —**Ant. 1.** safety.

1. Driving on dark country roads is a <u>hazard</u> of country living.

   part of speech _____

   sentence talks about _____

   meaning number _____

2. The golfer needed three tries to get beyond the <u>hazard</u> and on to the green.

   part of speech _____

   sentence talks about _____

   meaning number _____

mum[1] (mum), *adj.* **1.** silent; not saying a word: *to keep mum.* —*interj.* **2.** say nothing! be silent! **3. mum's the word**, do not reveal what you know. [ME *momme*, imit.]
mum[2] (mum), *v.i.*, **mummed, mum·ming.** to act as a mummer. Also, **mumm**. [ME *momme(n)*, v. use of MUM[1]; cf. MD *mommen* to act the mummer's part]
mum[3] (mum), *n. Informal.* chrysanthemum. [shortened form]
mum[4] (mum), *n. Chiefly Brit. Informal.* mother. [nursery word; see MOM]
mum[5] (mum), *n.* a strong beer or ale. [< G *Mumme*, said to have been named after the brewer who made it]

1. I'll only tell you what he said if you promise to keep <u>mum</u> about it.

   part of speech _____

   sentence talks about _____

   meaning number _____

2. The young man bought a dozen <u>mums</u> for his girlfriend.

   part of speech _____

   sentence talks about _____

   meaning number _____

val·et (val/it, val/ā, va lā/; Fr. vA le/), n., v., -et·ed, -et·ing. —n. 1. a male servant who attends to the personal needs of his employer, as by taking care of clothing; manservant. 2. a man who is employed to care for the clothing of patrons of a hotel, passengers on a ship, etc. 3. a stand or rack for holding coats, hats, etc. —v.t., v.i. 4. to serve as a valet. [< F; MF va(s)let squire = vas- (< ML vassus servant) + -let -LET; see VASSAL]

1. As soon as we register, let's call the <u>valet</u> and have him press our clothes.

   part of speech _____

   sentence talks about _____

   meaning number _____

2. James has been a <u>valet</u> to the Smiths for twenty years.

   part of speech _____

   sentence talks about _____

   meaning number _____

pan·el (pan/əl), n., v., -eled, -el·ing or (esp. Brit.) -elled, -el·ling. —n. 1. an area of a wall, door, ceiling, etc., that is distinct from the surrounding or adjoining areas. 2. any of various flat, thin pieces of material joined to form a surface or solid. 3. Painting. a. a flat, broad piece of wood on which a picture is painted. b. the picture itself. 4. a photograph much longer in one dimension than the other. 5. a broad, vertical strip of fabric set on a dress, skirt, etc. 6. Law. a. a list of persons summoned for service as jurors. b. the body of persons composing a jury. 7. a group of persons gathered to conduct a public discussion, serve as advisers, participate in a quiz game, or the like. 8. a public discussion by such a group. 9. a mount for or surface or section of a machine containing the controls and dials. 10. Elect. a switchboard or control board, or a division of a switchboard or control board containing a set of related cords, jacks, relays, etc. 11. Engineering, Building Trades. an area or section of a truss bounded by principal web members and chords. 12. Aeron. a. a lateral subdivision of an airfoil with internal girder construction. b. a section of the hull of a rigid airship marked off by a set of transverse and lateral girders. —v.t. 10. to arrange in or furnish with a panel or panels. 14. to set in a frame as a panel. [ME < OF panel a piece (of anything), dim. of pan piece of cloth or the like. See PANE]

1. The judge ordered the <u>panel</u> to leave the room while special testimony was heard.

   part of speech _____

   sentence talks about _____

   meaning number _____

2. On the <u>panel</u> was a photograph of the entire family.

   part of speech _____

   sentence talks about _____

   meaning number _____

Vocabulary Skills

Practice

Write the number of the dictionary entry that best defines the underlined word in each sentence.

Entries

re·volve (ri volv′), v., -volved, -volv·ing. —v.i. 1. to turn around or rotate, as on an axis. 2. to move in a circular or curving course or orbit. 3. to proceed or occur in a round or cycle; recur. 4. to be thought about or considered. —v.t. 5. to cause to turn around, as on an axis. 6. to cause to move in a circular or curving course, as about a central point. 7. to think about; consider. [ME revolve(n) < L revolv(ere) (to) roll back = re- **+** *volvere* to roll, turn round. See WALLOW] —**re·volv′a·ble**, *adj.* —**re·volv′a·bly**, *adv.* —Syn. 1. See **turn**. 2. **orbit**, **circle**. 7. **ponder**, **study**.

hook (hŏŏk), n. 1. a curved or angular piece of metal or other hard substance for catching, pulling, holding, or suspending something. 2. a fishhook. 3. something that catches; snare; trap. 4. something having a sharp curve, bend, or angle at one end, as a mark, symbol, etc. 5. a sharp curve or angle in the length or course of anything. 6. a curved spit of land. 7. a recurved and pointed organ or appendage of an animal or plant. 8. *Sports.* a. the path described by a ball, as in baseball, bowling, or golf, that curves in a direction opposite to the throwing hand or to the side of the ball from which it was struck. b. a ball describing such a path. 9. *Boxing.* a short, circular punch delivered with the elbow bent. 10. Also called **pennant**. *Music.* a stroke or line attached to the stem of eighth notes, sixteenth notes, etc. 11. **hooks**, *Slang.* hands or fingers. 12. **by hook or by crook**, by any means. Also, **by hook or crook**. 13. **hook, line, and sinker**, *Informal.* entirely; completely: *He fell for the story—hook, line, and sinker.* 14. **off the hook**, *Slang.* out of trouble; released from some difficulty or obligation. 15. **on one's own hook**, *Informal.* on one's own initiative or responsibility; independently. 16. **on the hook**, *Slang.* a. obliged; committed; involved. b. subjected to a delaying tactic; waiting. —v.t. 17. to seize, fasten, suspend from, pierce, or catch hold of and draw with or as with a hook. 18. to catch (fish) with a fishhook. 19. *Slang.* to steal or seize by stealth. 20. *Informal.* to catch or trick by artifice. 21. (of a bull or other horned animal) to catch on the horns or attack with the horns. 22. to catch hold of and draw (loops of yarn) through cloth with or as with a hook. 23. to make (a rug, garment, etc.) in this fashion. 24. *Sports.* to hit or throw (a ball) so that a hook results. 25. *Boxing.* to deliver a hook with. 26. to make hook-shaped; crook. —v.i. 27. to become attached or fastened by or as by a hook. 28. to curve or bend like a hook. 29. *Sports.* a. (of a player) to hook the ball. b. (of a ball) to describe a hook in course. 30. **hook up**, a. to fasten with a hook or hooks. b. to assemble, as a mechanical apparatus, and connect to a source of power. [ME *hoke*, OE *hōc*; c. D *hoek* hook, angle, corner; akin to G *Haken*, Icel *haki*] —**hook′less**, *adj.* —**hook′like′**, *adj.*

cop·y (kop′ē), n., pl. **cop·ies** for 1, 4–6, v., **cop·ied**, **cop·y·ing**. —n. 1. an imitation, reproduction, or transcript of an original. 2. written matter or artwork to be reproduced in printed form. 3. text to be read or heard, as distinguished from pictures to be seen, in newspapers, magazines, television commercials, etc. 4. one of the various examples or specimens of the same book, engraving, or the like. 5. *Brit. Informal.* (in schools) a composition; a written assignment. 6. *Archaic.* something that is to be reproduced; an example or pattern. —v.t. 7. to make a copy of; transcribe; reproduce. 8. to follow as a pattern or model. —v.i. 9. to make a copy or copies. 10. to make or do something in imitation of something else. [ME *copie* < ML *cōpia* abundance, something written, L: wealth, abundance; see COPIOUS] —Syn. 1. duplicate, carbon, facsimile. 8. See **imitate**.

tid·bit (tid′bit′), n. 1. a delicate bit or morsel of food. 2. a choice or pleasing bit of anything, as news or gossip. Also, *esp. Brit.*, **titbit**. [TID¹ (in sense of feast day) + BIT³]

Sentences

_____ 1. My thoughts keep revolving around the possible reasons we lost the contract.

_____ 2. I would improve my golf score if I could only get rid of my hook.

_____ 3. Change the copy; it doesn't describe our product accurately.

_____ 4. What a wonderful plate of tidbits you prepared for this afternoon's tea!

camp·er (kam′pər), *n.* **1.** a person who camps out for recreation, esp. in the wilderness. **2.** a person who attends a summer camp or day camp. **3.** a station wagon with enclosed sides or a pickup truck with a roomlike addition over the cab and truck bed, outfitted as temporary living quarters for use in camping or extended motor excursions.

_____ 5. The camper was loaded and ready for the long drive through the desert.

Practice

Using the dictionary entries for *revolve, hook, copy, tidbit,* and *camper,* select another meaning for each and write a sentence for it.

1. _____
2. _____
3. _____
4. _____
5. _____

Practice

The following dictionary entry for "drive" has thirty-seven basic definitions. Choose two noun and three verb meanings and write a sentence for each. Remember the part of speech and any special meaning the sentence must contain.

drive (driv), *v.*, **drove** or *(Archaic)* **drave; driv·en, driv·ing;** *n.* —*v.t.* **1.** to send, expel, or otherwise cause to move by force or compulsion (often fol. by *away, off,* etc.): *to drive away the flies.* **2.** to force to work or act; overwork. **3.** to cause and guide the movement of (a vehicle, an animal, etc.): *to drive a car; to drive a mule.* **4.** to transport in a vehicle, esp. an automobile: *He drove her to the station.* **5.** to keep (machinery) going. **6.** to impel; constrain; urge; compel. **7.** to carry (business, an agreement, etc.) vigorously through: *He drove a hard bargain.* **8.** (in mining, construction, etc.) to dig (a mine shaft, tunnel, etc.) horizontally. **9.** *Sports.* to hit or propel (a ball, puck, shuttlecock, etc.) very hard. **10.** *Golf.* to hit (a golf ball), esp. from the tee, as with a driver or driving iron. **11.** *Hunting.* **a.** to chase (game). **b.** to search (a district) for game. **12.** to float (logs) down a river or stream.
—*v.i.* **13.** to go along before an impelling force; be impelled: *The ship drove before the wind.* **14.** to rush or dash violently. **15.** to cause and guide the movement of a vehicle or animal. **16.** to know how to operate an automobile. **17.** to possess a valid driver's license: *In this state, you can't drive until you're 18 years old.* **18.** to go or travel in a driven vehicle; ride: *He drives to work with me.* **19.** *Golf.* to hit a golf ball, esp. from the tee, as with a driver or driving iron. **20.** to strive vigorously toward an objective. **21. drive at,** to attempt or intend to convey; allude to; suggest: *What is he driving at?*
—*n.* **22.** the act of driving. **23.** a trip in a vehicle, esp. a short pleasure trip. **24.** an impelling along, as of game, cattle, or floating logs, in a particular direction. **25.** the animals, logs, etc., thus driven. **26.** *Psychol.* an inner urge that stimulates a response, inciting or repressing action; a basic or instinctive need. **27.** a vigorous onset or onward course toward a goal or objective. **28.** a strong military offensive. **29.** a united effort to accomplish some specific purpose, esp. to raise money, as for a charity. **30.** energy and initiative: *a person with great drive.* **31.** vigorous pressure or effort, as in business. **32.** a road for vehicles, esp. a broad or scenic highway. **33.** *Mach.* a driving mechanism, as of an automobile: *gear drive; chain drive.* **34.** *Auto.* the point or points of power application to the roadway: *four-wheel drive.* **35.** *Sports.* a propelling, forcible stroke. **36.** *Golf.* a shot, esp. with a driver or driving iron from the tee, that is intended to carry a great distance. **37.** a hunt in which game is driven toward stationary hunters. [ME *drive(n),* OE *drīfan;* c. D *drijven,* Icel *drīfa,* Goth *-dreiban,* G *treiben*]
—**driv′a·ble, drive′a·ble,** *adj.*
—**Syn. 1.** push, force. **30.** enterprise.

(noun) 1. _____

(noun) 2. _____

(verb) 3. _____

(verb) 4. _____

(verb) 5. _____

Practice

Consider the context of the underlined word in each sentence. Two dictionary meanings and the part of speech are listed for each word. Write the letter of the meaning that is correct for the context.

_____ 1. I chartered the boat with all my chums and looked forward to having a wonderful afternoon.
   a) n. ground bait used to lure fish
   b) n. a friend

_____ 2. We held memorial services to honor those who had gone before us.
   a) adv. earlier
   b) adv. in front of

_____ 3. The old man's essence was totally evil.
   a) n. perfume
   b) n. basic nature

_____ 4. Use these supplies to trim the Christmas window.
   a) v. arrange goods in a store display
   b) v. cut to shape

_____ 5. The boy's errant behavior greatly concerned his family.
   a) adj. deviating from usual conduct
   b) adj. journeying in search of adventure

_____ 6. The embassy standard was lowered at sunset each day.
   a) n. model for comparison
   b) n. flag

_____ 7. The judge enjoined the landlord from bothering the tenants.
   a) v. prohibit
   b) v. direct someone to do something

_____ 8. I ran plump into my neighbors.
   a) adv. directly
   b) adj. fleshy

_____ 9. The new nation entered a stage which all new nations go through.
   a) n. platform in a theater
   b) n. phase in a process

_____ 10. Your pluck during these terrible times has pulled us together.
   a) n. courage
   b) v. to pull something off

Practice

Each dictionary entry provides more than one part of speech and several meanings for its word. Write a sentence using the part of speech requested.

lie¹ (lī), *n., v.,* **lied, ly·ing.** —*n.* **1.** a false statement made with deliberate intent to deceive; a falsehood. **2.** something intended or serving to convey a false impression; imposture. **3.** the charge or accusation of lying; a flat contradiction. **4. give the lie to, a.** to charge with lying; contradict. **b.** to prove or imply the falsity of; belie. —*v.i.* **5.** to speak falsely or utter untruth knowingly, as with intent to deceive. **6.** to express what is false, or convey a false impression. —*v.t.* **7.** to bring, take, put, etc., by lying (often used reflexively). **8. lie in one's throat** or **teeth,** to lie grossly or maliciously. [(n.) ME; OE *lyge;* c. G *Lüge,* Icel *lygi;* akin to Goth *liugn;* (v.) ME *lie(n),* OE *lēogan;* c. G *lügen,* Icel *ljūga,* Goth *liugan*] —**Syn. 1.** prevarication, falsification. See **falsehood. 5.** prevaricate, fib. —**Ant. 1.** truth.

lie² (lī), *v.,* **lay, lain, ly·ing,** *n.* —*v.i.* **1.** to be in or get into a recumbent or prostrate position; recline (often fol. by *down*). **2.** to be buried in a particular spot. **3.** (of objects) to rest on a surface, esp. in a horizontal position. **4.** to be or remain in a position or state of inactivity, subjection, restraint, concealment, etc. **5.** to be found or located in a particular area, place, or situation: *The fault lies here.* **6.** to be placed or situated. **7.** to be stretched out or extended. **8.** to consist or be grounded (usually fol. by *in*): *The remedy lies in education.* **9.** to be in or have a specified direction. **10.** *Law.* to be sustainable or admissible, as an action or appeal. **11.** *Archaic.* to lodge; stay the night; sojourn. **12. lie by, a.** to pause for rest; stop activities, work, etc., temporarily. **b.** to lie unused. **13. lie down on the job,** *Informal.* to do less than one could or should do; shirk one's obligations. **14. lie in,** to be confined in childbed. **15. lie low.** See **low¹** (def. 42). **16. lie over,** to be postponed for action at some future time. **17. lie to,** *Naut.* (of a ship) to lie comparatively stationary, usually with the head as near the wind as possible. **18. lie with, a.** to be the duty or function of: *The decision lies with him.* **b.** *Archaic.* to have sexual intercourse with. **19. take lying down,** *Informal.* to accept without objection or resistance: *I refuse to take that lying down!* —*n.* **20.** the manner of lying; the relative position or direction in which something lies. **21.** the haunt or covert of an animal. **22.** *Golf.* the position of the ball relative to how easy or how difficult it is to play. [ME *lie(n), liggen,* OE *licgan;* c. G *liegen,* D *liggen,* Icel *liggja,* Goth *ligan*] —**Syn. 1.** LIE, LAY, often confused, are not synonyms. LIE, meaning to recline or rest, does not require an object. Its principal parts, too, are irregular, and are therefore distinctive. LAY with its forms *laid, have laid, laying,* etc., means to put or place. If "put" or "place" can be substituted in a contemplated sentence, the verb to use is LAY. Moreover, since one must always "put" or "place" *something,* the verb LAY is used only when there is a grammatical object to complete the sense. **20.** place, location, site. —**Ant. 1, 3.** stand.

1. verb sentence: _____

_____

e·ven¹ (ē′vən), *adj.* **1.** level; flat; without irregularities; smooth: *an even surface.* **2.** on the same level; in the same plane or line; parallel: *even with the ground.* **3.** free from variations or fluctuations; regular: *even motion.* **4.** uniform in action, character, or quality: *an even color.* **5.** equal in measure or quantity: *even quantities of two substances.* **6.** divisible by two, as a number (opposed to *odd*). **7.** denoted by such a number: *the even pages of a book.* **8.** exactly expressible in integers, or in tens, hundreds, etc., without fractional parts: *an even mile; an even hundred.* **9.** equally balanced or divided; equal: *Check to see if the scales are even.* **10.** leaving no balance of debt on either side; square. **11.** calm; placid; not easily excited or angered: *an even temper.* **12.** equitable, impartial, or fair: *an even bargain.* —*adv.* **13.** evenly: *The road ran even over the fields.* **14.** still; yet (used to emphasize a comparative): *even more suitable.* **15.** (used to suggest that something mentioned as a possibility constitutes an extreme case or an unlikely instance): *Even the slightest noise disturbs him. Even if he attends, he may not participate.* **16.** just (used to emphasize occurrence, coincidence, or simultaneousness of occurrences): *Even as he lay dying, they argued over his estate.* **17.** fully or quite: *even to death.* **18.** indeed (used as an intensive for stressing the identity or truth of something): *He is willing, even eager, to do it.* **19.** *Archaic.* exactly or precisely: *It was even so.* **20. break even,** to have one's profits equal one's losses; neither gain nor lose. **21. get even,** to be revenged; retaliate. —*v.t.* **22.** to make even; level; smooth. **23.** to place in an even state as to claim or obligation; balance (often fol. by *up*): *to even up accounts.* —*v.i.* **24.** to become even: *The odds evened before the race.* [ME; OE *efen;* c. Goth *ibns,* OHG *eban,* ON *jafn* even, equal] —**e′ven·ly,** *adv.* —**e′ven·ness,** *n.* —**Syn. 1.** See **level. 11.** tranquil, peaceful.

2. adverb sentence: _____

_____

dis·pute (di spyo͞ot′), *v.,* **-put·ed, -put·ing,** *n.* —*v.i.* **1.** to engage in argument or debate. **2.** to argue vehemently; wrangle or quarrel. —*v.t.* **3.** to argue or debate about; discuss. **4.** to argue against; call in question: *to dispute a proposal.* **5.** to quarrel or fight about; contest. **6.** to strive against; oppose: *to dispute an advance of troops.* —*n.* **7.** a debate or controversy: *An increase in taxes was the subject of the dispute.* **8.** a quarrel. [ME < LL *disput(āre)* (to) dispute (L: to discuss) = *dis-* DIS-¹ + *putāre* to reckon, consider; see PUTATIVE] —**dis·put′er,** *n.* —**Syn. 8.** disputation, altercation, squabble. See **argument.**

3. noun sentence: _____

_____

pet¹ (pet), *n., adj., v.,* **pet·ted, pet·ting.** —*n.* **1.** any domesticated or tamed animal that is kept as a favorite and cared for affectionately. **2.** a person or thing especially cherished or indulged; favorite: *teacher's pet.* —*adj.* **3.** kept or treated as a pet: *a pet lamb.* **4.** cherished; favorite: *a pet theory.* **5.** showing affection: *a pet name.* —*v.t.* **6.** to treat as a pet; indulge. **7.** to fondle, caress, or stroke. —*v.i.* **8.** *Informal.* to make love by fondling and caressing. [? back formation from *pet lamb* cade lamb, ? syncopated var. of *petty lamb* little lamb; see PETTY] —**Syn. 6.** baby, humor, pamper.
pet² (pet), *n.* **1.** a fit of peevishness. —*v.i.* **2.** to be peevish; sulk. [appar. back formation from PETTISH] —**pet′ted·ly,** *adv.*

4. adjective sentence: _____

_____

Using the Dictionary 289

wash (wosh, wôsh), *v.t.* **1.** to free of dirt or other matter by application of or immersion in a liquid, esp. water or a solution of soap and water: *to wash a dress.* **2.** to remove (dirt or other matter) by this method: *She washed the mud off her dress.* **3.** to cleanse from defilement or guilt; purify. **4.** to move by means of water or other liquid: *The storm washed our boat ashore.* **5.** to wet or moisten, as with water. **6.** to wear or erode by the flow of a liquid, esp. water: *The storm washed gulleys in the mountain.* **7.** to cover with a thin layer, as of paint or metal.
—*v.i.* **8.** to wash oneself. **9.** to wash clothes. **10.** to cleanse anything with or in water or other liquid. **11.** to undergo washing without injury, esp. shrinking or fading. **12.** *Chiefly Brit. Informal.* to stand being put to the proof: *That story won't wash.* **13.** to be carried or driven by water: *The boat had washed ashore in the night.* **14.** to move along in or as in waves, or with a rushing movement, as water. **15.** to be removed by the action of water (often fol. by *away*): *This topsoil tends to wash away.* **16. wash down, a.** to clean completely by washing: *to wash down a car.* **b.** to facilitate the swallowing of (food) by drinking water or other liquid: *to wash chicken down with wine.* **17. wash out, a.** to be removed by washing: *This stain didn't wash out.* **b.** to demolish by the action of water: *The embankment was washed out by the storm.* **c.** *Slang.* to fail to qualify or continue; be eliminated: *He washed out after one semester.* **18. wash up, a.** to wash one's face and hands. **b.** to wash (dishes, pots, etc.): *I'll wash up the dishes.* **c.** to end, esp. ignominiously (usually in the passive): *He's all washed up in Wall Street.*
—*n.* **19.** the act or process of washing with water or other liquid: *to give the car a wash.* **20.** a quantity of things washed together. **21.** the flow, sweep, dash, or breaking of water. **22.** water moving along in waves or with a rushing movement. **23.** the rough or broken water or air left behind a moving ship, wing, propeller, etc. **24.** any of various liquids for grooming or cosmetic purposes: *a hair wash.* **25.** a lotion or other liquid having medicinal properties (often used in combination): *to apply wash to a skinned knee; eyewash.* **26.** a thin coating, as of paint or metal. **27.** a tract of land washed by the action of the sea or a river. **28.** a marsh, fen, or bog. **29.** a small stream or shallow pool. **30.** a shallow arm of the sea or a shallow part of a river. **31.** a depression or channel formed by flowing water. **32.** *Geol.* alluvial matter transferred and deposited by flowing water. **33.** Also called **dry wash.** *Western U.S.* the dry bed of an intermittent stream. **34.** waste liquid matter, refuse food, etc., from the kitchen, as for hogs; swill (often used in combination): *hogwash.* **35. come out in the wash,** to become known eventually.
—*adj.* **36.** capable of being washed without shrinking, fading, etc.; washable: *a wash dress.* [ME; OE *wasc(an)* (c. D *wasschen*, G *waschen*, Icel *vaska*) < Gmc **watskan* = *wat-* (see WATER) + *-sk-* v. suffix + *-an* inf. suffix]
—**Syn. 1, 2, 10.** clean, rinse, launder, scrub, mop. **5.** bedew, bathe. **19.** ablution, cleansing, bathing. **28.** swamp, morass.

5. verb sentence: _____

_____

scoop (skoop), *n.* **1.** a ladle or ladlelike utensil, esp. a small, deep-sided shovel with a short, horizontal handle, for taking up flour, sugar, etc. **2.** a utensil composed of a palm-sized, hollow hemisphere attached to a horizontal handle, for dishing out ice cream or other soft foods. **3.** the bucket of a dredge, steam shovel, etc. **4.** the quantity of material raised or held in such a utensil or bucket: *two scoops of chocolate ice cream.* **5.** a hollow or hollowed-out place. **6.** the act of ladling, dipping, dredging, etc. **7.** a news item revealed in one paper, magazine, newscast, etc., before any of its competitors can reveal it; beat. **8.** the act of gathering to oneself or lifting with the arms or hands. —*v.t.* **9.** to take up or out with or as with a scoop. **10.** to empty with a scoop. **11.** to form a hollow or hollows in. **12.** to form with or as if with a scoop. **13.** to reveal a news item before (one's competitors). **14.** to gather or put by a sweeping motion of one's arms or hands. —*v.i.* **15.** to remove or gather something with or as with a scoop. [ME *scope* < MD *schoepe*]

6. noun sentence: _____

_____

claw (klô), *n.* **1.** a sharp, usually curved, nail on the foot of an animal. **2.** a similar curved process at the end of the leg of an insect. **3.** the pincerlike extremity of specific limbs of certain arthropods: *lobster claws*. **4.** any part or thing resembling a claw, as the cleft end of the head of a hammer. —*v.t.* **5.** to tear, scratch, seize, pull, etc., with or as with claws: *The kitten clawed my sweater to shreds.* **6.** to make by or as by scratching, digging, etc., with hands or claws: *to claw a hole in the earth.* —*v.i.* **7.** to scratch, tear, or dig with or as with claws: *The cat clawed and hissed in fear.* **8.** *Scot.* to scratch gently, as to relieve itching. [(n.) ME; OE *clawu*, c. OHG *chlō(a)*, akin to D *klauw*, G *Klaue*; (v.) ME *claw(en)*, OE *claw(i)an* < *clawu* (n.); akin to D *klauwen*, G *klauen*] —**claw′er**, *n.* —**claw′less**, *adj.*

7. verb sentence: _____

hum·ble (hum′bəl, um′-), *adj.*, **-bler, -blest,** *v.*, **-bled, -bling.** —*adj.* **1.** not proud or arrogant; modest. **2.** having a feeling of insignificance, inferiority, subservience, etc. **3.** low in rank, importance, size, etc. **4.** courteously respectful. —*v.t.* **5.** to lower in condition, importance, or dignity; abase. **6.** to destroy the independence, power, or will of. **7.** to make meek. [ME (h)*umble* < OF < L *humil(is)* lowly, insignificant, on the ground. See HUMUS, -ILE] —**hum′ble·ness,** *n.* —**hum′bler,** *n.* —**hum′bling·ly,** *adv.* —**hum′bly,** *adv.* —**Syn.** **1.** unpretentious. **2.** submissive; meek. **3.** plain, common, poor. **4.** polite. **5.** mortify, shame. **6.** subdue, break. HUMBLE, DEGRADE, HUMILIATE suggest lowering or causing to seem lower. To HUMBLE is to bring down the pride of another or to reduce him to a state of abasement: *to humble an arrogant enemy*. To DEGRADE is to demote in rank or standing, or to reduce to a low level in condition, manners, or morals: *to degrade an officer; to degrade one's dependents*. To HUMILIATE is to make others feel or appear inadequate or unworthy, esp. in some public setting: *to humiliate a sensitive person*. —**Ant.** **1, 2.** proud. **3.** noble, exalted. **4.** insolent.

8. adjective sentence: _____

must[1] (must), *auxiliary verb.* **1.** to be compelled to, as by instinct or natural law: *One must eat.* **2.** to be required to, as because of coercion, moral obligation, or the promptings of reason or good sense: *You must not smoke here. You must keep your spirits up.* **3.** to feel a strong urge to: *I must try some of that pudding.* **4.** to be obliged to, in order to bring about certain results: *To succeed, you must have tried.* **5.** to be reasonably expected to; be bound to: *It must have stopped raining.* **6.** to be inevitably certain to: *Man must die.* —*v.i.* **7.** to be obliged; feel compelled: *Do I have to go? I must, I suppose.* **8.** *Archaic.* (sometimes used with ellipsis of *go, get,* or some similar verb readily understood from the context): *We must away.* —*n.* **9.** anything necessary or vital. [ME *most(e)*, OE *mōste* past tense; c. G *musste*. See MOTE[2]] —**Syn.** **1.** MUST, OUGHT, SHOULD express necessity or duty. MUST expresses necessity, or compulsion: *All men must die. I must attend to those patients first. Soldiers must obey orders.* OUGHT (weaker than MUST) expresses obligation, duty, desirability: *You ought to tell your mother.* SHOULD expresses obligation, expectation, or probability: *You are not behaving as you should. Children should be taught to speak the truth. They should arrive at one o'clock.* It also expresses the conditional: *I should be glad to play if I could;* and future intention: *I said I should be home next week.*
must[2] (must), *n.* new wine; the unfermented juice as pressed from the grape or other fruit. [ME, OE < L *must(um)*, short for *vinum mustum* new wine]

9. noun sentence: _____

10. verb sentence: _____

Practice

Consider the context of the underlined word in each sentence. Select the best dictionary meaning for the word and write its letter on the line.

_____ 1. Katie made such a strong impression during the interview that she got the job immediately.
   a) a mold taken of teeth
   b) a strong effect on someone

_____ 2. The jar of conserves lasted from July through December.
   a) to keep from decaying
   b) sweet food made from mixed fruit

_____ 3. Sergeant Maslanek detached a patrol on a house-to-house search for the missing woman.
   a) to send on a special mission
   b) not involved

_____ 4. The law school seniors set up a mock trial and followed the procedures perfectly.
   a) imitation
   b) to make fun of

_____ 5. If you parrot what I say, how will you develop your own style of expression?
   a) a hook-billed bird
   b) to repeat without understanding

_____ 6. The economic import of high taxes cannot be underestimated.
   a) consequence
   b) to bring in merchandise from another country for the purpose of selling locally

_____ 7. Excessive repetition in one's work can sap the creative energies of even the most talented employee.
   a) the juice of a woody plant
   b) to weaken

_____ 8. A peep through the window will tell you whether the gardener has finished cutting the grass.
   a) a short, high cry or sound
   b) a quick look

_____ 9. The artist quickly hatched the panel surface with a delicate design.
   a) to mark with fine, parallel lines
   b) to bring forth

_____ 10. At a given signal, the drivers scrambled to their cars and roared from the starting line.
   a) to move quickly
   b) to cook eggs

CHAPTER 13

Using Context Clues

Preview

Read the following words and check those that you know.

_____ alleviate   _____ jarring
_____ altercation   _____ logged
_____ banister   _____ medium
_____ banned   _____ meticulously
_____ base   _____ ousted
_____ bland   _____ pilfered
_____ boycott   _____ placards
_____ breweries   _____ refuge
_____ brusquely   _____ running risks
_____ cane   _____ salient
_____ chair   _____ sensation
_____ concerted   _____ squandered
_____ concourse   _____ staple
_____ cranny   _____ stars
_____ crudely   _____ stoop
_____ cryptic   _____ stuff
_____ exhilarating   _____ succinctly
_____ fire

Using Sense-of-the-Sentence Context Clues

You have used a word's part of speech and the subject of its sentence to locate its definition in the dictionary. But how will you decide on the meaning of a word when you do not have a dictionary available? In the following example, answer the questions without using a dictionary.

Example

The soldier gave the order to fire at the enemy.

Questions

1. What part of speech is "fire"? _____
2. Does the sentence talk about business, war, or a blaze? _____
3. What words in the sentence helped you to answer Question 2?

   _____ and _____

4. Fire means _____
   a) to let someone go from a job.
   b) to shoot at.
   c) red-hot flames.

The sentence contains two clues to the meaning of "fire." First, "fire" is a verb. Second, the sentence talks about war; the words "soldier" and "enemy" help you to understand this. You can immediately eliminate the choice "red-hot flames," since it is a noun answer that refers to a blaze. Although the choice "to let someone go from a job" is a verb answer, it refers to business, and should be eliminated. The choice "to shoot at" is a verb answer that talks about fighting; it is the correct answer.

Example

The boy scouts lit a fire using only flint and wood.

Questions

1. What part of speech is "fire"? _____
2. Does the sentence talk about war, business, or a blaze? _____
3. What words helped you to answer Question 2? _____, _____, _____, and _____
4. Fire means _____
   a) to let someone go from a job.
   b) to shoot at.
   c) red-hot flames.

In this example "fire" is a noun in a sentence that talks about a blaze. You can immediately eliminate choices *a)* and *b)*, verb answers that talk about business and fighting. Choice *c)*, "red-hot flames," is a noun answer that refers to a blaze; it is the correct answer.

> The meaning of a word can change as it is used in different sentences. The phrase, sentence, or paragraph in which a word is located and its part of speech in that location are called the **context of the word**. You can determine the meaning of a new word by looking at its context, that is, what part of speech it is and what the sentence or paragraph talks about.

Practice

Consider the context of each underlined word. First, write its part of speech on the line. Then, choose the best meaning and write the letter of that meaning on the line.

_b_ 1. The fire blazed for hours and nearly destroyed the old house.

In this sentence, fire is a(an) _noun_. It means

a) to shoot at.

b) red-hot flames.

c) a match.

d) to let someone go from a job.

___ 2. The workers gathered cane in the fields.

In this sentence, cane is a(an) _____. It means

a) a stick used as support in walking.

b) a sugar stalk.

c) to hit with a piece of wood.

d) to weave wood pieces, as in a chair.

___ 3. The supervisor asked everyone to make a concerted effort to maintain company production goals.

In this sentence, concerted is a(an) _____. It means

a) to act as one.

b) a musical performance.

c) bodies.

d) unified.

___ 4. The chair recognized each speaker at the meeting.

In this sentence, chair is a(an) _____. It means

a) a piece of furniture.

b) sitting.

c) a leader.

d) to direct a session.

_____ 5. Rice is considered a staple in many countries.

   In this sentence, staple is a(an) _____. It means

   a) a basic food substance.

   b) to fasten papers.

   c) a metal clip used to attach items.

   d) to supply with food.

Practice

Read each sentence carefully and write the part of speech for the underlined word. Then write the meaning of the word.

1. Sam was fired because he could not fulfill his work requirements.

   In this sentence, fired is a(an) _____.
   (part of speech)

   Fired means _____.

2. The elderly patient used a cane to help her walk.

   In this sentence, cane is a(an) _____.

   Cane means _____.

3. Mayor Arnold canceled the concert when the band failed to arrive.

   In this sentence, concert is a(an) _____.

   Concert means _____.

4. New material gave the chair a refreshing look.

   In this sentence, chair is a(an) _____.

   Chair means _____.

5. "Randy, can you staple these papers so they won't fall apart?" asked Anita.

   In this sentence, staple is a(an) _____.

   Staple means _____.

Practice

Use the context of the underlined word to help you determine its meaning. Do not use a dictionary.

1. Captain Edwards <u>logged</u> the ship's mileage in his book and added a description of the weather conditions.

    In this sentence, logged is a(an) _____.
    (part of speech)

    Logged means _____.

2. The newly cut <u>log</u> burned brightly in the fireplace.

    In this sentence, log is a(an) _____.

    Log means _____.

3. I like a <u>medium</u>-broiled steak that is pink on the inside.

    In this sentence, medium is a(an) _____.

    Medium means _____.

4. The <u>medium</u> stared into her crystal ball and predicted the future.

    In this sentence, medium is a(an) _____.

    Medium means _____.

5. After the doctor tapped my knee, I felt a funny <u>sensation</u>.

    In this sentence, sensation is a(an) _____.

    Sensation means _____.

6. The newest dancer in the company triumphed in her first appearance and was called an instant <u>sensation</u>.

    In this sentence, sensation is a(an) _____.

    Sensation means _____.

7. How can you be so <u>base</u> as to rob a blind person?

    In this sentence, base is a(an) _____.

    Base means _____.

8. The company of soldiers left their <u>base</u> to patrol the countryside.

    In this sentence, base is a(an) _____.

    Base means _____.

9. In the clear mountain sky, you can see hundreds of <u>stars</u> each night.

   In this sentence, stars is a(an) _____.

   Stars means _____.

10. At the opening of the new movie, you will see hundreds of <u>stars</u>.

    In this sentence, stars is a(an) _____.

    Stars means _____.

Practice

Consider the context of each underlined word and use it in two ways: to eliminate incorrect choices and to determine the correct answer. Do not use a dictionary.

_____ 1. Alex <u>pilfered</u> money and goods from his company for several years before the losses were discovered.

   In this sentence, pilfered is a(an) _____. It means

   a) thieves.
   b) taking from.
   c) stole.
   d) is arrested.

_____ 2. The main <u>concourse</u> of the shopping center contained walks, fountains, benches, and trees.

   In this sentence, concourse is a(an) _____. It means

   a) open area.
   b) was meeting.
   c) plazas.
   d) filled.

_____ 3. The <u>cryptic</u> message made the agents wonder whether or not their code had been revealed.

   In this sentence, cryptic is a(an) _____. It means

   a) hiding.
   b) mysteries.
   c) vaguely.
   d) mysterious.

_____ 4. Dr. Holmes tried to <u>alleviate</u> Marcia's fear by explaining the operation to her.

   In this sentence, alleviate is a(an) _____. It means

   a) easing.
   b) lessen.
   c) brightens.
   d) increasing.

_____ 5. I'm sure you can succinctly explain your project before you make the full presentation next week.

In this sentence, succinctly is a(an) _____. It means

a) thorough.
b) little.
c) briefly.
d) shortening.

Practice

Use the context of the underlined word to help you eliminate incorrect choices and to select the correct answer.

_____ 1. Thousands of products have been banned because government officials judged them to be dangerous.

In this sentence, banned is a(an) _____. It means

a) offered.
b) supported.
c) flags.
d) prohibited.

_____ 2. Do we need laws that prevent us from running risks with our lives?

In this sentence, running risks is a(an) _____. It means

a) unwise.
b) taking chances.
c) moving quickly.
d) dangerous.

_____ 3. The government once passed a law closing all liquor stores, bars, and breweries in this country.

In this sentence, breweries is a(an) _____. It means

a) places where liquor is made.
b) processing beer and liquor.
c) a factory.
d) alcohol.

_____ 4. The boys quickly hid the stuff under the seats of the car.

In this sentence, stuff is a(an) _____. It means

a) items.
b) selling.
c) completely filled.
d) packing firmly.

_____ 5. If you eat food that is <u>crudely</u> prepared, you may become violently ill.

In this sentence, crudely is a(an) _____. It means

a) lacking in manners.   c) poorly.

b) filtering.   d) finely.

Practice

The underlined words come from sentences in a selection entitled "Spending a Few Days With the Kid that You Once Were." Determine the context for each new word and write the correct meaning on the line.

1. Think about what it would be like if you were turned loose in the house where you grew up. It was <u>jarring</u> . . . . weird.
   Jarring means *disturbing*_____.
   a) a small container.   c) laughing.
   b) disturbing.   d) many rooms.

2. It would be confusing and <u>exhilarating</u> and happy and sad, all at the same time.
   Exhilarating means _____.
   a) stimulating.   c) to be safe.
   b) to leave.   d) correcting.

3. . . . sitting on the front <u>stoop</u> waiting for the paper boy to arrive.
   Stoop means _____.
   a) to bend over.   c) sitting down.
   b) a basement.   d) set of steps.

4. In the upstairs hallway was a little <u>cranny</u> built into the wall to hold a telephone.
   Cranny means _____.
   a) a hole.   c) indented.
   b) to sit in a booth.   d) a receiver.

5. And the banister that runs up the stairway and then curves around next to the bedrooms.

   Banister means _____.

   a) steps.
   b) inclining.
   c) hand rail.
   d) went up.

Practice

Consider the context of each underlined word and define it.

1. I noticed her blue eyes immediately. They were her most salient feature.

   Salient means _____.

2. Since you have stomach problems, you must eat only bland food instead of your usual diet.

   Bland means _____.

3. Placards were taped to every store window so that customers could read about the coming sale.

   Placards means _____.

4. In one year, Boris squandered his entire inheritance on foolish things like boats, wild parties, and expensive trips.

   Squandered means _____.

5. The boycott of union products grew from a demand for better working conditions and higher salaries.

   Boycott means _____.

6. For an hour, the cat meticulously cleaned the kitten's paws, face, and body.

   Meticulously means _____.

7.–8. Ousted by the revolutionary group, the fleeing dictator asked for refuge in a neighboring country.

   Ousted means _____.

   Refuge means _____.

9.–10. Following the accident, each driver angrily accused the other of being at fault and an altercation began. It ended when one of the drivers brusquely slammed his door and drove away.

Altercation means _____.

Brusquely means _____.

Preview

Read the following list of words and check those you know.

_____ adept
_____ ameliorate
_____ apartheid
_____ arbiter
_____ boutique
_____ cerebrovascular accident
_____ chaos
_____ cupola
_____ debacles
_____ deluded
_____ disparity
_____ entomology
_____ excruciating
_____ gist
_____ humdrum
_____ increments
_____ indelible
_____ insurrection

_____ inveterate
_____ menace
_____ mired
_____ nebulous
_____ parameters
_____ recluse
_____ restitution
_____ Rubella
_____ skyrocketing
_____ slammer
_____ sphygmomanometer
_____ sporadic
_____ squalid
_____ symposium
_____ terminations
_____ vita
_____ voided

Using Synonym Context Clues

You have practiced locating the correct dictionary meaning of a word by using its part of speech and determining the subject of a sentence. You have also applied these skills to understanding new words without using the dictionary. Consider the following sentences and review how you can use a word's general context to understand its meaning.

Example

1. The private marched with the soldiers in his troop.
2. This is a private conversation which only you can hear.

Questions

1. In Sentence 1, what part of speech is "private"? _____
2. In Sentence 2, what part of speech is "private"? _____
3. What does Sentence 1 talk about? _____
4. What does Sentence 2 talk about? _____
5. What does "private" mean in Sentence 1? _____
6. What does "private" mean in Sentence 2? _____

In Sentence One, "private" is a singular noun that relates to the military. In Sentence Two, "private" is an adjective that relates to one person hearing a conversation. "Private" has a different meaning in each example: "a soldier" and "personal or not intended for anyone to hear." The meaning of "private" changes when its part of speech and context change.

> **Context** is a group of words—the phrase, sentence, or paragraph—in which a word is located. As the context of a word changes, its meaning can change.

There are often specific words in a sentence or paragraph that can help you determine the meaning of an unfamiliar word.

Example

1. The couple arrived at the <u>party</u> in time to enjoy the social gathering.
2. The telephone operator connected one <u>party</u>, or speaker, with the person on the other phone.

Questions

1. In Sentence 1, what part of speech is "party"? _____
2. In Sentence 1, is there another noun or noun phrase that has the same meaning as "party"? _____
3. In Sentence 2, what part of speech is "party"? _____
4. In Sentence 2, what singular noun has the same meaning as "party"? _____

"Party" is a singular noun in both sentences. In Sentence 1, the phrase that has the same meaning is "social gathering." In Sentence 2, the word that has the same meaning is "speaker." Each sentence contains a word or phrase that has the same meaning and part of speech as "party." These words are synonyms for "party."

> Sentences with difficult words often contain synonyms for those words. **Synonyms** are words or phrases that are similar in meaning to other words. You can recognize some synonyms because they are set apart by commas, dashes, or parentheses. Usually, a synonym context clue appears as the same part of speech as the new word. A synonym is one type of context clue that helps you to determine the meanings of unfamiliar words.

In the exercises that follow, the unfamiliar word and its synonym have the same function or part of speech in the sentence. As you become more familiar with the skill of identifying synonym clues, you will practice using synonym clues that are less obvious because they have different parts of speech than the new word.

Practice

Determine the meaning of the underlined word by identifying its part of speech and by locating its synonym.

1. The job applicant sat in the personnel office and filled out a <u>vita</u>. When she finished the résumé, she gave it to the secretary.

   Vita is a(an) _noun_.   Its synonym is _résumé_.
       (part of speech)

2. John led the <u>symposium</u> on job opportunities, and was thrilled to learn that four hundred people had attended the panel discussion.

   Symposium is a(an) _____.   Its synonym is _____.

3. The teenager was ordered to make full <u>restitution</u> to the owner of the damaged car. He swiftly made full payment for damages to the auto he had hit.

   Restitution is a(an) _____.   Its synonym is _____.

Using Context Clues 307

4. "Don't get mired down in details," cautioned Professor Ames. "Don't get stuck writing every little fact."

   Mired is a(an) _____. Its synonym is _____.

5. Sylvia did a fine job managing the boutique and was able to attract many new customers to the specialty store.

   Boutique is a(an) _____. Its synonym is _____.

6. The cost of a college education is skyrocketing. Since tuition costs are rapidly rising, many students must take jobs to help meet expenses.

   Skyrocketing is a(an) _____. Its synonym is _____.

7. Some political campaigns turn into debacles. Mismanagement, illegal funding, and serious debts are characteristic of these disasters.

   Debacles is a(an) _____. Its synonym is _____.

8. Adept advertisements attract new customers. These clever ads promise whatever the customers desire and more.

   Adept is a(an) _____. Its synonym is _____.

9. Inmates recently released from the slammer do not want to return to prison again.

   Slammer is a(an) _____. Its synonym is _____.

10. Police attempted to force out the recluse when he refused to leave the condemned building. The lone shut-in had lived in the building for years and claimed he had nowhere else to go.

    Recluse is a(an) _____. Its synonym is _____.

Vocabulary Skills

Practice

Each of the following sentences contains a synonym clue to help you understand the meaning of the underlined word. Be aware of the new word's part of speech. Circle its synonym in the sentence and write the letter of its meaning on the line.

1. The instructor failed the student because of his <u>sporadic</u> attendance record. (Occasional) attendance in class was unacceptable to the teacher.
   Sporadic means __b__
   a) acceptable. b) infrequent. c) failure.

2. The detectives were <u>deluded</u> by all the false evidence. They were completely deceived and they arrested the wrong person.
   Deluded means ____
   a) wrong. b) arrested. c) misled.

3. Discomfort suffered from a broken leg can be so <u>excruciating</u> that drugs are often prescribed to relieve the agony.
   Excruciating means ____
   a) painful. b) suffering. c) hurt.

4. <u>Inveterate</u> gamblers are habitual customers at the race track betting windows.
   Inveterate means ____
   a) betting. b) regular. c) gambler.

5. Our plane tickets were <u>voided</u> when the airline ticket agent declared that the airport was closed. Therefore, all reservations were canceled.
   Voided means ____
   a) reserved. b) closed. c) eliminated.

6. Although the <u>insurrection</u> began in the rural areas, the rebellion quickly spread throughout the cities.
   Insurrection means ____
   a) spreading. b) revolt. c) rebels.

7. Hired troublemakers created chaos in the convention hall. Everything in the auditorium was in total confusion by the time they left.

   Chaos means ———

   a) complete disorder.   b) troublemakers.   c) noise.

8. After ten years in one job, Mike decided that his paperwork was humdrum and that his telephone sales job was dull.

   Humdrum means ———

   a) workable.   b) tired.   c) boring.

9. Moving closer to school can both ameliorate your commuting problem and improve your social life.

   Ameliorate means ———

   a) make better.   b) move.   c) combine.

10. Laundry owners use indelible marking pencils on their customers' clothing. They use permanent markers that will not wash off the garments.

    Indelible means ———

    a) removable   b) lasting.   c) stained.

Practice

Determine the meaning of the underlined word through its part of speech and synonym clue.

1. The arbiter in the second murder trial was the same judge as in the first trial.

   Arbiter means ———————————————.

2. The disparity between the estimate and the actual bill was over $200. This difference amazed the homeowner.

   Disparity means ———————————————.

3. Research in the field of entomology has resulted in new ideas in the study of insects.

   Entomology means ———————————————.

4. Monthly <u>increments</u> in your salary will begin next year. The increases will continue for three years.

   Increments means _____.

5. If you understand the <u>gist</u> of the story, you should be able to tell me the main idea.

   Gist means _____.

6. Your ideas are so <u>nebulous</u> that your point is unclear to me.

   Nebulous means _____.

7. Drunk drivers are a <u>menace</u> because they are a threat to the safety of other drivers.

   Menace means _____.

8. The building's roof is in the shape of a <u>cupola</u>, or dome, and is similar to the one on the top of the city hall.

   Cupola means _____.

9. Apartment buildings in slum areas provide only <u>squalid</u> living conditions. These rundown homes are often barely livable.

   Squalid means _____.

10. The <u>Rubella</u> vaccine protects us from German measles. One injection helps us build an immunity to the disease.

    Rubella means _____.

Practice

The following underlined words have been taken from textbooks. Circle the synonym clue for the meaning of the underlined word and try to restate that meaning in your own words.

1. <u>Terminations</u>, or discharges, are permanent separations resulting from inability to perform the work, repeated violations of work rules, excessive absenteeism, elimination of jobs, or the closing of work facilities (BOONE AND KURTZ, 192).

   Terminations means _____
   _____.

2. A stroke, also called a <u>cerebrovascular accident</u>, occurs when the blood supply to the brain is cut off (INSEL AND ROTH, 424).

   Cerebrovascular accident means _____.

3. Blood pressure is checked by means of a stethoscope and an instrument called a <u>sphygomomanometer</u>, or more commonly, a blood pressure cuff (INSEL AND ROTH, 394).

   Sphygmomanometer means _____.

4. <u>Apartheid</u>—separation of the races—in South Africa is based on a caste system, as is the denial of civil rights to Native Indians in many parts of North and South America (HESS, 197).

   Apartheid means _____.

5. Although role performance is never static, as individuals are constantly interpreting and defining one another's behavior, there are certain boundaries, or <u>parameters</u>, within which we enact our conventional roles without a great deal of thought (HESS, 83).

   Parameters means _____.

Vocabulary Skills

Preview

Read the following list and check those words that you know.

_____ acme	_____ ignominy
_____ ancestry	_____ infractions
_____ antipathy	_____ interval
_____ breeding	_____ modes
_____ cacophony	_____ needle
_____ caulk	_____ ostensible
_____ circumvented	_____ redundant
_____ cooptation	_____ remnants
_____ destitute	_____ rooted
_____ devastation	_____ self-actualized
_____ disposition	_____ self-estrangement
_____ dissenters	_____ shambles
_____ distraught	_____ squelched
_____ erratic	_____ tangible property
_____ flustered	_____ tirade
_____ frills	_____ unethical
_____ hierarchy	_____ waning

Using Example Context Clues

Using example context clues is another method of understanding new words. Example context clues are words or phrases that illustrate the meaning of a new word. They should not be mistaken for synonyms or definitions. Read the following carefully to see how example clues provide illustrations of the meaning of the new word.

Example

The <u>remuneration</u> for many jobs can vary greatly. For example, one can earn the <u>minimum</u> wage at the Pizza Pub, $5.50 an hour at a department store, or $4.50 an hour at the Bargain Toy Store.

Questions

1. What signal indicates that there is a listing of examples that describes "remuneration"? _____

2. What are the three illustrations of "remuneration"?

   _____

   _____

   _____

3. What is the meaning of "remuneration"? _____

> An **example context clue** is a word or a phrase that illustrates a difficult word rather than defines the word. You can use the examples to derive the correct meaning of an unfamiliar word.

Practice

Each sentence contains examples of the underlined word. Circle the example clues and write the meaning of the word on the line.

1. I liked to needle him by (telling everyone about the time he was thrown out of class) and about the (awful name we gave him.)
   Needle means *tease or irritate*.

2. After the tornado, there was devastation everywhere. Houses were destroyed, roads were cracked, and cars were wrecked.
   Devastation means _____.

3. I can trace my ancestry through my parents, grandparents, and even to my great-grandparents.
   Ancestry means _____.

4. I'm puzzled by your classwork. You do well on the home assignments, yet you have failed most of the quizzes. At times, your attendance is perfect, but occasionally you miss an entire week. Your erratic behavior indicates a need for counseling.
   Erratic means _____.

5. At the acme of her athletic career, she established new world records, was chosen for the Olympic team, and was elected president of the runners' association.

   Acme means _____.

6. During the electrical blackout, the neighborhood was in a shambles. People stole from unprotected stores, traffic was backed up for miles, and many were trapped in elevators for hours.

   Shambles means _____.

7. The strong wind is decreasing in force, the heavy snow is moving away from the city, and the gray skies are turning blue again. I can't believe that the storm is finally waning.

   Waning means _____.

8. Excessive lateness and absence are infractions of the attendance rules.

   Infractions means _____.

9. The child's fine breeding was apparent in his perfect speech, his excellent manners, and his appreciation of the arts.

   Breeding means _____.

10. In your term paper you've stated the same idea three times and have used several adjectives repeatedly. You should be aware that your writing is often redundant.

    Redundant means _____.

Practice

In each of the following, circle the example context clue(s) and define the underlined word.

1. The employees' angry words and physical threats were a part of their tirade against the administration.

   Tirade means _____.

2. His being well-dressed, speaking well, and displaying fine manners are some of the ostensible reasons for saying he is a gentleman.

   Ostensible means _____.

Using Context Clues

3. The cacophony wasn't loud enough to waken the sleeping student: the buzzing alarm clock and the ringing phone failed to disturb him.
   Cacophony means _____.

4. In our government, the hierarchy of power starts with the President, proceeds to the Vice President, and moves down to the Speaker of the House.
   Hierarchy means _____.

5. In the excitement of winning the state lottery, the winner was so flustered that he forgot his wife's name, gave an incorrect address, and misread his Social Security number.
   Flustered means _____.

6. The distraught woman couldn't sit patiently waiting for her husband to arrive at the hospital. She nervously paced the floor, bit her fingernails, and anxiously smoked one cigarette after another.
   Distraught means _____.

7. Ignominy was brought upon the family when their son was arrested and expelled from school. The newspaper printed the embarrassing story, and soon their friends stopped talking to them.
   Ignominy means _____.

8. The fans rooted for the home team by waving banners and cheering loudly.
   Rooted means _____.

9. By suppressing opposing viewpoints in the newspaper, canceling radio and television commentaries, and banning all public speeches, the dictator squelched all criticism of his illegal activities.
   Squelched means _____.

10. The tired housekeeper left some of the remnants of the evening meal on the table. The next morning she wrapped the few pieces of pie, washed the serving trays and glasses, and cleaned the crumbs from the table.
    Remnants means _____.

Practice

Circle the example clue(s) and define each underlined word.

1. We circumvented the necessity of buying new furniture by borrowing chairs from friends and by building tables and beds from lumber we already owned.
   Circumvented means _____.

2. She screamed and ran out of the house when she saw the snakes. Her antipathy for the reptiles was obvious.
   Antipathy means _____.

3. We applied cement to the spaces between the window and the wall, placed a strip of carpet under the front door, and similarly caulked any other areas where heat was escaping from the house.
   Caulked means _____.

4. Her delightful disposition was evident in her cheerful mood and her easygoing manner. She always smiled and said pleasant things to everyone.
   Disposition means _____.

5. After the vote to approve the school budget, a few dissenters voiced their objections and petitioned the school board for a revote.
   Dissenters means _____.

6. Whoever added the lace, ribbons, and imitation jewels to her dress knows little about simple clothing that needs no such frills.
   Frills means _____.

7. During the two-hour interval between my first and second class, I either spend time in the library, eat my lunch in the cafeteria, or complete my homework.
   Interval means _____.

8. Traveling by stagecoach, by horse, or by foot were the usual modes of transportation for the early pioneers.
   Modes means _____.

9. It is <u>unethical</u> for politicians to take bribes, students to cheat on exams, or teachers to date their students.

   Unethical means _____.

10. With no source of income and no place to sleep, the <u>destitute</u> man begged for food on the street and slept in cold doorways.

    Destitute means _____.

Practice

The following examples appear in textbooks. Circle the example clue(s) for each word, and, then, briefly define the underlined word.

1. At the extreme, members of modern society can become alienated even from themselves; that is, to feel detached from one's own activity, like a robot, just going through the gestures of living—an orientation referred to as <u>self-estrangement</u> (HESS, 327).

   Self-estrangement means _____.

2. <u>Cooptation</u> can be seen when a feminist elected to Parliament becomes part of the power élite against which he or she had previously fought (HESS, 556).

   Cooptation means _____.

3. Property can be divided into several categories, one of which is <u>tangible property</u>. Every business is concerned with this kind of property, which includes equipment, supplies, and delivery vehicles (BOONE AND KURTZ, 587).

   Tangible property means _____.

4. <u>Self-actualized</u> people are not frightened by the unknown. They do not feel it necessary to reduce uncertainty or avoid it. They are in fact attracted to the unknown. They also have a lack of fear of their own insides, of their own impulses, thoughts (INSEL AND ROTH, 66).

   Self-actualized means _____.

Vocabulary Skills

Preview

Read the following list of words and check those that you know.

_____ anxiety	_____ indigenous
_____ catalyst	_____ inordinate
_____ circuitous	_____ jagged
_____ commodious	_____ judiciously
_____ conservative	_____ lunatic
_____ contaminated	_____ mass-produced
_____ controversy	_____ nonchalant
_____ conventional	_____ nondescript
_____ demolish	_____ penury
_____ diverse	_____ pertinent
_____ docile	_____ pondered
_____ evasive	_____ prior to
_____ frank	_____ prominent
_____ griped	_____ reckless
_____ henpecked	_____ reflective
_____ imbued	_____ rote
_____ impeccable	_____ thwart
_____ improvising	_____ vigorous
_____ inadvertently	_____ vilify
_____ incline	_____ vociferous
_____ indefatigable	_____ weary
_____ indifferent	

Using Antonym Context Clues

Still another type of context clue is the antonym clue. You learned that synonym clues provide nearly the same meaning as the new words, and that example clues are illustrations of the new words. Consider the following example to see how antonym context clues provide the opposite meanings of new words.

Using Context Clues

Example

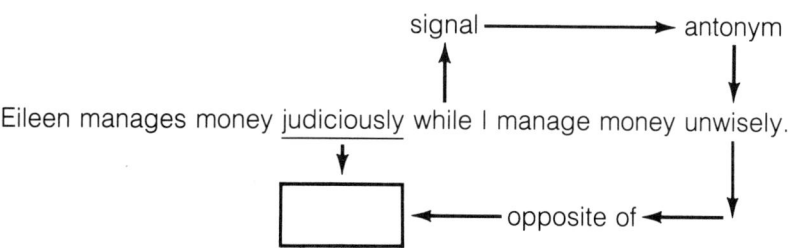

Eileen manages money judiciously while I manage money unwisely.

Question

What does "judiciously" mean? Write the meaning in the box.

The word "while" signals the antonym "unwisely." You can reason that "unwisely" is the antonym or opposite of "judiciously." Thus, "judiciously" means "wisely."

> **Antonyms** are words or phrases that have opposite meanings to other words or phrases. Recognizing that certain words often signal an antonym clue can help you to understand new words. Authors frequently use words and phrases, such as, "on the other hand," "as opposed to," "but," and "while" to signal antonym clues.

Practice

Each of the following sentences contains an antonym clue for the underlined word. Locate the word or phrase that signals the antonym clue and circle it. Then, circle the antonym clue. Finally, select the best meaning for the underlined word.

1. Professor English's attitude showed his (care and concern.) The students' attitudes, (on the other hand,) were very nonchalant.
   Nonchalant means __c__
   a) attitude.   b) concerned.   c) casual.

2. She has a love of rote work, but no fondness for creative jobs.
   Rote means _____
   a) creative.   b) mechanical.   c) fondness.

3. Some students were inadvertently late for class while a few were purposely late.

   Inadvertently means _____
   a) purposely.   b) accidently.   c) always.

4. In many nations there are two financial extremes, from penury to great wealth.

   Penury means _____
   a) wealth.   b) poverty.   c) middle income.

5. It is better to be reflective about problems than to be thoughtless.

   Reflective means _____
   a) thoughtful.   b) uncaring.   c) problems.

6. Today's teenagers seem to be more liberal in their ideas than their conservative grandparents.

   Conservative means _____
   a) free-thinking.   b) traditional.   c) old.

7. Oranges are indigenous to Southern California but foreign to New York farms.

   Indigenous means _____
   a) native.   b) unknown.   c) alien.

8. Our commodious house has more advantages than our overcrowded apartment.

   Commodious means _____
   a) small.   b) different.   c) spacious.

9. Rather than carefully planning, the speaker relied on improvising the speech as he addressed the audience.

   Improvising means _____
   a) joking.   b) making up.   c) planning.

10. Why did you spend such an inordinate amount of time on the first question? Ten minutes would have been more reasonable.

    Inordinate means _____
    a) tiny.   b) difficult.   c) excessive.

Practice

Each of the following sentences contains an antonym clue for the underlined word. First, circle the signal word or phrase and the antonym clue. Then, write the meaning of the underlined word on the line.

1. Michael was vigorous and able to excel in sports, while his brother, John, was unenergetic and performed poorly on the athletic field.
   Vigorous means _____.

2. Outwardly, Emily seemed indifferent to her school work, but in reality she cared a great deal about her assignments.
   Indifferent means _____.

3. One usually chooses a career major prior to, rather than after one's junior year.
   Prior to means _____.

4. Carefully smooth down the wood bench with a planing tool. A bench must have even edges, not jagged ones.
   Jagged means _____.

5. Today, Elton is a prominent rock star, but only a few years ago he was unknown.
   Prominent means _____.

6. Most people like Ellen because they know she is frank with them. On the other hand, they distrust her sister because she is always secretive.
   Frank means _____.

7. Even though he was usually a careful driver, he was arrested after yesterday's party for reckless driving.
   Reckless means _____.

8. Most members of the committee pondered the serious issue, while a few ignored it completely.
   Pondered means _____.

9. Rather than demolish the tenement building, the construction workers started to build a housing project using the tenement's frame and wood supply.
   Demolish means _____.

10. Yesterday, David became weary after walking only one mile, but today after walking two miles, he still feels energetic.

    Weary means _____.

Practice

Read each sentence and circle the word or phrase that signals an antonym clue and the antonym. Then, define the underlined word.

1. Instead of trying to thwart the project, why don't you help us to achieve a workable plan?

    Thwart means _____.

2. After weeks of training, the aggressive and dangerous dog became docile.

    Docile means _____.

3. Production output was at a standstill until the new foreman acted as a catalyst to increase productivity.

    Catalyst means _____.

4. Clean storage and cooking conditions rarely result in foods becoming contaminated.

    Contaminated means _____.

5. The pertinent facts were emphasized while the less important details were hardly mentioned.

    Pertinent means _____.

6. We took a circuitous route to school rather than a direct path.

    Circuitous means _____.

7. During her office hours her work was impeccable, but when she was at home, her work was sloppy and filled with errors.

    Impeccable means _____.

8. Why do you tire so easily when most competitors in tennis are indefatigable at this pace?

    Indefatigable means _____.

9. Please speak in a whisper while you are in the hospital room; any vociferous complaints will disturb the patient.
   Vociferous means _____.
10. Can't you praise her occasionally instead of vilifying everything she does?
    Vilifying means _____.

Practice

Read the following sentences and define the underlined words.

1. Her writing was imbued with creativity but totally lacked precision.
   Imbued means _____.
2. There is still controversy over the exact boundaries of the parcel of land, but there is total agreement over the size of the property.
   Controversy means _____.
3. Most businessmen wear conventional suits, but a few wear nonconformist jeans and sweaters.
   Conventional means _____.
4. The members of our discussion group come from diverse backgrounds, but the members of our religion class have similar backgrounds.
   Diverse means _____.
5. Some students griped when they saw their final exam schedule, but others were happy.
   Griped means _____.
6. The henpecked husband, never the dominant type, always let his wife order him around.
   Henpecked means _____.
7. When there is ice on the ground, it is more difficult to drive on an inclined road than on a flat one.
   Inclined means _____.

8. The response was <u>evasive</u> instead of being to the point.

    Evasive means _____.

9. No sane person would commit such a <u>lunatic</u> crime.

    Lunatic means _____.

10. The <u>nondescript</u> stranger blended into the crowd so well that no one mistook him for my unusual-looking friend.

    Nondescript means _____.

Practice

Define the following underlined words.

1. Contrary to general belief, 75 percent of U.S. industry's products are not <u>mass-produced</u> in long production runs but are assembled in small batches as styles and sizes change (BOONE AND KURTZ, 334).

    Mass-produced means _____.

2. The situation that originally provoked the most <u>anxiety</u> now elicits only relaxation (HILGARD, 495).

    Anxiety means _____.

Recognizing Stated Definitions

As you read textbooks, you will encounter unfamiliar subject terms that are defined directly in the passage. These new terms are usually placed in *italics* or **boldface print** since they are directly related to the subject. Textbook authors want you to understand these terms, and so they provide complete definitions. Therefore, it is important for you to take the time to read these difficult subject terms and consider their complete definitions. Consider the following example from a psychology text.

Example

Human beings have, during the course of history, wasted an enormous amount of time and money hunting <u>aphrodisiacs</u>—drugs that will arouse or influence sexual passions (MCCONNELL, 334).

Questions

1. Can you fully define an "aphrodisiac" as a drug? _____
2. What is the complete definition of "aphrodisiacs" as stated in the example? _____

Authors want their readers to understand **subject terms**—or the language of the course. Recognizing that subject terms are set off visually in a passage, by italics, boldface print, or marginal notations, helps you to identify the important course vocabulary. Carefully reading and noting complete definitions stated in the text helps you to learn the course content.

Practice

Each of the following passages from textbooks contains a stated definition for the underlined subject term. Highlight the complete definition.

1. Hazardous wastes are any industrial by-products of no current economic value that pose a threat, either now or in the future, to humans, animals, or plants (SINACORE, 430).

2. According to the definition of Chinese traditional medicine, acupuncture is the treatment of disease—not just the alleviation of pain—by inserting very fine needles into the body at specific points called loci (INSEL AND ROTH, 347).

3. In recent years, a new type of gentry has been identified: those middle and upper income individuals who leave the suburbs to move into the city. Gentrification is the term used to describe the migration of these people into urban centers and their renovation of existing housing (HESS, 528).

4. Reciprocity—a privilege renounced or a gift given at one point in time, obligates the receiver to return something of equal value at some future date (HESS, 282).

5. In terms of personality, much is being written today of androgyny, the combination of feminine and masculine traits that are found in every individual (HESS, 227).

6. If the blood supply to your brain is choked off by what is sometimes called "hardening of the arteries," you may enter a child-like state commonly called a <u>senile psychosis</u>, or senility (MCCONNELL, 626).

7. Psychologists usually divide memory into three distinct types: sensory, short-term, and long-term. <u>Sensory memory</u> is the momentary lingering of sensory information we experience after a stimulus has been removed (WORTMAN, 177).

8. Some problems can best be solved by a strategy called an <u>algorithm</u>: a precisely stated set of rules that usually works for solving problems of a particular type (WORTMAN, 217).

9. The <u>foramen magnum</u> (the large opening in the skull), through which the spinal cord passes and connects to the brain, is an important clue to evolutionary relationships (HAVILAND, 82).

10. The development of similar cultural adaptations to similar environmental conditions by peoples of quite different cultural backgrounds is called <u>convergent evolution</u> (HAVILAND, 360).

Practice

Highlight the stated definitions of the underlined subject terms.

1. <u>Allegory</u> is a technique for expanding the meaning of a literary work by having the characters, and sometimes the setting and events, represent certain general abstract ideas, qualities, or concepts, usually moral, religious, or political in nature (PICKERING, 77).

2. This same process of partial recognition may account for the phenomenon called <u>déjà vu</u>—the distinct feeling that something is familiar even though we have never encountered it before. In this case we may be partially matching a novel experience with a very similar but unidentifiable past event (WORTMAN, 184).

3. <u>Vestigial structures</u> are reduced and generally useless structures that are found in many plants and animals.

4. Those economists who specialize in the use and development of statistical techniques to analyze economic problems are <u>econometricians</u> (NIGRO, 95).

5. When there is only one producer, and no other potential producers, we say this industry is a <u>monopoly</u> (NIGRO, 231).

6. When agreement cannot be reached, <u>binding arbitration</u>, is entered into. This involves each side giving up freedom of decision and calling in a third party to make a decision that is binding on both sides whether they like the decision or not (NIGRO, 381).

7. A round lot is the basic unit for a transaction, and for stock it is usually 100 shares (MAYO, 115).

8. The investor may purchase the security on margin, which is purchasing the security on credit supplied by the broker (MAYO, 119).

9. Liquidity is the ease with which assets may be converted into cash without loss. If a firm is liquid, it will be able to meet its bills as they come due (MAYO, 234).

10. The term underwriting refers to the process of selling new securities (MAYO, 106).

Practice

Read the following paragraph from a theater text. Then, define each of the underlined words.

Sometimes other kinds of settings are used in the theatre. The backdrop, or drop, usually theatrical canvas that stretches across the stage, is weighted at the bottom and painted to represent either indoor or outdoor scenes. With drops, top curtains called teasers and side curtains called tormentors mask the backstage areas and the fly space, the area behind the top of the arch above the floor of the stage (CASSADY, 174).

Backdrop means _____

_____.

Teasers means _____

_____.

Tormentors means _____

_____.

Fly space means _____

_____.

INDEX

A

Antonym context clues
  introduction, 318–319
  practice in general sentences, 319–324
  practice in text sentences, 324
  summary of words used, 318
Assumptions. *See* Comparisons and contrasts; Descriptive listing

C

Causes and effects
  application in selections, 143–165
  conclusions
    from causes, 139
    from effects, 140–141
    introduction, 137
    practice, 139–141
  distinguishing between causes and effects
    introduction, 130–131
    practice, 131–134
    recognizing causes, 133–134
    recognizing effects, 131–132
  fact and opinion
    introduction, 134–135
    practice, 135–136
    to support a point of view, 134–136
  following directions
    introduction, 127–128
    practice, 128–130
  point of view
    introduction, 134–135
    position statement, 135
    practice, 135–136
    supported by causes and/or effects, 135–136

(continued)
  recognizing causes and effects in argumentative writing, 123–124
  signal words. *See* Signal words; Essay tests
  supporting a position
    with causes, 137
    with effects, 138
    introduction, 134
    practice, 135–136
  writing assignments, 149, 155, 161, 165, 167
Comparisons and contrasts
  application in selections, 101–120
  assumptions
    application in comparisons and contrasts, 96–97
    practice, 97–99
  fact and opinion
    introduction, 99
    practice, 100
  following directions
    introduction, 88–89
    practice, 89–90
  point of view
    introduction, 99
    practice, 100
  predictions
    application of comparisons and contrasts, 96–97
    practice, 97–99
  recognizing comparisons and contrasts in analytical writing, 84–86
  shared traits
    common characteristics, 91
    introduction, 90–91
    practice, 91–93

(continued)
signal words. *See* Signal words; Essay tests
types of comparisons and contrasts
    introduction, 94–95
    parts, space, and sequence, 95
    practice, 95–96
writing assignments, 107, 111, 117, 120, 122
Conclusions. *See* Causes and effects
Context clues. *See* Antonym context clues; Example context clues; Sense of the sentence context clues; Stated definitions; Synonym context clues
    introduction, 294–295
    See also Parts of speech

D

Descriptive listing of ideas
    application in selections, 60–81
    assumptions
        in comparisons and contrasts. *See* Comparisons and contrasts
        introduction, 56–58
        practice, 58–59
    distinguishing between comparisons and listings
        introduction, 84–85
        practice, 85
        recognizing descriptions, 41–42
    fact and opinion
        introduction, 54–55
        practice, 55–56
        to support a point of view, 54–56
    following directions
        introduction, 47
        practice, 48–49
    generalizations
        introduction, 56–58
        from listed characteristics, 54–56
        practice, 58–59
    listed characteristics
        introduction, 42–43
        practice, 43–44
    signal words. *See* Signal words; Essay tests
    types of descriptions
        introduction, 50–51
        practice, 52–53
        quality, space, sequence, 50–51
    writing assignments, 65, 71, 76, 81, 83

(continued)
Details
    identifying in a paragraph, 199–202
    in causes and effects, 123–126, 128–130
    in comparisons and contrasts, 85–86, 88–93
    in listings, 43–49
    relationship to the main idea, 192–193, 198–199
    in a sequence, 5, 7–9
    See also Outline
Dictionary
    introduction, 260–262
    multiple meanings in an entry. *See* Multiple meanings
    parts of speech. *See* Parts of speech
Directional words. *See* Essay tests; Multiple-choice; True-false

E

Essay tests
    creating essay outlines, 229
    introduction, 228
    practice, 229–234
    recognizing directional words, 228–229
        causes and effects, 229
        comparisons and contrasts, 229
        descriptive listings, 228
        sequence of ideas, 228
    See also Signal words; Studying for tests
Example context clues
    introduction, 312–313
    practice in general sentences, 313–317
    practice in text sentences and paragraphs, 317
    summary of words used, 312
Expository writing. *See* Details; Main ideas; Outlines; Topics

F

Fact and opinion. *See* Causes and effects; Comparisons and contrasts; Descriptive listings; Sequence of ideas
Flashback. *See* Sequence of ideas
Following directions. *See* Causes and effects; Comparisons and contrasts; Descriptive listings; Sequence of ideas

G

Generalizations. *See* Descriptive listing

I

Idioms
  definition, 238
  introduction, 238
  practice, 239–248, 250–258
  preview, 237, 249
  summary of idioms used, 237, 249

M

Main idea
  introduction, 192–193, 194–195
  noting. *See* Outlining
  practice in identifying, 195–197, 199–201
  relationship to details, 192–193, 198–199
  relationship to the topic, 192–193
  various locations in the paragraph, 195–197
  unstated main ideas, 194–195
Multiple meanings of words
  introduction, 278–279
  parts of speech and what the sentence talks about, 278, 279, 294, 295
    to locate meanings in a dictionary, 278–283
    to locate meanings without a dictionary, 294–302
  practice, 280–292
  summary of words used, 277

O

Objective tests
  multiple-choice
    all-of-the-above answers, 221
    directional words, 222
    most complete answers, 221
    practice questions, 223–225
    specific determiners, 222–223
  true-false
    completely true statements, 225–226
    partially true statements, 225–226
    practice questions, 226–228

(continued)
    specific determiners, 226
Outlines
  on essay tests, 229
  form of the chapter outline, 205
  introduction, 204–205
  paragraph outline, 209–216
  practice with lists, 206–208
  practice with text passages, 209–216
  relationship of the main idea and details, 204
  relationship to highlighting, 204–205

P

Parts of speech
  introduction, 260–262
  to locate meanings in a dictionary practice, 262–276
  to locate meanings without a dictionary practice, 294–301
  in sense of the sentence context clues, 294–301
  in synonym context clues, 306–310
  summary of words used, 259
Point of view. *See* Causes and effects; Comparisons and contrasts; Descriptive listings; Sequence of ideas
Predictions. *See* Comparisons and contrasts; Sequence of ideas
Previewing
  chapter
    introduction, 174–175
    review and questions, 175
    subtitles, 175
    summary, 175
    title, 172
    visual aids, 175
  introduction, 171
  text
    appendix, 173
    chapter parts, 172–173
    copyright page, 172
    glossary, 173
    index, 173
    preface, 172
    table of contents, 172
  text preview practice
    psychology, 174–178
    reading, 173
    sociology, 179–184

R

Role-Playing
  situations, 39–40, 82–83, 121–122, 166–167

S

Selections with questions and writing assignments
  "America in Solitary," 156–161
  "... And, on Shaky Grounds," 17–22
  "Cheating," 150–155
  "The Feminine Physique," 101–107
  "How America Lives," 112–117
  "How to Recognize An Aries," 77–81
  "In Praise of Plains," 72–76
  "Leo and Cancer Personalities," 108–111
  "Mind Over Matter," 162–165
  The Old-Time Bakery: A Still-Palpable Thrill," 23–29
  "On the Pressures and Politics of Waiting in Line," 143–149
  "Prohibition: The 'Noble Experiment' That Failed," 66–71
  "Sleep Cycles," 36–38
  "Spending a Few Days with the Kid that You Once Were," 60–65
  "Welcome Back, Baby," 30–35
  "What is an American," 118–120
Selectivity of ideas. See Sequence of ideas
Sense-of-the-sentence context clues
  introduction, 294–295
  parts of speech and what the sentence talks about, 294–301
  practice, 296–303
  summary of words used, 293
Sequence of ideas
  application in selections, 17–38
  chronological order, 3–5
  comparisons and contrasts of sequence. See Comparisons and contrasts
  descriptions of sequence. See Descriptive listing
  distinguishing between sequence and a listing, 41, 42
  fact and opinion
    introduction, 12–13
    practice, 13
    understanding who the narrator is, 11–12

(continued)
  flashback
    introduction, 9–10
    practice, 10–11
  following directions
    introduction, 6
    practice, 6–7
    See also Essay tests; Studying for tests
  introduction, 3–4
  point of view
    introduction, 11–12
    narrator, 11–12
    opinion *vs.* fact, 12
    practice, 12–13
  predictions
    introduction, 14–15
    practice, 15–16
    See also Comparisons and contrasts
  recognizing sequence in narrative writing, 3–4
  selectivity of ideas
    introduction, 7–8
    practice, 8–9
  signal words. *See* Signal words; Essay tests; writing assignments
  writing assignments, 22, 29, 35, 38, 40
Signal words
  causes and effects
    introduction, 125–126
    practice, 126–127
    signals of causes, 125
    signals of effects, 126
  comparisons and contrasts
    introduction, 86–87
    practice, 87–88
  descriptive listing
    introduction, 45
    practice, 46
    recognizing a listing, 45–46
  sequence of ideas
    chronological order, 5–6
    introduction, 4
    practice, 5
  test-taking. *See also* Objective tests; Essay tests
Specific determiners. *See* Multiple-choice; True-false
Stated definitions
  introduction, 324
  practice in text passages, 324–327
Styles of writing
  Analytical. *See* Comparisons and contrasts
  Argumentative. *See* Causes and effects

(continued)
   Descriptive. *See* Descriptive listing of ideas
   Narrative. *See* Sequences of ideas
Synonym context clues
   introduction, 304–306
   parts of speech and what the sentence talks about, 306–310
   practice in general sentences, 306–310
   practice in text sentences, 310–312
   summary of words used, 304

T

Taking notes. *See* Details; Main ideas; Outlines; Taking tests
Taking tests
   approaches to tests
      allowing time related to point values, 219–220
      reading directions, 220
      rereading, 220
   See Objective tests; Essay tests
   Studying for tests

(continued)
      applying understandings of writing styles, 218–219
      asking questions in class, 217
      creating test questions, 218–219
      reading notes, 217–219
      reciting, 218
      time for study, 218
      using index cards, 217–218
      See also Causes and effects; Comparisons and contrasts; Descriptive listings; Sequence of ideas
Text paragraphs. *See* Details; Main ideas; Outlines
Topics
   introduction, 185–186
   of a list
      practice naming, 187
      practice selecting, 186
   of a passage
      practice identifying, 188–191
   relationship to the main idea, 192–193
   of a text paragraph
      practice identifying, 188–191